Public Library
Youth Services:
A Public Policy Approach

Information Management, Policy, and Services
Charles R. McClure and Peter Hernon, Editors

Public Library
Youth Services:
A Public Policy Approach

Holly G. Willett

ABLEX PUBLISHING CORPORATION
NORWOOD, NEW JERSEY

Copyright © 1995 by Ablex Publishing Corporation

Printed in the United States of America.

Library of Congress Cataloging-in-Publication Data

Willett, Holly G.
    Public library youth services : a public policy approach / Holly
G. Willett.
        p. cm. – (Information management, policy, and services)
    Includes bibliographical references and indexes.
    ISBN 1-56750-122-2. – ISBN 1-56750-123-0 (pbk.)
    1. Children's libraries–Government policy–United States.
    2. Public libraries–Services to teenagers–United States.
    I. Title. II. Series.
    Z718.2.U6W55   1995
    027.62'6–dc20   94-15773
                                                                CIP

Ablex Publishing Corporation
355 Chestnut Street
Norwood, NJ 07648

To

John Boll, Charles Bunge, Edwin Cortez, James Krikelas,
Jane Robbins, Richard Walker, Darlene Weingand,
Wayne Wiegand, and Douglas Zweizig

Contents

Acknowledgments

Writing is a lonely occupation, but one couldn't do it without other people's help. Thus, I am delighted to acknowledge the assistance of many people, beginning with the faculty of the Bush Institute for Child and Family Policy at the University of North Carolina at Chapel Hill, who, from 1983 to 1985, provided a broad social policy foundation for my work, helped me refine both my problem and my arguments, poked holes in my logic, and suggested alternative approaches and sources of information. I am particularly grateful to have had the support and advice of Ron Haskins, Joan Lipsitz, and James Gallagher. The other participants in the policy analysis training program, my fellow Fellows, as it were, made valuable contributions. The Bush Foundation of St. Paul, Minnesota, deserves my thanks for funding the Bush Institute, the success of which can be measured by the fact that the University of North Carolina at Chapel Hill continues to support it as the Carolina Institute for Child and Family Policy. I wish to thank the current director of the Institute, Richard Clifford, for his support and assistance with this work and other research.

I am also grateful to the Graduate School of the University of Wisconsin–Madison for summer research funds that helped me complete the first draft of the book. My graduate student assistants, Ruth Cleven Doran (UW–Madison), Linda McVey, and Dana Fogg (Texas Woman's University), located materials in several libraries and saved my time in many, many ways. Merri V. Lindgren, editorial assistant extraordinaire, not only found the typographical errors, the grammatical errors, and the places where I had left the reader in confusion, but also served as a cheering squad.

Lorraine Adkins and John Peters, government publications librarians at the State Historical Society of Wisconsin, *always* found answers to my demographic queries, as did the government documents staff of the Willis Library at the University of North Texas. The historical material in Chapter 5 was considerably strengthened by the scrutiny and contributions of Wayne Wiegand. Editors Charles McClure and Peter Hernon were the souls of patience and understanding—thanks for the latitude.

Throughout the writing of this book, I had recourse to the personal knowledge and expertise of many people who are cited for "personal communication." I am grateful that they found time in their busy workdays to locate and update stray facts and contribute their perspectives. And last, but never least, I am very grateful to many people at Texas Woman's University, including Dean B. Keith Swigger, Ann Barnett, and the interlibrary loan staff who made completion of the manuscript possible and pleasant.

Of course, I must also enter the traditional *mea culpa*: Whatever errors and omissions are found in the text, they are my responsibility alone.

Preface: What Is Public Policy Analysis?

Thomas R. Dye defined public policy as "whatever governments choose to do or not to do" (1987, p. 3). Although many observers would include whatever governments *say* they will or will not do, meaningful public policies are those that have an impact on people's lives. In this book, the actions of government agencies will be more important than written policy statements.

One of the things local governments in the United States have chosen to do is provide public libraries, and the state and federal governments have chosen to support local efforts. It is true that from the point of view of librarians, the support is modest at best, but nevertheless, the full spectrum of governments have policies of supplying public libraries to citizens, including children and adolescents. This book is an analysis of the policy of providing public library services for young people. Following a model proposed by MacRae and Haskins (1981), it examines criteria and evidence supporting the existing service, explores possible alternative policies, and makes recommendations for public policy regarding youth services in public libraries.

There are a number of reasons for analyzing any governmental policy, most of them having to do with spending public money in prudent and socially useful ways. Implementing a new policy proposal carries with it the expenditure of public funds and the possible construction of a new bureaucracy that may be difficult to dismantle once it is in place. A policy analysis made before a policy is effected attempts to predict the policy's usefulness and the extent to which it is likely to attain its goals and have the desired impact. Policy analyses of this kind are made with the intention of helping policymakers decide whether or not to implement a particular policy or whether to modify the proposed policy.

On the other hand, analyses (such as this one) that seek to appraise a policy that has been in effect for a period of time look at what has been done to discover how well the policy has been implemented, to examine how funds have been spent, to assess the policy's effectiveness in achieving its intended outcomes, to determine if the policy is justified, and to uncover any unintended effects. Again, the intention is to assist policymakers in their deliberations about retaining, modifying, or discarding a particular policy.

 Public policy analysis is, then, a process of information gathering and interpretation to abet government decision making. MacRae and Haskins described it as "the application of reason, evidence, and a valuative framework to public decisions" (1981, p. 2). The process itself might be carried out in a number of systematic ways, but most analyses will include the following components, as noted by MacRae and Haskins (1981), MacRae and Wilde (1979), and Stokey and Zeckhauser (1978), and modified by the present author:

1. *Definition of the problem and the context*. Public policies are promulgated to address real-life situations. The more specific and precise our understanding of the situation, the more likely we are to be able to carry out the other steps necessary to choosing an appropriate policy or policies to accommodate reality. Social policies such as providing public library services to children and teenagers may at first appear to be defined by simple and straightforward objectives, such as being sure that young people have access to books. Behind such objectives, however, we find a number of assumptions and values concerning both young people and books, for example, assumptions about the usefulness of reading and the need for adults to select the materials that young people read. Everyone involved in a situation may not hold to the same set of "truths" about it. To be truly useful, a statement of a problem must define the conflicts, objectives, assumptions, and values involved in the status quo.

2. *Selection of the criteria for choice*. The statement of the problem leads to a set of lenses through which the problem may be viewed and a set of criteria, tests, or standards against which alternative policies must be measured; in other words, the evidence and the valuative framework mentioned earlier. One's choice of lenses and criteria depends on the nature of the policy being analyzed, the kinds of data available from which to make the analysis, the policy's objectives, and the analyst's own values. Some public policy objectives rest on maximizing the efficiency of projects that have measurable, quantifiable outputs. These are situations in which mathematical models provided by such methods

as systems analysis, operations research, linear programming, statistical probability, and computer simulations are applicable. Some examples of such projects would be capital improvements such as roads or hydroelectric dams.

Social policies are also susceptible to this kind of analysis when they lead to measurable results. The analysis of a policy of reducing benefits to recipients of Aid to Families with Dependent Children (AFDC) if their children are truant from school would certainly include a statistical comparison of the attendance rates of AFDC child recipients before and after the policy was implemented. Many social policies are not amenable to precise mathematical evaluation and must be judged on the basis of ethical criteria, such as cost-benefit analysis or equity considerations. Where feasible, a combination of mathematical and ethical criteria is desirable. In addition, political feasibility is often used as a pragmatic criterion because a policy to be implemented must be acceptable to policymakers, who, by and large, are politicians.

3. *Discussion of alternative policies.* Rare is the public policy situation that can be met with only one possible course of action. A variety of alternatives is usually available, including maintaining the status quo. Designing or discovering these alternatives may be the most creative and demanding part of public policy analysis. Sources of inspiration may be found in the way that policies dealing with related problems are handled in our own country, in the approaches to the same problem used by foreign countries, or in the analyst's originality. The consequences of each alternative are developed, as far as is predictable, and each one is submitted to judgment against the criteria developed in Step 2. The alternatives are compared with each other.

4. *Choice of recommended policy or modifications.* The application of "reason, evidence, and a valuative framework" should result in specific recommendations, whether for a particular policy in its entirety or modifications to a proposed or existing policy. The decisions should follow logically from the other components of the process that should have demonstrated clearly the reasons for preferring the recommended policies over the alternatives.

The astute reader has noticed that the process described here is similar to that recommended for planning and evaluation (see, for example, McClure, Owen, Zweizig, Lynch, & Van House, 1987), and it bears a resemblance to the research process as well. Both policy analysis and evaluation are done for the sake of making decisions and both are political processes. In both policy analysis and evaluation, politics may determine the goals and objectives of the analysis, the goals and objectives of the agency or policy under examination, the sources investigated, the recommendations made, and whether anything changes as a result of the analysis. It is difficult, if not impossible, to do an evaluation or a policy analysis in the real world without recognition of the specific political situation involved. In fact, an analysis "uncontaminated" by political awareness might not be worth very much because a large part of the context in which policies exist would be left out. In recent years, public librarians have had to become more aware of the political nature of library support.

The techniques of policy analysis and evaluation are also similar. In both policy analysis and evaluation, the status quo is described and compared to a set of relevant criteria agreed to before the comparison is made. Evaluators have recognized that planning and evaluation is an iterative cycle; so, too, an analysis may need to be repeated after a policy has been in place for a few years.

At first glance, public policy analysis might well be thought of as evaluation at a macro level, taking an overall look at a policy rather than at an individual institution or agency that carries out the policy locally, especially when a policy has been in force for a period of time (MacRae & Wilde, 1979). In fact, it is only partly the case that policy analysis looks at the big picture whereas evaluation focuses on the local. In this regard, librarians might compare R.D. Leigh's (1950) *The Public Library in the United States*, which attempted to assess the overall situation of public libraries in the United States, with Levy, Meltsner, and Wildavsky's (1974) examination of the Oakland Public Library. Although Leigh's work focused on the public library as a national phenomenon and described the situation and alternative roles for the public library, it developed recommendations from an unquestioning point of view, assuming that public libraries were carrying out the intended policy and that the policy itself was valid. In contrast, Levy, Meltsner, and Wildavsky not only evaluated the performance of a single municipal library but also critiqued the entire input-based method of public library evaluation employed by librarians at the time, noting that evaluation based on outputs and outcomes was preferable. Within the limitations of the available social science methodology of their times, both of these works might well be considered policy analyses, even though one is national and the other local in focus.

If differences between the two fields exist, they are likely to rest on the tools, the assumptions, and the viewpoints taken. Policy analysis often ranges more widely than evaluation, bringing in information, perspectives, and models from a number of disciplines, rather than focusing solely on an organization from an insider's perspective. In fact, a policy analysis may study a policy implementation across several organizations or bureaucracies, because the policy is the focus, not the agency, and policies may be implemented by various agencies. Policy analysis may involve looking at longer periods of time, both past and future, than the usual planning and evaluation cycle accounts for. Assumptions differ as well. Planning and evaluation take place in a context in which the agency's existence is not questioned. Policy analysis scrutinizes the very underpinnings of a policy and is concerned about the *outcomes* of the policy, as well as the services provided through implementation of the policy.

Policy analysis may be thought of as a form of applied research. The process of asking questions, designing a means of testing the questions, setting decision rules, gathering evidence to be tested against the decision criteria, and deciding if the criteria have been satisfied is, indeed, like research. Sometimes a policy analysis requires original research, as in the example given earlier of the AFDC policy. Perhaps more frequently, policy analysts make use of evidence already accumulated, theories already tested, models previously applied in other contexts, and prior analyses. Policy analysis is eclectic when appropriate; it allows for the synthesis and integration of research from many fields. And, it may uncover areas needing further study and information, a typical outcome of research.

Like any other endeavor, a policy analysis may be done well or poorly, and those who use a policy analysis are entitled to judge its worth. Human selectivity in information use being what it is, it is important to know who gathered the information and how those individuals acquired and used the information. Many groups of people may be involved in discussions of policy, but there are three groups of people who are most likely to actually analyze public policy—those who must make decisions (legislators and bureaucrats), those who make their livings analyzing policy (private sector organizations and consultants), and those interested in public policy from a research point of view (college and university faculty). MacRae (1981) added a fourth group: the civic-minded citizen who carefully analyzes policies in order to ensure that they are ethical and effective.

Each of these groups has reasons for making analyses that may lead to particular results and recommendations. For example, most readers will be familiar with the differences in outlook between the Brookings Institution and the American Enterprise Institute. These organizations exist for the express purpose of representing particular political and ideological values. Their values influence the sources analysts choose to examine and their interpretations of data. A policy analysis done by either of these groups can be expected to espouse recommendations based on specific political beliefs, which is not to say that their work should be ignored or denigrated. On the contrary, the obvious use of an ideological framework can assist policymakers in decision making by serving as one screen for the selection of information. Policymakers make decisions within a political context that includes a great deal of information and many voices crying to be heard. When suffering from information overload, one needs some mechanism for determining to which sources one will attend.

When a university or college faculty member produces a policy analysis (such as this one), the analyst intends to be objective, not a supporter of a partisan political position or a parochial professional ideology that must be defended at all costs. Ideally, academic policy analysts make recommendations but do not advocate, leaving decisions to politicians and administrators. The objective frame of mind that guides research should inform a policy analysis. In fact, of course, few humans are completely objective about their work, especially if they spend large portions of their lives thinking about and studying a particular field. Even scientists, upon whom the burden of objectivity lies most heavily, will admit that they care deeply about their work. Advocacy can be seen in the choice of policies that scholars consider, the kinds and sources of data they assume to be germane to the analysis, and in their recommendations.

Scholarly policy analysts have an obligation to be aware of their biases, to the extent that such awareness is humanly possible, and the scrutiny of other scholars presumably roots out the most blatant prejudices. Despite the opportunities for correction, people nevertheless look through the lens of their own consciousness and live in a personal political situation. Consequently, it may help the reader to know something about the author of the policy analysis in hand. For 9 years I worked as a children's librarian in public libraries in California and Massachusetts. I experienced both Proposition 13 in 1978 and Proposition 2 1/2 in 1980, property tax limitation measures that had far-reaching impacts on public agencies in those states. I can easily take the side of librarians and "go native," as an anthropologist might say, because, after all, I *am* a native. On the other hand, no one criticizes libraries and librarianship as much as librarians themselves do, and I entered academia because I had many questions that I knew would never be answered if I remained a practicing librarian. This book represents some of the tentative answers I have found thus far.

Arriving at answers was not an entirely random process, although serendipity sometimes took a hand, as it so often does in human affairs. The approach I have chosen is one of many possible procedures for carrying out a policy analysis, and it adheres closely to the process described earlier. In my view, youth services in public libraries are at an important time in their development; some commentators believe that this is true of the public library in general (see Robinson, 1992, for example). Youth services faces a number of challenges that make a policy analysis an important step at this time. The first chapter describes these challenges. Later chapters describe the services as they exist today and develop the criteria and the lenses through which the current services can be analyzed. These lenses include the history of the services, the view through the lens of public goods theory, and the perspectives provided by child development and learning theories. Alternative policies are discussed in Chapter 8 and recommendations are found in Chapters 9 through 12.

CHAPTER 1

The Challenges Facing Youth Services

INTRODUCTION

Public librarians and library supporters believe that library services have a positive impact on library users' education, information, recreation, and culture. They believe that the library promotes the free flow of ideas in a democratic society, and therefore, its benefits extend to the community in general, even to those who do not use the library (North Carolina Department of Cultural Resources, Division of State Library, 1983; Public Library Association, 1979). In the minds of many people, the goal of positive influence is pursued mainly through the provision of books and other print materials. A major tenet of librarianship, sometimes called the *library faith*, is the notion that reading is good for you, and reading good books is better. Those who serve specific groups, such as children, teenagers, ethnic minorities, business, the elderly, or the handicapped, share this ideal and state it in a manner relevant to the specific clientele.

In this book, we examine the policy of providing public library services to children and teenagers. It needs to be stated at the outset how the librarians serving these groups view the ideal of library services for these age groups. Certainly, librarians serving children and teenagers believe that the books, materials, and activities they provide enhance the cognitive, affective, and social development of young people. They also believe that reading is important for young people's continued development and library use in adulthood as well as for their development in youth. Chelton (1990) summarized the desired impacts and their developmental connections.

1

Library use by preschool children should develop prereading skills associated with receptive language ability (learning about the organization of written language through listening), establishing habits conducive to reading and learning (sitting quietly), understanding how books and stories operate (physical structure of books, intellectual structure of stories, integration of text and pictures), and associating reading with pleasure. For children in elementary school, the goals are to build reading competence, not only in terms of skill but also comprehension and motivation to read. Maintaining or increasing self-esteem and acquiring the skills needed to do simple independent research, including self-directed inquiry, are also goals for the school-age child. Youth services goals for secondary school pupils include knowledge of oneself as an individual and as a citizen of the local community, the nation, and the world; the ability to conduct research using a variety of media and distinguishing fact from opinion; and knowledge and skills to participate in employment and personal relationships. Reading as a tool for lifelong learning and enjoyment and knowledge of where and how to find information are also goals of services to young adults (Chelton, 1990).

No one can argue with the worthiness of the desire to have a positive impact on the development of reading and what we might call life skills. For more than a hundred years, youth librarians, like other public librarians, have pursued their goals with little systematic study about the effectiveness of what they do, relying on the library faith and its acceptance by library supporters, library administrators, and public officials to support their activities. That these goals overlap considerably with those of the public schools has also not been a concern for librarians.

THE CHALLENGES FACING PUBLIC LIBRARY YOUTH SERVICES

Recent social trends signal that the support for youth services may need to be placed on a different basis. Those involved in public library services must consider their priorities, methods, and results in order for the public library and its youth services to continue a viable existence. These trends include funding restraints, labor shortages, ambivalence toward changing technology, demographic shifts, concern for educational achievement and literacy, legitimacy, and the status of young people in our society, all of which are discussed in the remainder of this chapter. The discussion of these trends is aided by defining some terms. Throughout this book, whenever the words *youth* or *young people* occur,

they refer to the entire group of persons between
school graduation. When the term *children* appears,
group generally designated by public librarians as ch
tion varies according to local use, but most comm...
defined as those up to age 12 (sixth grade) or up to age 14 (eighth g...
Depending, again, on local decision, *young adults* are those from 12 or 14
through high school, although a very few libraries include those in their
early 20s in the definition of young adults. This application of the term
young adult varies from the one in general use, which usually means the
early years of adulthood, after high school graduation through the 30s.

Funding Restraints

1980-90 funding doubled

During the 1988–1989 fiscal year, federal, state, and local governments
spent $4.25 billion on public libraries. Nevertheless, expenditures for
public libraries represented a tiny proportion of government spending—
.21% of total government expenditures, which were $2.03 trillion (U.S.
Bureau of the Census, 1991). Over the years, the proportion of government spending represented by public libraries has changed little. In 1977
spending on public libraries amounted to .24% of all government
expenditures; public library expenditures were .18% of government
outlays in 1982; and .19% in 1984 (Goldhor, 1985; Public Library
Association, 1985; U.S. Bureau of the Census, 1986; White, 1983). Even
at the local government level, which is the major source of public library
funding, libraries receive less than 1% of all expenditures; in 1984-1985,
local governments in the United States spent .63% of their outlays on
public libraries ("Library expenditures by state and local governments,
1984-1985," 1988). Nevertheless, like all government agencies, public
libraries have been affected by the vicissitudes of public finance during
the past 15 years. As a service that is not essential to the protection of
lives and property, the public library has been vulnerable to tax
reduction measures, efforts to stabilize local government funding, and
the loss of federal revenue sharing funds. The property tax issue is
especially serious because public libraries frequently receive 80% or
more of their funding from local property tax revenue (California State
Library, 1979; Public Library Association, 1985). Between 1978 and 1980,
43 states enacted some form of property tax limitation or new property
tax relief (Citrin, 1984).

The most widely publicized of these measures were Proposition 13 in
California in 1978 and Proposition 2 1/2 in Massachusetts in 1980.
Library services were affected in both states. In California, Clark
(personal communication, 1984) estimated that public libraries experienced reductions of 20% overall, and these reductions remained several

ears after the passage of Proposition 13. In a series of longitudinal case studies of four California public libraries, I found that 1988–1989 expenditures in one of the libraries was only 61% of that same library's expenditures in 1977–1978 when inflation was taken into account. In Massachusetts, one study found that library budgets in 33 cities were reduced initially to a greater degree than the overall budgets for those cities (Massachusetts Municipal Association, 1982). Another study found that in 17 libraries where allocations had increased during the second and third years after the passage of Proposition 2 1/2, the increases did not match inflation and negotiated wage increases during the same period, leaving a net loss (J.M. Greiner, 1984).

As a locally supported public service, the library is particularly vulnerable to local fiscal conditions and policies, and there is a good deal of variation in local and state economies across the nation. When Wisconsin has a state budget surplus, Massachusetts may be in recession. In the library press one may read of successful attempts to increase library funding and pass library construction bond issues, and, indeed, one annual study (C. Palmer, 1991) showed that expenditures on public libraries (based on a representative sample of 53 libraries) more than doubled between 1980 and 1990. Because of inflation, the increase is really 41%, based on 1980 dollars. However, one may also read of reductions and failures to pass funding increases. During the recession of the 1970s, many youth librarians had the perception that, under conditions of retrenchment, services to young people were being reduced disproportionately to services for adults. Farrell (1977), Rollock (1978), and Silver (1980) cited the elimination or downgrading of personnel and services in the children's and young adult areas of public libraries during periods of fiscal stringency in various locales.

Although studies of youth services in Massachusetts have not been done, case studies of California public libraries after Proposition 13 found evidence of reductions in children's and young adult services (Shoham, 1984; Willett, 1987). It is difficult to assess the permanence, disproportionality, or impact of these reductions. Rubin, Medrich, Lewittes, and Berg (1980) and Willett (1987) found that although cuts had been made in services to youth immediately after Proposition 13, over time the cuts did not remain disproportionate to reductions in services for adults. Because one cannot generalize from case studies, it is possible that disproportionate reductions have remained in other locales in California or other states. At this writing, claims of disproportionate impact on young adult services are being made, as many libraries are suffering budget reductions.

Ironically, the social situation of its audience may put youth services and the public library in general at even greater risk of losing funding.

Daily, it seems, the media broadcast a news story about the plight of young people in American society. The concerns for education and literacy are discussed separately, but the statistics about crime, drugs, poverty, homelessness, child abuse, runaways, and health among people under 18 are appalling.

Here is a sample: Drug abuse among American youth is declining, but still the highest in the industrialized world. About 42% of young women and 25% of young men between the ages of 15 and 24 have thought seriously about committing suicide. Infant mortality rates in the United States are higher than in most other industrialized countries and black infants are twice as likely to die in the first month of life as white infants due to lack of prenatal care. Although crimes committed by children and young adults are increasing, young people aged 12 to 19 are the victims of crime twice as often as adults (Foster, Jacobs, & Siegel, 1989). The Children's Defense Fund estimates that 14.3 million American children lived in poverty in 1991, about 21.8% of the under-18 population and nearly 25% of children under 6. One third of the homeless population consists of families with children (Children's Defense Fund, 1992). The seriousness of these problems may make funding the public library seem irrelevant. It can be difficult to defend federal funding for public libraries at a Congressional hearing, for instance, if the person before you has been pleading for AIDS babies (Mary Costabile, personal communication, January 5, 1993).

As part of a profession that claims to improve the quality of young people's lives, youth-serving librarians are concerned about children and young adults, whether library users or not. However, as an institution with a primarily middle-class clientele, the public library may be in danger of seeming irrelevant to the people who fund it when they face social problems to solve with a dwindling public exchequer. If funding restraints continue, even the meager funds supporting the public library may seem to have a better use. Hypothetically, any reductions (or stagnation while the population grows) in public library budgets may impede the library's ability to have a positive impact on the development of young people because the reductions result in the loss of the basic components of library service: staff, hours, and materials budgets. Whatever the fate of the public library, youth services will share it.

Changing Personnel Structures

It is ironic that after discussing the budget restrictions many public libraries experienced in the 1970s and 1980s, it is also necessary to point out that from the late 1980s through 1990, public library directors reported a shortage of trained children's librarians, and some of the large city libraries had difficulty recruiting young adult librarians. At the 1986 Public Library Association convention, of the 148 vacancies advertised, 49 were for children's librarians, the largest category of vacancies ("53 applicants for 148 jobs," 1986). The labor market for librarians is subject to the same tides of the local and national economies as library budgets. This is being written during a slow recovery from a recession, and the number of jobs currently advertised for all types of librarians has been reduced over those available in 1991. On the other hand, some urban libraries continue to need children's librarians, and others have difficulty recruiting at the middle management level. Although the current labor market reflects the poor national economy, it is possible that unfilled positions have been "frozen." When the recession is over, there may again be insufficient numbers of trained youth services librarians.

The numbers tell us that there may well be a need for more youth services librarians. A recent national survey found that only 42% of the responding libraries employed someone designated to serve children (ages 0 to 14) and about half of these persons had a Master's of Library Science degree (Lewis & Farris, 1990). A similar survey found that only 11% of the public libraries had a person on staff designated to serve young adults aged 12 to 18 (National Center for Education Statistics, 1988). Whereas many libraries are too small to employ specialized staff, others may not be able to find suitable people to hire.

Numerous explanations are advanced for the shortage of trained children's and young adult librarians, and each explanation may contribute to our understanding of this challenge to public library youth services. At the gatekeeper level – education for youth services – the lack of full-time faculty may hinder recruitment. This writer has been able to identify only 23 full-time faculty with public library background teaching in the youth services area at the more than 50 accredited schools of library and information studies in the United States and Canada. In the other schools, working librarians teach the courses on a part-time basis, which results in little advisement or recruitment for the specialty. Faculties that do not include a full-time public library youth services person may lack an adequate perspective of the field, which may have consequences for the curriculum as well as for the numbers of students entering youth services.

In addition, various perceptions convey a negative image of public library youth services as a career. Residual notions from the articles about youth librarians being laid off during the recession in the 1970s may lead possible recruits to be reluctant to take jobs that may be vulnerable to reductions in force. Those who have an initial interest in the field may feel discouraged by the low salaries paid to youth services librarians. The American Library Association (ALA) salary studies indicate that children's and young adult librarians have the lowest mean salaries among librarians in public and academic libraries, whether one looks at scheduled starting salaries, posted maximum salaries, or salaries actually paid (Lynch & Myers, 1986; Lynch, Myers, & Guy, 1984). The most recent American Library Association salary study (Lynch, Myers, & Guy, 1991) indicated that children's librarians earn less than librarians in other specialties such as cataloging, reference, and collection development, and the discrepancy ranges from less than $50 per year to more than $2,000 per year, depending on the position and the size of library.

For those wishing to work with young people, school library positions may be far more attractive than public library work. School librarians frequently earn more for 9 months' work than children's librarians do for 12 months. The annual survey of recent graduates of American Library Association accredited schools found that the median annual salary of beginning school library media specialists in 1988 and 1989 was $3,000 more than the median salary of beginning public librarians in those years (Learmont & Van Houten, 1989, 1990). The most recent data suggest that things may have equalized during 1990, but entering school library media specialists still made $500 more than public librarians (Zipkowitz, 1991). In addition, school librarians know that they will receive salary increments for continuing education, whereas public librarians do not. Job conditions may also be more attractive; school librarians rarely work evenings, weekends, or summers as public librarians do. The only difference between the two specializations is that school librarians are certified as teachers as well as librarians and may have the equivalent of an additional year of education.

Another suggested reason for the unwillingness of new librarians to enter the field of youth librarianship is the low status of the specialization that the salary levels indicate. Youth librarianship shares this status with other occupations whose clients are principally children, such as day-care workers and elementary and secondary school teachers. This low status leads people to believe that it is difficult to advance within the specialty or to go into general public library administration, despite numerous outstanding examples to the contrary, such as Mary Somerville, once the coordinator of children's services for the Miami-Dade County Public Library, now that library's assistant director; Regina Minudri, a former young adult librarian who retired as director of the Berkeley (CA) Public Library; and Karen Krueger, director of the Janesville (WI) Public Library, who began her career as a children's librarian.

Additionally, it is surmised that the women's movement has encouraged women to seek vocations in fields less traditionally female than youth librarianship. Surveys of the American Library Association membership have shown that 80% of public librarians are women, but children's librarians are 97% female (Estabrook & Heim, 1980; Lynch & Myers, 1986). College-educated women have many more options than they did 15 years ago, and many of them are going into business, law, and medicine. Like elementary education, youth librarianship has to compete for the best and the brightest with other occupations with higher salaries and greater prestige. Can the public library be said to be doing its best to have a positive impact on the development of young people when it cannot attract qualified full-time staff to take charge of services to children and teenagers?

Ambivalence Toward Changing Technologies

A variety of information technologies are having a major impact on late 20th-century society. It is probably not necessary to give the reader a laundry list of these technologies; such a list might well be out of date by the time this book is published. Observers of the larger culture express various delights and concerns about the rapidity of the changes and their impacts on the ways that people work and play and view themselves. For a concise summary of the issues being debated by philosophers, psychologists, and computer scientists, the reader is invited to consult Chapter 7 of David Lyon's *The Information Society: Issues and Illusions* (1988). For our purposes, it is enough to note that all kinds of librarians are moving to incorporate technological advances into their services, but for many librarians, the changes are not entirely comfortable and they lead to much discussion over basic professional values. Two of these technologies, computers and television, will be discussed here because of their particular relevance to youth services librarians.

Computers. Ideally, computers can relieve library staffs of much of the mundane, routine clerical work required by an inventory control system, which is a major function of any public library. Furthermore, computerized information services can be faster and more accurate than manual methods, if properly designed and used. It is not surprising that librarians began using computers in the 1960s and today use both midsized computers (usually called minicomputers) and microcomputers. Most of the largest public libraries are automated (F.R. Bridge, personal communication, January 3, 1992). Yet, computers are still not employed in all libraries because of various obstacles. The expense of installing and maintaining an automated system using a minicomputer may squeeze other areas of library budgets, but librarians also feel some necessity to automate because of competition from other information providers, especially the commercial database services, such as DIALOG. There is also an urgency to automate because of increased circulation combined with pressure to avoid staff increases. Bridge, who writes an annual update on library automation for the *Library Journal*, also noted that librarians may feel compelled to automate simply to maintain the appearance of being an up-to-date public library (personal communication, January 3, 1992).

Therefore, computers are attractive to many librarians, and the professional journals are full of articles and advertisements about computer products and services. However, minicomputers continue to be relatively expensive (about $100,000 for a small 8-terminal system), and the number of public libraries that have purchased them is relatively small. By the end of 1990, library automation vendors had sold approximately 700 minicomputer-based systems to public libraries in the United States. These figures do not include microcomputer systems or systems designed inhouse, nor do they indicate how many of these systems went to multilibrary cooperatives. Bridge estimated that perhaps as many as 10,000 microcomputer-based library systems have been sold to public libraries (personal communication, January 3, 1992), indicating that approximately 5,000 to 8,000 of the nation's 16,000 to 19,000 public libraries are not yet automated.

For those libraries that have automated, the budget consequences can be considerable, and both positive and negative. There is only anecdotal evidence to suggest what the costs and benefits may be. On the negative side, there may be a tendency for library directors to concentrate on automation to the exclusion of concern for public services. Ideally, the addition of computer technology should allow public libraries to serve more people more accurately and faster; however, much of the attention seems to be on internal library processes, rather than public service. In an interview with the author, Collin Clark of the California State Library commented in July 1984 that recent requests for federal Library Services and Construction Act (LSCA) funds were most often for computer conversion of library records and microcomputer projects, rather than for extending service to underserved groups, which had been the original purpose of the LSCA. Two other consultants at the California State Library, who were in touch with many library directors in the state, felt that library directors in general were less interested in public service than they had been in the 1970s (John Amend, personal communication, August 9, 1984; Cy Silver, personal communication, July 18, 1984).

Library directors may continue to have their attention focused on technology and away from services because computer technology is notorious for needing constant upgrades and adaptations to new means of communication and information storage, CD-ROM being one recent example and connection to the Internet another. Of the four libraries in the author's case study research, three of them were facing computer expansion in 1989. One library was planning its third integrated automated system, and the other two were preparing for their second systems since 1984 and 1985, respectively (Willett, 1992).

This could have deleterious consequences for youth services as well as service to other groups. At this time there seems to be only anecdotal evidence of the impact of the cost of computerization. One California library did not replace the coordinator of young adult services when she resigned, using the salary savings to help pay for computerization (John Kallenberg, personal communication, 1984). On the other hand, another California library found that computerization saved staff time so that clerical workers could be reassigned and branch libraries could be open longer hours (Willett, 1987), which would have had beneficial consequences for the entire community.

At those libraries that have minicomputers, children may have little access to them or may not benefit from them. Whereas some of the computerized systems for purchasing, cataloging, and checking out materials have indirect benefits for children, the change that is most immediate to library users is the online public access catalog that has replaced the card catalog in a number of libraries. Some libraries have included the children's and young adult collections in their online catalogs, but most systems were not designed for use specifically by young people. A study at an Illinois public library looked at the use of an online catalog by fourth-, sixth-, and eighth-grade students and tentatively concluded that the online system used there was developmentally inappropriate for these students and librarians needed to be ready to help young people use the catalog (Edmonds, 1987; Edmonds, Moore, & Balcom, 1990). The new Kid's Catalog interface, discussed later, may radically improve the online catalog situation for children.

When we consider microcomputers, a quite different problem appears. Micros are relatively inexpensive and children are being trained to use them as readily as the telephone. By Fall 1985, 92.2% of all public schools, 82.9% of Catholic schools, and 61.9% of other private schools owned microcomputers (Snyder, 1987). Of course, having them in the schools does not mean all children use computers. In 1989, it was estimated that 46% of children aged 3 to 17 used a computer at school, with the greatest use by 9- to 12-year-olds, about 60% of whom used a computer at school (Kominski, 1991). The 1989 study also found that

24.2% of 3- to 17-year-olds lived in a home furnished with a computer. The 1989 study confirmed earlier reports that family income, householder's education, and race are related to home computer ownership; children in white families with college-educated parents who earned middle-class incomes were more likely to have access to a home computer than other children. Schools, both public and private, help to equalize the disparity. For many young people, computers are familiar tools. And they can serve the public library's goals as well as the school's.

Public access microcomputers can be used for reading readiness software for preschoolers, educational and games software for older children, and word processing and bulletin boards for teenagers, as well as for access to library materials through an online catalog. Other applications of electronic technology appropriate for youth services include the careers database and the INFOTRAC index to magazine articles that are of interest to teenagers. There are a few CD-ROM products of use to children, and Internet access for children and young adults will continue to expand. It has to be pointed out that these services are also of interest to adults and were not designed with young people in mind. Such uses of computer technology undoubtedly support development in a number of ways, but few libraries have micros available for public use. A survey completed in 1984 found that out of 19,191 public libraries (this number includes main libraries and branches), 4,990 owned microcomputers (Avallone, 1985). A more recent national survey (Lewis & Farris, 1990) found that of the 820 responding libraries, only 28% made personal computers available to the public and 26% made software available. Of those libraries with microcomputers, 88% allowed at least some children (ages 14 and under) to use the microcomputers and software.

Because microcomputers can also be used for library administration functions such as inventory control and catalog access in small libraries, their familiarity to children and teenagers, as well as adults, makes them doubly attractive options. In regards to cataloging information, the same situation occurs with microcomputers as with minicomputers: Unless the library staff has the expertise in cataloging, computers, and child development to design homemade catalogs and databases, librarians must make do with the programs available on the market. At the time this was written, only one online catalog program specifically for children was available for purchase. Some school librarians report that a number of the general catalog programs for microcomputers work quite well with elementary children (Neah Lohr, personal communication, February 13, 1992). However, in systematic observational research of one of these systems, Solomon (1991) found that elementary school students were unsuccessful at 34% of their attempts to use the online catalog. Most of the problems were the result of the system not being capable of making allowances for children's less-than-perfect knowledge and skills.

Slowly this may change. Research being conducted at the University of California at Los Angeles using Apple Macintosh hardware and Hypercard software shows promise of developing an online catalog that is truly appropriate for children (Walter & Borgman, 1991). This catalog is being designed by university researchers, not corporate engineers. Information from this project and further qualitative research with children at the Denver Public Library resulted in CARL Systems, Inc.'s Kid's Catalog, which became available in late 1992 (Pam Sandlian, personal communication, March 8, 1993). The Kid's Catalog is an interface designed to allow children access to the main catalog in ways that they can understand and physically manipulate, using mouse technology and graphic images as well as print.

Because it is built to NISO's standard for command language, the Kid's Catalog may be usable on more than one kind of system. Although manufacturers have recognized the size of the potential market for software for young people, it has taken a long while for them to realize that elementary schools and public libraries may be a very large market for child-friendly catalog programs and information databases. It is too soon to tell how successful the Kid's Catalog will become, but it is certainly a step toward filling a major gap.

Even as one applauds the appearance of the Kid's Catalog, the potential impact of computerization raises issues of possible loss of funds due to diversion to purchasing computer equipment, the evidence that few available systems are designed to accommodate children's developing capacities, and equity issues around access to computer services for young people in poverty areas such as inner cities and rural communities. A further potential problem has to do with the public library's image. If young people become accustomed to using computers in everyday life, will uncomputerized libraries seem to be a viable part of the real world?

Television.   Another technology that has changed the lives of children and is of major concern to librarians is television, in both broadcast and videocassette forms. Since its introduction in the 1950s, television has been the object of intense scrutiny and comment. Popular opinion deplores the quality of the shows, yet few homes are without a television set, and the number of homes with videocassette recorders (VCRs) grows daily. Parents, teachers, and librarians are concerned about the relationship between television viewing and various intellectual, physical, and social skills. For our purposes, the relationship between watching television and reading ability is the most salient issue to examine, if we take as a given that librarians remain dedicated "people of the book." Following the lead of such antitelevision writers as Neil Postman and Marie Winn, children's librarians encourage parents to restrict children's access to television and sponsor community-wide television turn-off days. For example, the Minnesota Library Association published a bibliography called *TV: Beware! A List of Sources on Taming the One-Eyed Monster* (Dodge, 1989).

Unfortunately for librarians, most of what is written in the popular press about children and television is not grounded in the research on the topic, is inadequately supported, or is oversimplified (D.R. Anderson & Collins, 1988). What follows is a summary of what is known about the relationship of television and reading. Researchers are not entirely certain about the nature of the relationship, but they do agree that television viewing is correlated with reading in a complex way (Beentjes & Van der Voort, 1988; Gerbner, Gross, Morgan, & Signorielli, 1984; Neuman, 1984, 1988; Reinking & Wu, 1990). One of the issues is that television viewing may occupy time that the child would otherwise spend reading. A second issue is whether reading achievement is influenced by the amount of television a child watches.

Because reading is a set of skills that require much practice in order to acquire facility, the popular notion is that television viewing diminishes reading skills by competing with the time children have for leisure reading. According to figures produced by the A.C. Nielsen Company using their "people meter" equipment, the average child aged 2 to 11 spent 3 hours and 20 minutes per day watching television in 1990 (Television Bureau of Advertising, 1991, February). Teenagers aged 12 to 17 spent slightly less of their daily schedule in front of the television, 3 hours and 15 minutes. Neuman (1988) and other studies corroborated the finding that teens spend less time watching television. Many people think this is a lot of time in front of the television set, but persons over 18 actually spent more time watching television than younger people, according to Nielsen. Men over 18 spent 3 hours and 51 minutes, women over 18, 4 hours and 28 minutes. These figures include broadcast television and cable, but not use of videocassettes, apparently.

Measuring the time children spend reading is more difficult, because there are no practical ways of unobtrusively observing children's leisure reading. The earliest studies of television's impact on amount of reading found little change in book reading (Himmelweit, Oppenheim, & Vince, 1958; Schramm, Lyle, & Parker, 1961). Studies using the most reliable methods in which children keep daily time-use diaries estimate that the average fifth-grade child spends no more than 15 minutes per day reading materials other than school textbooks (R.C. Anderson, Wilson, & Fielding, 1986; Greaney, 1980). However, there is wide variation among children: Some do no leisure reading, others read for more than an hour per day.

Although television viewing and leisure reading occupy such differing amounts of time in the lives of most children, there seems to be little evidence that children would spend more time reading books if they spent less time watching television (R.C. Anderson, Wilson, & Fielding, 1986; Greaney, 1980; Neuman, 1988) In fact, R.C. Anderson, Wilson, and Fielding stated, "there was no strong evidence that any out-of-school activity interfered with book reading" (1986, p. 20). Major reviews of the research on television and cognitive development conclude that television seems to have displaced comic book reading, listening to the radio, going to the movies, and participation in outdoor activities with only a small displacement of reading and homework (D.R. Anderson & Collins, 1988; Beentjes & Van der Voort, 1988). Neuman (1988) believed her findings indicated that television and reading gratify different needs and one is not a substitute for the other. Furthermore, the *perceived* difficulty of reading compared with watching television may influence children's choice of activities, despite the fact that the cognitive skills required for each activity are very similar.

On the other hand, broadcast dramatizations of books do lead some viewers to read the books, which is the rationale for public television's "Reading Rainbow" program for children. Some teachers use television to teach the concepts of narrative structure, which can then be applied to stories in print (Greenfield, 1984; Himmelweit, Oppenheim, & Vince, 1958). However, Beentjes and Van der Voort (1988) pointed out that there is no evidence that being influenced to read a particular book after seeing a televised version of it leads to increased reading in general. And Neuman (1988) reminded us that we do not really know whether televised narrative structures are the same as those in print stories.

The second question that is asked about television and reading—what is the relationship between viewing and reading achievement—seems to have an even more complicated and as yet incomplete answer (D.R. Anderson & Collins, 1988; Beentjes & Van der Voort, 1988). The National Assessment of Educational Progress (NAEP) for 1970-1971, 1979-1980, 1983-1984, and 1987-1988 associated higher levels of daily television viewing with lower scores in reading proficiency and other areas of scholastic achievement (Snyder & Hoffman, 1990). More sophisticated statistical techniques have found that the relationship is actually a curvilinear one, not a linear relationship. That is, television viewing may be helpful to students of lower ability and harmful to more capable students. For example, Gerbner, Gross, Morgan, and Signorielli

(1984) found that low-ability children who were heavy television viewers scored *higher* on reading comprehension than low-ability children who watched low levels of television. However, high-ability children who were heavy television viewers scored *lower* than their peers who watched less television.

The reading skills of children in lower socioeconomic groups also may benefit from a moderate amount of television (not more than 4 hours per day) because it may give them knowledge of the world not available in their home environments (Neuman, 1988; Reinking & Wu, 1990). In fact, Neuman (1988) found that children who watched 2 hours of television per day had slightly higher reading achievement scores than those who watched no television. Greenfield (1984) also cited research showing that young children's learning about dynamic processes, such as growth, is facilitated by the use of television because moving visual images are more concrete than verbal explanations.

Because most studies are correlational, it is possible that high levels of television viewing and low reading scores are themselves caused or affected by other variables. Researchers have suggested a lengthy list of possibilities, including IQ, age, socioeconomic status, personality, media availability, gender, and home environment factors such as parental encouragement, parental education, parental attitudes toward television and reading, and the degree to which children are permitted to explore the world outside the home (Neuman, 1986; Reinking & Wu, 1990). According to the NAEP, parental education and owning a variety of reading materials correlate positively with children's reading achievement. Other factors that might have an impact on the relationship between reading and television include the form and content of programs watched, teachers' beliefs about television, how much attention is paid to the television, whether other activities are occurring while the television is on, and interaction with other people while watching (Beentjes & Van der Voort, 1988; Neuman, 1988; Reinking & Wu, 1990).

Television per se is neither good nor bad; its value depends on the qualities of particular shows and how they are viewed (Greenfield, 1984), yet there are few studies that try to assess the impact of the content or form of television watched on reading achievement. Furthermore, the characteristics of the viewer must also be taken into account. For example, studies in which IQ is controlled usually find that the negative impact of television viewing on reading achievement becomes statistically insignificant.

Although librarians continue, possibly mistakenly, to deplore television viewing and its supposed effects on young people's reading habits and skills, they have also responded to the popular demand for visual entertainment and information by providing collections of videocassettes. By the end of 1989, 85% of public libraries serving populations of 25,000 or more were circulating videocassettes. At some libraries, videocassettes accounted for 20% of the circulation, with one library in Michigan claiming that videos were 43% of the circulation (Pitman, 1990). The American Library Association has entered into two large grant projects with the Carnegie Corporation to provide quality videos to public libraries, one of which was specifically for children's videos. In 1991, the Association for Library Service to Children (ALSC) awarded the first Carnegie Medal for excellence in children's video, elevating video to the same status accorded to children's books, for which the ALSC awards the Newbery and Caldecott Medals. Clearly, many, if not most, public librarians have accepted videocassettes as legitimate library materials.

The question of the perceived value of print vs. video has not been faced openly, however. Pitman (1990) commented, "The 1990s may see shifts that will challenge the philosophical bedrock of public libraries" (p. 249). Despite the apparent acceptance of video, rarely is the audiovisual budget as large as the budget for print materials, and the audiovisual budget is susceptible to cuts in fiscal crises. In case studies of three libraries affected by Proposition 13, Willett (1987) found that the audiovisual budgets were one of the first areas cut. Shoham (1984) reported similar findings in six other California libraries.

The only statewide studies of expenditures for children's materials that requested information about audiovisual purchases are relatively old, but they reveal that the proportions of money spent on audiovisuals for children were quite small at the time the surveys were taken (Grover & Moore, ca. 1981; Richardson, 1978; Wisconsin Department of Public Instruction, 1981). A more recent study in New Jersey found that multimedia collections for children could be rated "strong" because 100% of the libraries owned records, 70% had audiocassettes and filmstrips, 50% had toys, and 40% had computer software for children (Razzano, 1986a).

The most recent national information about the availability of non-print materials for children is contained in Lewis and Farris (1990). This survey found that 65% of the libraries made videocassettes available for use or circulation, but 44% of them did not make videocassettes available to any children 14 or under, which means that at those libraries, only adults could check out videos made specifically for children. A number of librarians commented that videocassettes were too expensive to trust to children, an argument that is losing force as many videos for children are now quite comparable in price to four-color picture books that often cost $15 apiece. In contrast, of the 79% of libraries that made audiocassettes available, 86% allowed children to use them. Nothing is said about the number of items or the quality or usefulness of the materials.

Collections for young adults appear to be more limited to print materials than children's collections. Of the 794 libraries that responded to the National Center for Education Statistics (1988) national survey of young adult services, 84% owned collections of materials designated for young adults (defined as 12-18-year-olds). However, 91% of the average collection consisted of books and only 3% of the collection was audio-visuals. Razzano's (1986b) study in New Jersey found that 60% of the libraries owned records for teens and 50% had audiocassettes, but her study did not indicate the proportion of the collections devoted to such materials. Neither of these surveys collected information about circulation policies regarding young adult access to audiovisuals, but in some libraries persons under 18 are not allowed to check them out. These restrictions, combined with the relatively small proportion of budget support for audiovisuals, give us reason to be concerned that public libraries are not "keeping up with the times" when it comes to the changes in communication media that affect young people.

The message given seems to be a double one: Don't watch television, but if you cannot help it, we will provide you with "the best" things to watch. The arguments about television are reminiscent of arguments about the place of novels in public libraries in the latter part of the 19th century, when librarians debated whether adults, let alone children, should have the fiction that they so frequently requested. Mark West (1988) showed how elements of society that consider themselves elite (including librarians) have attacked popular mass media for more than a century in the United States. Television and its companion, video games, are only the latest in a long line of popular entertainments (such as dime novels and comic books) to receive the opprobrium of those who believe they know best for other people. No doubt the critics will attack virtual reality entertainment as it becomes more available.

Demographic Changes

At least three aspects of American demography have implications for public libraries: the increase in working mothers, the decreasing proportion of children, and the increasing proportion of ethnic and racial minorities. Of these three factors, working mothers have had the most immediate impact on youth librarians. In 1970, 38.8% of children under 18 had a working mother (Bureau of Labor Statistics, 1989). In 1990, 56.6% of children under 6 lived in a household in which all resident parents were in the labor force (Children's Defense Fund, 1992). While mothers work, their preschool children are in some kind of childcare arrangement, whether it is a preschool, a day-care center, a family day-care situation, or in the care of relatives. School-age children may be in after-school care or left on their own—the latter are sometimes called latchkey children. These changed conditions require some changes in patterns of library services for preschoolers and elementary school children because parents are not available to bring children to the library at the times they once did.

Public librarians have adjusted to the situation by adapting their strategies for reaching preschool children. Because many mothers are no longer available to bring children individually to the library, children are bused in groups to the library or library staff travels to the day-care center or preschool. There is an advantage to this in that the librarian may be able to influence more (and different) children and their caregivers than would have come to the library in the past. However, the librarian may not have as much contact with parents of preschoolers. If public education expands to include 4-year-olds, the public librarian's strategy will have to change yet again.

The situation with latchkey children seems to be more ambivalent. U.S. Census Bureau reports vary on the percentage of school-age children lacking adult supervision before and/or after school. In a 1984 study, 7.2% of children aged 5 to 13 were without supervision after school (Bruno, 1987). According to a study in 1987, 22% of children aged 5 to 14 cared for themselves after school (U.S. Bureau of the Census, 1990). Other researchers report up to 45% of all elementary school children spend some part of their day in self-care (Dowd, 1991). Undoubtedly, the problems associated with collecting the data affect their accuracy; that is, parents may say they are caring for a child when the contact is only by telephone or parents may be unwilling to admit a child is home alone, either for the child's safety or to avoid the legal problems of being open to a charge of child neglect. Nevertheless, somewhere between 2.9 and 15 million school-age children are without supervision when school lets out (Dowd, 1991).

Because children come to public library children's areas in great numbers after school, many children's librarians believe that some parents use the public library for free childcare. Sometimes they have anecdotal evidence in the child who stays at the library's front door after closing time, saying, "My mother told me to wait here until she came to pick me up." In 1988, a survey of public libraries serving populations of 100,000 or more attempted to give dimension to the situation. Of the 91 respondents, 69 (75.8%) reported unattended children using the library on weekdays and 45 (49.5%) reported unattended children in the library on weekends. More than half of the libraries reported that the presence of unattended children resulted in difficulty in serving other patrons, vandalism, disturbances due to inappropriate behavior, complaints from other patrons, limited seating, and delays at closing time. The problems Dowd's respondents described suggest that the librarians had defined inappropriate library use but may have needed behavior management training. Librarians at 63 libraries said they felt unsure how best to serve the latchkey child (Dowd, 1989).

Dowd repeated her survey in 1990, using a different sample of libraries serving 100,000 or more people. Virtually all of the 110 responding librarians reported unattended children using the library after school or on weekends, and most reported that this use had an impact on services and personnel. Only 20% regarded the impact as "high," however. Adverse impacts similar to those reported in the earlier survey were reported again: delays at closing, need for increased security, medical or legal problems, and need to reallocate staff to cover the after-school hours. Most of the respondents reported that the number of unattended children was not increasing; 15% reported increasing numbers of latchkey children, and 15% reported decreasing numbers. The attention paid to the issue in the professional literature and the professional associations seems to have helped librarians cope with the situation: 78% felt competent to handle latchkey children (Dowd, 1991). In addition, Dowd found and described several successful after-school programs established by public libraries in different areas of the country.

Dowd's groundbreaking research seems to indicate that after-school use of public libraries by unattended children is a common national phenomenon. On the other hand, the fact that using the public library is voluntary obscures the issue. Aside from shopping malls, fast food restaurants, and parks, the public library is one of the few places that children may visit without adult escort, and youngsters may come and go when they desire. This fact makes it difficult to sort out how many children are using the public library as after-school childcare—that is, have no one to go home to—and how many are in the library after school because they want to be there, whether or not there is an adult at home. Dowd did not clearly separate these two types of after-school child patrons.

In one of my California case study libraries, I found that the children's librarian, noting the large numbers of children in the library after school, began making a point of being in the children's room at that time to provide reference assistance and occasional activities. For several months she kept attendance, and all through the period that she was available in the room, more and more children came to the library after school. This probably does not mean that the number of unattended children increased in her town. It most likely means that when the children's librarian paid attention to the children, they wanted to come to the library and they brought their friends.

The libraries in Dowd's studies represented 42 states and the District of Columbia, but it is difficult to determine if the results apply to smaller libraries in suburban and rural settings as well as cities. The studies do not tell us if the situation is actually more difficult than it was in the 1970s or if it is any different from the situation during the baby boom. The library literature of the 1960s is replete with reports by librarians feeling overwhelmed by the number of children and adolescents using the library. The current situation could be the result of the echo of the baby boom; it could be the result of the libraries having done a successful job of promoting themselves; it could actually be that parents do find the public library a safe, appropriate place for after-school care; it could be some combination of these factors or even none of them.

A third aspect of the impact of working parents has to do with library hours. Librarians like to encourage parents to accompany their children to the library, but library hours may be inconvenient for parents who work full time. Conventional hours at central libraries tend to be 9:00 a.m. to 9:00 p.m. Monday through Thursday, and 9:00 a.m. to 5:00 p.m. on Friday and Saturday. There is wide variation, however. Many small town libraries are open only 2 or 3 days per week and may have no evening or weekend hours at all. Branch libraries in cities and suburbs usually have shorter hours than central libraries. There are situations in which the children's room is closed when the rest of the library is open in the evening. Thus the library loses potential users: parents and children, but also working adults who do not have children. A few libraries are open on Sundays, but only a few. A national survey of public libraries found that only 7.5% of public libraries were open 7 days per week (Public Library Association, 1985). Common sense suggests that a library that is not available at times and for purposes useful to its constituents can have little impact on children, youth, or adults.

The second demographic trend that has implications for youth services is the decreasing proportion of children in the United States. The median age of the population has been increasing for nearly 200 years, with the exception of the baby boom, as the birthrate has fallen and life expectancy has risen (Pifer & Bronte, 1986). The U.S. Bureau of the Census projections for the next 100 years show that this trend may continue until the under-18 population, which represented 25.57% of the whole in 1990, is 20.3% in 2080. In comparison, the over-65 population will rise to 23.5% in 2080 from 11.3% in 1980 (Bogue, 1985; Spencer, 1984; U.S. Bureau of the Census, 1992). Many observers speculate that this could lead to age polarization in the competition for scarce resources.

In 1990 the Bureau of the Census estimated that only 37% of United States households included children under 18. Because young people do not vote but the elderly do, and because fewer and fewer adults are parents who can represent the interests of children and teenagers, young people's needs may be given short shrift by policymakers and voters. Richman and Stagner (1986) indicated this has begun to happen, pointing to a lack of a national day-care policy, declining support for public education among elderly voters, and diminishing support for children in poverty. Other observers believe that interest in education and children's issues is increasing since the 1988 presidential campaign and former President Bush's promise to be the "Education President." Whether children's issues are being ignored or promoted, library services to young people cannot avoid the challenges of the changing proportions of age groups. At least one article (Falcigno & Guynup, 1984) appeared in the library press suggesting that public libraries need not pay as much attention to youth services in the future as they presently do. Interestingly, as the proportion of children in the population has dropped, the circulation of children's materials has risen. C. Palmer (1991) reported that children's materials accounted for 37% of total circulation in 1990, up from 31% in 1980, and the median circulation of children's materials increased by 68% since 1980, based on a national sample of public libraries serving over 25,000 persons. Unfortunately, we do not have information on the circulation that can be attributed to young adult use of the public library.

The third aspect of our changing demographics is the growing presence of racial and ethnic minorities as a proportion of total population and the youth population. By 1990 24.4% of the U.S. population belonged to a minority group (U.S. Bureau of the Census, 1992), and by 2080 50% of the population may be minorities (Usdan, 1984). Already minority children account for more than 40% of the school-age population in California, New Mexico, and Texas (Usdan, 1984). Owing to their high birthrates, Hispanics and African Americans are becoming major segments of the population. In fact, the Hispanic population is expected to double between 1985 and 2020 because of its high birth and immigration rates (Exter, 1987). Both of these groups will have high proportions of young people. By 2010, approximately 26% of the total population will be under 20, but 32% of the African-American population and 36% of the Hispanic population will be under 20 (Bogue, 1985; Exter, 1987). The phenomenon will not affect all areas of the United States equally. Minority birth rates and white flight will affect urban areas more than other areas.

The problems public libraries may experience as a result of these trends are twofold; both stem from the library's image as a white, middle-class institution. First, the public library may lose some public support because the two fastest growing groups, blacks and Hispanics, are not well represented among the middle class, the class that supports the public library. Both of these groups have generally lower incomes and education levels than the usual public library clientele, although these levels are expected to increase gradually over the next 50 years (Gibson, 1986; Torres-Gil, 1986). If the large cities become pockets of poor, undereducated people, urban libraries might be adversely affected if city governments have financial difficulties. Second, by and large, the staff, materials, and services of the public library have been tailored to the interests and demands of a white middle-class clientele. This has come about because the white middle class is most active in support of the library, provides most of the staff of the public library, and controls most of the publication and communication industry, making it difficult to find minority staff and materials appropriate to other cultural groups.

For instance, the proportion of librarians who belong to minority groups is smaller than their representation in the general population (Estabrook & Heim, 1980). Though no figures are available for the racial composition of youth librarians, within the past decade, most of the prominent African-American children's librarians have retired, and only a few younger ones have come forward to take their places. Hispanic and Asian librarians are similarly few in number. Library education does not seem to have recruited minorities to the profession, either; of those who graduated from library school in 1988, only 6.2% belonged to one of the four minority groups (Moen & Heim, 1988). In addition, minority group members are underrepresented among the authors, publishers, and producers of media for children (Children's Television Workshop may be the exception). Horning and Kruse of the Cooperative Children's Book Center of Madison, Wisconsin, found that of the approximately 2,500 trade children's books published in 1986 in the United States, only 18 were by African-American authors. In 1987, about 3,000 trade children's books were published and 30 were by African Americans. In 1988, 38 children's books by African Americans were published. In 1989, 4,000 books were published for children and 48 were by African-American authors and illustrators. The trend continued in 1990, when approximately 5,000 new titles were published for children and 51 were by African-American authors and illustrators (Horning & Kruse, 1989, 1990; Horning, Kruse, & Lindgren, 1991). Even fewer children's authors or illustrators of Hispanic, Asian, or Native American descent are published.

For youth services, the demographic challenge is to maintain their visibility as legitimate parts of the public library while adjusting to changes in family life, age structure, and racial/ethnic composition of the population. Not only does this mean adjusting library hours, it also means that new materials and modes of services must be introduced to fit varying cultural expectations.

Education and Literacy

Public librarians consider themselves to be part of the educational system. Of the four major missions of the public library (education, information, recreation, and culture), education is the one most often cited by librarians as justifying the existence of the library. There is some support for the notion. Every court that has ever had to decide if the public library is an educational institution has found that the public library *is* an educational institution (Terrie & Summers, 1987). In many states, though not in all, state-level responsibility for public libraries resides in the state department of public instruction. In the federal government, library programs are administered through the Department of Education. However, there is evidence that teachers and other educators do not consider the public library part of the educational system.

When *A Nation at Risk* (National Commission on Excellence in Education, 1983) was published, it added to a national debate about the state of educational achievement in this country. The Commission compared achievement test scores in the United States with those in other industrialized nations and found the comparison unfavorable. It estimated that functional illiteracy affected 23 million adults and 13% of 17-year-olds, with higher rates among minorities (National Commission on Excellence in Education, 1983). Various reforms were proposed and debated by the educational community, but few of the proposals mentioned the role of library services for young people, neither school library media centers nor public libraries. *A Nation at Risk* and other official statements on education merely indicate that the library is a source of books and ignore the use of other media and the expertise of librarians (Commission on Reading, 1985; National Commission on Excellence in Education, 1983; U.S. Department of Education, 1986).

Clearly the education establishment does not see the public library as an educational institution. White (1983), an economist, believed that the general adult public does not see the public library as a source of education by the way that it uses the library as a source of entertainment materials. Nevertheless, there are at least three general ways in which public libraries theoretically contribute to the formal education of children and teenagers in the United States: prevention of illiteracy, support for school curricula, and support of home schooling. It is not only the library's collections that potentially contribute to education but also the skill and knowledge of library staff in matching materials to needs and interests.

Unfortunately, public librarians have made few attempts to demonstrate the educational outcomes of what they do, partly because of a strong ethic against prying into and judging individual uses of library materials. As a practical matter, it is difficult to sort out the effects of library use when people have access to many sources of education and information: television, newspapers and magazines, videocassettes, bookstores, radio, movies, computer discussion groups, other people, and their own experiences, to name the most obvious. In consequence, much of library research has been descriptive, enumerating and describing library programs. For example, two studies of public library adult literacy projects have taken this approach (Terrie & Summers, 1987; Zweizig, Johnson, & Robbins, 1990), though Zweizig, Johnson, and Robbins attempted to analyze the projects to determine what factors aided success. In the case of youth services, we have only limited data on the educational impact of public libraries on young people, which are presented in the chapter on education. If it could be shown that the public library has positive effects on children's reading and other media skills and the prevention of adult illiteracy, the political, social, and economic justification for the public library would be stronger.

Acceptance of Young Adult Services

The challenges discussed thus far have applied variously to both children's services and services for young adults. Children's services have one advantage that young adult services do not: Despite the challenges to children's services, they are more generally accepted as a legitimate function of public libraries. National surveys show that 42% of public libraries have a staff member designated to serve children, but only 11% have a staff member who serves young adults, in spite of the fact that 25% of public library patrons are between the ages of 12 and 18 (Lewis & Farris, 1990; National Center for Education Statistics, 1988). During the fiscal crises of the 1970s and 1980s, many of the supervisory and leadership positions in public library young adult services were dropped, and they have not been reinstated. The numbers of young adult librarians have shrunk so drastically that the Young Adult Library Services Association, a division of the American Library Association, has come perilously close to disappearing because its membership has, in recent times, been almost too small to maintain its status within the ALA (Flum, 1988). The organization has been sustained by its secondary school librarian members.

Young adult librarians place the responsibility for the situation on the value that society has for teenagers, or rather, on the lack of value for teenagers. Children, though not valued as highly as adults, as noted earlier, are at least considered lovable, worth helping on humanitarian grounds, and "politically correct." Teenagers, however, "are often viewed narrowly and with revulsion and are only seen as noisy sarcastic creatures filled with an abundance of sexual energy" (Flum, 1988, p. 4). They do not vote or pay property taxes, and it may seem safe to pay little attention to their needs or interests.

A Delphi study conducted in 1978 gave evidence of public library directors' ambivalence toward services to young adults: 81% of the respondents thought it desirable to continue and expand services to young adults, but only 41% thought it was likely that the services would continue and expand (Downen, 1979). Because the directors in the study were in a position to affect continuation and expansion of services to young adults, the study may have become a self-fulfilling prophecy. Young adult librarians do not feel the situation has changed in the past few years. In a 1992 survey of the Young Adult Library Services Association members, 35% of respondents to an open-ended question about the most critical needs of young adult services cited lack of recognition by library administrators, staff, and the community as a pressing need, and 45.6% said money (Young Adult Library Services Association, ca. 1992).

In my own view, lack of understanding of adolescent development on the part of the general adult population, and library staff in particular, contributes to a belief that teenagers do not need specialized public library services. Either they are viewed as an abnormal "problem" population, rife with crime, drug abuse, pregnancy, illiteracy, truancy, and unemployment, or they are seen as needing the same kinds of services provided to adults with the same kind of staff provided for adults. Depending on the view subscribed to, library staff may feel anxious to control teenagers on the one hand or complacent about the value of services given on the other. In either case, adults miss seeing adolescents as individuals moving through a particular time in their lives, a time that has its own pace and requirements. Unless librarians recognize their needs and treat teens with respect and sympathy (and firm expectations about behavior), they are unlikely to enhance adolescent development.

SUMMARY

In 1950, when the results of a major national study of public libraries were published, children's services were called "the classic success of the public library" (R.D. Leigh, 1950, p. 100). So successful, apparently, that they merited little specific attention in the study itself, and services for young adults were not given separate attention. Today, even that nominal success is being challenged by changes and new situations in the public library's external environment. Taxpayers are reluctant to increase funding even as costs rise. The costs and problems of introducing technology into the library, even as that technology provides competition for the library's products and services, has deflected attention from public services. Library collections remain overwhelmingly print oriented as the society increasingly uses audiovisual and electronic sources of information and recreation. People who might once have entered the field of children's librarianship are not attracted to it, and only the largest libraries provide staff designated to serve teenagers.

Meanwhile, the library has responded only partially to the changes in the American family and is only beginning to prepare to serve an increasing minority population. Neither the general public nor professional educators are convinced that the public library has an important role in educating children, teenagers, or adults. In addition, internal constraints in the form of low salaries for youth services librarians and lack of acceptance of young adult services continue to challenge those who provide public library services to young people.

Children's librarians and young adult librarians are often urged to analyze and evaluate their services in order to demonstrate their value and their effectiveness (Chelton, 1987; Flum, 1988; Robbins, Willett, Wiseman, & Zweizig, 1990). Evaluations of a specific institution may have an important impact on that library but tell us little about the ability of public libraries to meet the goals of service to young people. For that reason, a comprehensive review is indicated to assess the contributions of youth services to the development of children.

Because youth librarianship is just beginning to be researched, it is necessary to look for assistance with these issues from other fields. In the following chapters, evidence from child development, education, and economics, as well as from librarianship, is applied for its possible usefulness to the issues facing youth librarianship. The history of youth services will aid our understanding of the changing values expressed by those who developed the services. Enhancing child development, providing and supporting education, meeting the criteria of microeconomic theory, and supporting appropriate social values will be important criteria in judging current policies and in recommending policy changes.

CHAPTER 2

Relevant Concepts From the Field of Child Development

INTRODUCTION

The study of child development is rich with theories and research approaches. Zigler and Finn-Stevenson (1987) noted two general categories of theories—epigenetic and environmental—and four major theories—psychoanalytic, psychosocial, cognitive-developmental, and social learning. It would be impossible within the scope of this chapter to do justice to all of these theories, though research contributions from each of these points of view have produced information useful to anyone living or working with children. However, librarians see themselves as providing an environment that stimulates the child's developing cognitive abilities through oral, print, and graphic media. Therefore, it is most salient to consider the evidence that relates to environmental factors in cognitive development, particularly the development of language. Where appropriate, information regarding social and physical development is brought in, too, but most of the following discussion presents Jean Piaget's theory of cognitive development. It is based on information easily found in standard textbooks on the subject, such as Zigler and Finn-Stevenson (1987). Social cognitive theory is discussed in Chapter 3.

COGNITIVE DEVELOPMENT AND LANGUAGE

Although later researchers have criticized and modified some specifics of his work, Piaget's theory of the cognitive development of children continues to be widely influential. Piaget believed that the nature of children's thinking differed from that of adults. It was not merely that children had less experience and knowledge than adults that made them different, but that their cognitive processes worked on different principles of order. Piaget described a sequence of development leading to the achievement of adult ways of thinking. His four basic stages are the following:

1. Sensorimotor (ages birth to approximately age 2)
2. Preoperations (approximately ages 2 to 7)
3. Concrete operations (approximately ages 7 to 12)
4. Formal operations (approximately ages 12 to adulthood)

Not all child development theorists agree that there are stages in children's development. Some believe that development is gradual and stages cannot be easily defined and that the notion of stages masks the importance of an individual's abilities as they contribute to one's development. For purposes of discussion, however, it is helpful to demarcate periods of development.

In the sensorimotor stage, children learn through sensory perception; that is, through touch, taste, feel, smell, vision, and hearing, and through movement. In Piaget's view, touch and movement are particularly important. The child begins to differentiate its perceptions of the world and itself into mental patterns through a cycle of experience and assimilation, initially through reflex actions, which are gradually replaced by purposeful activity. For example, the infant "experiments" with objects, grasping them, putting them into its mouth, or throwing them in different directions to see what happens (Piaget, 1967).

The development of language begins at birth with the child's attention to the speech of the adults around it. Language development continues with the appearance of babbling at about the age of 6 months. At 12 months the child may be using single words and at 24 months, at the end of the sensorimotor stage, the child may speak in sentences of two or three words (nouns, verbs, and adjectives only). Encouragement and reinforcement from the young child's parents and other adults is extremely important at this stage. Although children do not merely imitate or parrot adults, they do learn through interacting verbally with them. The child's ability to retain a mental image of objects and events has also developed by the end of the sensorimotor phase. Contemporary researchers believe that memory may be crucial to cognitive development.

Piaget's second stage is the preoperational stage, which encompasses the preschool years. *Preoperational* refers to the fact that the child's thinking is not yet logical. The child's ideas are, from an adult's point of view, distorted, incomplete, and egocentric, and the child's thinking is still based on what the child has experienced and perceived. The child ascribes cause and effect to unrelated events. The child may believe that everything that moves is alive, that everything has a purpose, and that everything was made by someone. Fantasy and reality are interchangeable. During this stage, the child's increasing ability to remember mental pictures or symbols allows the child to engage in symbolic and imitative play using imaginary objects or real objects in pretend situations. It is believed that through play the child gradually acquires more mature ways of thinking and that imaginative play may be related to creativity and individuality later in life (Zigler & Finn-Stevenson, 1987).

During the preoperational stage, the child begins to develop concepts of classification and conservation. The notion of classification is important because human beings would be overwhelmed by detail if all events and objects were perceived as unique instead of as parts of larger categories. The concept of conservation relates to understanding appearance and reality and to memory. The classic example is the two glasses of liquid that are the same shape. If the contents of one glass are poured into a vessel of a different shape, preoperational children will say that the *volume* of liquid has changed, even if they have seen that nothing was added or taken away. Preoperational children are not able to mentally reverse the action of pouring or think about more than one aspect of an object at a time, that is, the appearance as well as the volume. Contemporary researchers believe that children acquire conservation at about the ages of 5 or 6, earlier than Piaget thought they did.

During the preoperational period, children's use and understanding of language grow rapidly. Children easily pick up new words and are fascinated by words, but they may not always know their meaning. They may even make up words and expect others to understand them! Sentence length increases so that the average 5-year-old speaks in sentences of 6 to 8 words. By the time children are 6 years old, they may have a vocabulary of several thousand words and a basic understanding of their native language's syntax, phonology, and grammar, though not the fine points. Children also learn to understand tone of voice; even 2-year-olds use intonation to convey meaning, raising their voices at the end of a word to ask a question, for example. As children's memory improves, they are able to remember more of what they are told. A 4-year-old can follow a more complex sequence of events, such as a story, than a 2-year-old can.

During this period, language becomes a communication tool because children can pay attention to others and respond to them. They can also determine if someone listening understands their message. It should be noted that during this period children's receptive vocabulary is greater than their expressive vocabulary; that is, their understanding of what is said to them is twice as great as what they can say.

During Piaget's third stage, concrete operations, which he believed began at about the age of 7, thinking gradually becomes more logical, flexible, and organized. At this stage children are often labeled "school age" because most of them are in school. Their thinking is no longer dominated by visual impressions, but they are still thinking about concrete, tangible objects and signs of the objects (such as arithmetic word problems) rather than abstract concepts. They are aware of rules of logic and can manipulate data. In the United States, most children are learning to read at the beginning of this stage. Concrete operations children understand conservation and various types of relationships such as hierarchies and series. These abilities make it possible for them to see that individuals have various social roles.

Children also become more flexible in their use of language. During the course of middle childhood, children progress in their ability to monitor their understanding of what is said to them—they know when they do not understand. Their knowledge of syntax improves as does their precision in understanding word meanings. Early in the middle childhood period, there is a great advance in verbal humor, and toward the end of the period, children can explain metaphors as well as use them. Librarians are well aware that second and third graders love jokes, riddles, word play, and double entendres. A moderate amount of intellectual challenge results in surprise and delight at being able to quickly understand the joke. Both metaphors and verbal humor are possible because the concrete operations child can hold two meanings in mind at the same time, and many children enjoy their ability to do so.

At this stage language becomes a means of instruction as well as communication. Children are able to profit from being in classrooms because of their increased competence with language and reasoning, longer attention spans, and ability to sit for longer periods. Their social development at this age includes the ability to follow rules and some independence from their parents (though not completely apart from adults), and these abilities, too, are necessary for group instruction.

Piaget believed that experience and interaction with the environment were necessary for cognitive development. Because schooling provides certain kinds of experience, it may have an impact on developing language, memory, and other cognitive skills. In other words, there may be a cycle of reciprocity, with development enabling a child to use instruction and instruction reinforcing and advancing development that enables the child to take advantage of further instruction. In most cultures children begin school or are expected to take on increased responsibilities between the ages of 5 and 7, evidence that adults generally recognize the concrete operations child's competence and that Piaget's stages apply cross-culturally.

Piaget's final stage is called formal operations. It is achieved at about the age of 12 and roughly coincides with adolescence. Cognitive development at this stage is characterized by the ability to use complex logical operations and abstract concepts and to think from a variety of perspectives. Not everyone achieves formal operations, although all normal humans in all cultures achieve concrete operations. Piaget believed that one had to interact with people who have attained formal operations in order to reach this stage, and formal operations apparently are not achieved by people in nontechnological societies. Thus, achieving formal operations appears to require schooling, unlike the other stages. There is some controversy over formal operations because it may be a sociocultural phenomenon rather than a purely developmental one. Also, Piaget's concept of formal operations may be biased toward scientific rationalism and not apply to other kinds of thinking processes.

Adolescents who have reached formal operations can think about statements and ideas as well as tangible objects. They know that logical rules apply to hypothetical situations as well as actual ones and can judge whether an argument is valid. Their thinking is reflective and systematic. They are capable of thinking about very broad issues, including how the world is, how it ought to be, and what they might do in it. In fact, the young person at the formal operations stages is said to be able to think about thinking. Information processing researchers have concluded that the adolescent's brain is physiologically more mature than the child's, but the adolescent's greatest advantage is the strides made in problem-solving strategies.

It appears that research about the adolescent years concentrates on the physical, emotional, and social aspects of adolescence (Nielsen, 1987). Research on cognitive development is generally focused on intelligence, creativity, and so on. Language development per se is not discussed in the adolescent development literature (surprising but true!). One suspects that the development of skills in speaking, writing, and reading does not cease at the age of 12, but perhaps it is a matter of gradually and constantly improving the skills one has rather than making fundamental additions to one's repertoire of skills. There is more to say about language and adolescents when we discuss education and reading.

THE PUBLIC LIBRARY AS AN INTERVENTION IN CHILD DEVELOPMENT

It is clear from Piagetian child development literature that certain groups – parents, teachers, caregivers, and peers – play key roles in child development. Contemporary American researchers testing the work of Lev Vygotsky, a Russian theorist who believed that psychological development was the result of the individual's interaction with other people, confirm the importance of parents, particularly, in the development of language and cognition (Ratner, 1991). However, Zigler and Finn-Stevenson (1987) pointed out that children and teenagers learn from all their experiences, not just those they have with parents, teachers, and peers. Researchers have also found that there are three periods when intervention may be most effective in stimulating cognitive development: prenatal, preschool, and adolescence. Theoretically, it is possible that children's and young adult librarians at public libraries may have an influence on the development of young people both indirectly, by assisting parents, teachers, and caregivers in their interactions with children, and directly, by relating to young people themselves. Possible interventions by public library staff are described later. Chapter 3 expands on these concepts in the discussion of social learning. In Chapter 4, the results of available research on these topics are discussed.

Potential Indirect Impacts

Even before a child is born, the public library may have an impact on a child's life through the materials and services it provides parents in the prenatal period. Public libraries generally carry a stock of materials on fetal development, child development, childbirth, child health, parenting, the ever-popular "what to name the baby" books, and a great many other materials for parents whatever the age of their children. Some libraries promote themselves by giving new parents a gift packet shortly after their child is born. Such a packet might include a library card application, bibliographies of materials for parents and children, and a book suitable for a very young child. Similar materials are available for teachers and caregivers: materials on education, child development, activities and curriculum, books to read to and with children, and in some libraries, toys, puppets, and multimedia kits. Although it is certainly difficult to demonstrate through research, these materials can help parents, teachers, and caregivers do their jobs better, thus enhancing the development of the children under their care.

In recent years, children's librarians have assumed a more direct teaching function regarding adults living and working with children. Examples include offering read-aloud workshops for parents and teachers or making presentations at childbirth classes to describe the materials and services available to parents before and after a child's birth and the importance of talking, singing, and reading with the very young child. Another method of teaching adults is to provide demonstrations modeling how to read and tell stories with children and how to talk with children, such as 2-year-old storytimes where parents assist their children to participate. Librarians who offer such services do so because they believe that adults who live and work with children can provide more experiences for more children than librarians can by themselves. By training parents, teachers, and caregivers in the importance and methods of reading with children, the librarian's efforts are more efficient (Mahmoodi & Wronka, 1989).

Potential Direct Impacts

Nevertheless, librarians continue to work directly with children and teenagers, providing programs and materials (which are described in Chapter 4). If we subscribe to the Piagetian notion that intelligence is partly the result of children's interaction and adaptation to their environment, it is possible that programs, books and other library materials, and even the physical environment of the library are sources of new experiences for children to assimilate into their cognitive patterns, no matter what the age of the child. By offering experiences that are different from those offered by the school and the home, the library and its staff provide alternative opportunities for cognitive development. For children whose homes or schools are not providing enough stimulation, public libraries potentially may make an important difference.

Young people develop concurrently along social, emotional, and physical dimensions as well as cognitively. Although cognitive development may be most important in librarians' minds, the public library may be a place where social, emotional, and physical development can be encouraged. Children's librarians are most conscious of their role in social development when they state as a goal for preschool story hours that children will become accustomed to being in a group of children without their parents. The librarian's recognition that the library has potential for enhancing social development sometimes seems to stop with that age level. Libraries are, however, likely places for young people to meet and interact with their peers in both group activities planned by library staff and informally. Interaction with peers is very important for the social development of school-age children and young adults as well as preschoolers. The so-called latchkey children may be those who recognize that the public library is a relatively safe place with moderate supervision where they can meet their peers.

Given that public library staff seldom become intimate with many of their clients, it may seem unlikely that emotional development could be directly enhanced through library use. However, the writer knows of instances when a youngster relied on library staff to provide some of the support lacking at home or at school. Zigler and Finn-Stevenson (1987) noted that the attention of a single caring adult can make up for lack of attention in other places. If the atmosphere in the library is positive and accepting of young people, then the library may contribute to young people's feeling that the world is a safe and trustworthy place.

Of all the aspects of development, physical development may seem the least likely to be supported by public library services. However, the physical abilities of young people must be attended to in any kind of programming or selection of materials for them. For instance, the limited fine motor skills of toddlers and preschoolers indicate the need for books with cardboard pages that they can grasp and turn. Finger plays done in preschool story hours may reinforce budding abilities to control the arms and hands. By providing the opportunity for very young children to practice motor skills, the library abets the child's development.

For school-age children, learning new things that they can *do* is an important part of their physical development and growing sense of competence. Materials and programs that introduce new skills or allow children to extend previously learned proficiencies, such as crafts and hobbies, contribute to school-age children's physical development.

Adolescence is a time of tremendous physical growth and skills development, second only to the preschool period. High school students are often extremely good at physical tasks (sports, music, crafts, etc.) as well as at cognitive tasks. The public library could help by not only providing information about activities requiring physical competence but also by offering opportunities for adolescents to show their skills by featuring teens in programs for their peers, families, and younger children. One of the defining characteristics of adolescence is sexual maturation. The social and psychological aspects of this process can be assisted through the provision of accurate, up-to-date information in a variety of formats, including speakers and audiovisuals.

SUMMARY

Although Piaget's work is now frequently critiqued by child development experts, his developmental stages—sensorimotor, preoperations, concrete operations, and formal operations—remain useful markers for discussions of child development. Piaget explained that development occurs as assimilation and equilibration. He believed that as children mature, their brains are able to acquire new ideas that compete with older ideas of how the world works. Initially, new concepts are unsettling, but through assimilation, the old ideas are adjusted to incorporate the new ones, and a new balance is made (Piaget, 1967). In contrast, Vygotsky believed that development occurs as new concepts replace old ones; in other words, there is discontinuity in development (Ratner, 1991). Although psychologists who study child development may not agree on the precise mechanisms by which development is accomplished, it seems clear that children's and teens' social lives play a large role. Imitating adult behavior, interacting with other people, and experimenting with language, concepts, and the physical world, in combination with the genetic forces that govern development, move the child along the path to adulthood.

Parents and teachers are key figures in the journey, but the influence of other adults should not be discounted. I have suggested several possible ways in which public library materials, staff, and activities might have an influence on the development of children and teenagers. Libraries provide places to acquire intellectual, aesthetic, and emotional experiences, practice physical skills, observe adults in their working roles, explore language and ideas, and become involved in social situations outside the school and family. To what extent these potential impacts of public library services to young people are realized is evaluated in Chapter 4, which examines research emanating from scholars of librarianship.

Before looking at this research, it is helpful to spend some time considering the educational needs of children and teenagers. Public libraries are considered educational institutions by the courts and by librarians. In order to judge their effectiveness as educational institutions, it is necessary to consider insights from learning theory that can tell us about the prerequisites and processes for learning. We also take a look at the development of reading and literacy because this is an area of particular interest to librarians, who tend to be print oriented. Material on the nature of learning from audiovisual and computer software is introduced to help us judge the appropriateness of newer formats collected by libraries.

CHAPTER 3

Relevant Concepts from Learning Theory and Education

INTRODUCTION

In some ways it is rather artificial to distinguish child development from the education of children and young adults. In fact, both child psychologists and educational psychologists lay claim to the work of cognitive-developmental, social cognitive, and information processing theories. The reason for separating learning from development is to be able to discuss the contributions the public library makes to children from both points of view. Public librarians see their work as having an impact on the individual in a number of areas, including education; it is through its impact on the individual that the public library has an impact on society. Because education is a very salient issue in American society, it needs to be discussed separately from development.

This chapter presents an educational model that may offer some understanding of the ways in which educational possibilities can be found in public libraries—Albert Bandura's social cognitive theory (formerly social learning theory). The second part of the chapter focuses on reading as a particular educational benefit public librarians hope to foster. Jean Chall's model of the stages of reading development illustrates the potential contributions of librarians and libraries. Because most people recognize that learning materials come in many formats and a variety of technologies, the third section of this chapter concerns the educational value of other types of library materials.

SOCIAL COGNITIVE THEORY

Youth services librarians rarely find themselves in the position of providing formal educational experiences, by which is meant a teacher instructing at least one student via a structured set of activities designed by the teacher to produce specific outcomes on the part of the student. Sometimes youth librarians must teach information seeking skills to children and teenagers, either because school personnel have not done so or cannot do so or because the public library has materials the school library media center does not own. Youth librarians sometimes find themselves teaching adults either part time in library schools or through workshops for parents and other adults. Far more often, however, youth librarians are engaged in promoting informal education, the kind of learning that takes place because the learner is independently pursuing a personal agenda or because the environment provides the opportunity. Most learning theories concern themselves with what happens in the classroom rather than the types of learning that interest librarians. Bandura's theory of social cognition is, however, applicable to public libraries because it focuses not on classroom instruction but on the learning that can occur in any social situation.

Bandura is interested in learning that takes place in *naturalistic* settings, that is, learning that occurs in the everyday environment rather than in a laboratory (Bandura, 1986; Bell-Gredler, 1986). For example, television, books, and daily experience provide us with role models that may influence our behavior, and in fact, many social cognitive theorists have looked at the impact of television. Social cognitive theory is a refinement of behaviorism, and as such makes use of the concepts of stimulus and response. Rather than taking a mechanical point of view about stimulus and response, social cognitive theory includes the learner/observer's values, decisions, and thought processes, positing that individuals choose to reproduce or not reproduce the observed behavior. According to the theory, when individuals perform an observed behavior, they may do so in their own way, deliberately modifying the behavior and thereby creating the complex variety of human activity. In addition, human beings very sensibly change their behavior to suit the situation (Bandura, 1986).

Storytelling provides an example. Librarians frequently learn stories from written sources, rather than in a traditional oral mode, but after they have told a story for a while, they are sometimes surprised at how they have changed, added, or subtracted from the original written source in response to the audiences they have told the story to. Storytellers are conscious of modifying stories to suit an audience, telling a simple version to preschoolers and using another tone and other details for older children. Observing other tellers may influence not only the stories one has in one's repertory but also the gestures, vocalizations, and postures one uses overall as a storyteller. In all these processes, individual storytellers actively use their intellect, judgment, and values to decide how to change their storytelling behavior. Storytellers learn from the social event of participating in storytelling as performer and audience.

Another aspect of social cognitive theory is that environment, behavior, and personal factors have an impact on each other. This interaction is hypothesized to take place in a reciprocal, triangular fashion, with each aspect influencing and being influenced by the other two. Personal factors such as values and expectations may lead to particular behaviors that may alter one's self-evaluation. Other personal factors such as age and race may lead to differential social treatment by others in one's environment, the consequences of which may also change one's self-concept. Behavior and environment are mutually influencing in that a particular environment may allow for some kinds of behavior that can lead to change in the environment and vice versa (Bandura, 1986). A simple example may serve to illustrate the process.

Let us take a hypothetical teenager who asks a librarian to purchase rock music on compact discs (CDs). If the librarian complies, the teen will have changed a part of his environment, may be more favorable toward that environmental component (the library) such that he uses the library more often, and he may also have a more positive sense of his ability to have an impact on the environment. If the librarian does not comply with the request for CDs, the environment is not changed, and the teenager's personal factors (his attitudes toward the library and himself) may be negatively reinforced such that he comes to regard the piece of the environment represented by the library as unchangeable and his control of the environment as nil.

None of this is certain to happen because other variables also play a role, such as the teenager's motivation, depth of feeling on the issue, general level of self-esteem, and previous experiences with libraries. The librarian's manner also plays a part, as does the teenager's response to her as a human being. In terms of the outcome for the teenager, it matters whether the librarian is understanding or irritated when the teenager makes his request. If she does not comply with the request for CDs but is understanding, the teenager may still feel comfortable making other requests in the future. Depending on his reactions to the librarian, if she is irritated by his request, he may not make another one, whether or not she purchases rock CDs. For the teenager's peers and siblings, the transaction between him and the librarian provides a model of potential behavior and its outcomes for themselves. They may imitate his behavior (i.e., make requests for library materials) if they value him, admire his behavior, and like the outcomes (or rewards) he receives.

For the librarian involved, personal factors, such as previous experiences with teenagers, and environmental factors, such as the library's budget priorities, may condition or influence her response to the request. Her own response behavior may reinforce personal and environmental factors; if she responds in some positive manner, whether or not she agrees to purchase rock CDs, she may reinforce her own positive attitude toward teens.

Public libraries are places where models for social learning abound. Ordinarily, we think of such models as residing in the materials the library owns, the books, recordings, films, videos, and so on, because social cognitive theory provides that behavioral models may be found in visual and verbal sources as well as living persons. Although Sabine and Sabine (1983) did not intend to test social cognitive theory, their study provided many examples of books acting as behavioral models. Sabine and Sabine contacted people from various walks of life and asked them what book made the greatest difference in their lives and what was that difference. Many responses demonstrated that people found models of behavior that influenced their lives in profound ways, such as the waitress whose reading of Benjamin Spock's *Baby and Child Care* showed her that she did not have to abuse her children as she had been abused herself. Reading *My Friend Flicka* by Mary O'Hara as a child inspired one informant to move to Wyoming, to teach high school English, and to write children's books.

There is in the Sabine and Sabine study little evidence that the interviewees found these personally important books at public libraries or any other type of library. Books are more widely available in our society now than they were when public libraries were developing in the 18th and 19th centuries; every drugstore, grocery store, and discount department store offers a selection of books that would make Benjamin Franklin envious. Furthermore, it is evident that most of the Sabines' respondents were looking for a way to make changes in their lives at the moment they encountered their significant book, indicating the importance of individual motivation.

Public libraries are more than a single book; they are a concatenation of many books, many people, many ideas brought together in an organized fashion. Toth and Coughlan (1991) compiled a volume of writings about public libraries—poetry, fiction, essays, and memoirs. Some entries are poignant, some portray librarians and libraries in negative ways, others are humorous. Those entries that deal with the writers' personal childhood experiences are, by and large, positive. At the age of 8, novelist Amy Tan wrote that learning seemed "to turn on a light in the little room in my mind" and the books she checked out of the public library "seem to open many windows in my little room" (pp. 423–424). Scholar Alfred Kazin found that the buildings he saw on his walks to the library and the books he read there during his adolescence helped him realize his interest in literary history: "I had at last opened the great trunk of forgotten time in New York in which I, too, I thought, would someday find the source of my unrest" (p. 438).

Writer Pete Hamill said of the library he used in childhood, "for a long time in my young life it was the true center of the world" (p. 212). It was a refuge in a dangerous neighborhood and a place that refined the images of popular culture. "In short, the library was a place where most of the things I came to value as an adult had their beginnings" (p. 217). Growing up in Pittsburgh, poet and essayist Annie Dillard found in the Homewood Library the books that opened the natural world to her and discovered, too, that there were other readers who shared her favorite books, though she did not know them (pp. 223–228).

That access to the books in a library can have serious, even frightening consequences was made plain by Richard Wright. As a 19-year-old in the segregated South, he convinced a white co-worker to loan him a library card with which he finagled books from the whites-only library:

> My reading had created a vast sense of distance between me and the world in which I lived and tried to make a living, and that sense of distance was increasing each day. My days and nights were one long, quiet, continuously contained dream of terror, tension, and anxiety. I wondered how long I could bear it. (p. 452)

We cannot be surprised that writers have fond or strong memories of youthful public library use. It is their gift to observe, record, and share experience in words, and an institution that provides books is a writer's natural ally and support system. However, the testimony of writers does not exclude the possibility that other users who leave no record of their experiences also find revelation, inspiration, safety, and anxiety in what they read (or hear or view) through a public library.

The portraits of librarians presented by Toth and Coughlan clearly show that the behavior of library staff is noted and remembered, just as social cognitive theory suggests it should be, providing grist for writers' mills, with sometimes embarrassing results. Social cognitive theory suggests, and the writers in Toth and Coughlan bear supportive witness, that if public librarians wish to enhance the education of children and young adults, the library must offer more than a store of recorded knowledge. It must offer also a variety of services to assist and encourage young people to consider the library as an aid in their personal knowledge seeking, and it must provide a human and physical environment conducive to the search.

The following chapter describes library services that may provide assistance and encouragement, including reference assistance, visiting classrooms, and activities such as story hours and film programs. In all of these situations, the library staff are themselves potential behavioral models at the same time that the materials and activities provide other possible models for children, young adults, parents, and teachers to imitate, avoid, or modify. Furthermore, library staff are responsible for selecting the materials and activities that contain potential models, although they are not responsible for the ways individuals make use of the materials and activities. Because it is difficult, if not impossible, to predict what influence a book, a film, or a television program might have because individuals construct their own meanings and choose their behavior, librarians should offer a broad selection of choices.

Because young people are believed to need protection in our society, there may be fewer selections showing unacceptable or marginally acceptable behavior in young people's collections than one would find in adult collections. Nevertheless, the public library is likelier to have a wider range of material than school libraries, partly because of more intense community scrutiny of school libraries and partly because communities distinguish between the required use nature of schools and the voluntary use of public libraries. Furthermore, the public library offers a selection of voices and role models that would not be found in the kinds of books, videos, and mass media commercially available for children in most communities because libraries do not buy only the most popular materials and they keep materials that are no longer available for purchase.

In sum, social cognitive theory shows how learning takes place in many situations, not only formal classroom instruction. The materials and activities of public libraries provide opportunities for social learning, opportunities not found in other settings. Social cognitive theory also provides support for public librarians' very strongly held belief in the efficacy of individual agendas for learning among people of all ages.

In addition to the rather general notion of contributing to education, librarians believe the public library plays a role in children's acquisition and development of a major intellectual skill needed for educational achievement, namely, reading. In order to see how this might be, the following section focuses on how children learn to read and how the public library might contribute to reading skills.

READING

"Reading is the process of constructing meaning from written texts" (R.C. Anderson, Hiebert, Scott, & Wilkinson, 1985, p. 7). Since the early

1980s, the ability of American students to understand what they read has been a topic of public concern in the debate over education in the United States. (Achievement in math and science has also been an issue in the discussion.) Why we should be concerned about individual and aggregate reading scores is clearly stated in *Becoming a Nation of Readers: The Report of the Commission on Reading* (R.C. Anderson, Hiebert, Scott, & Wilkinson, 1985): "Reading is a basic life skill. It is a cornerstone for a child's success in school and, indeed, throughout life. Without the ability to read well, opportunities for personal fulfillment and job success inevitably will be lost" (p. 1).

From a social policy standpoint, reading is of great interest because of American society's changing needs for a literate populace. As civilization has become more technical and complex, the economic and industrial system has required workers with higher level reading skills than formerly. Where once a fifth-grade reading level was the requirement for many jobs, today's more technical jobs require the ability to read at the eleventh- or twelfth-grade level (Chall, 1983). At the same time, there is concern over the so-called *baby bust*, the demographic change that may see a larger proportion of the population in the category of nonworking dependents (elderly and children) supported by a smaller proportion in the category of working producers. By the end of the first quarter of the 21st century, the United States may need all of its workers functioning at as high an intellectual level as possible. Despite the pervasiveness of audiovisuals and computers, reading continues to be a necessary skill for working and learning.

Reading is one of the most studied aspects of education; it would be impossible to summarize everything that is known or unknown about it within the scope of this chapter. For our purposes, it is most germane to understand something about how reading normally is learned and from there to investigate what and how public library youth services could contribute to learning to read. Each semester that I teach children's literature, I ask my students if they remember learning to read. Most do not. Over the years, I have found only two students who had an experience similar to my own. Some time during my kindergarten year, I asked an adult cousin to read an alphabet book to me. Her response was, "You know how to read that." I looked down at the page, and suddenly the letters seemed to move into new shapes as I understood for the first time that they had meaning. Afterward I went around sucking up print the way a thirsty person gulps water. I had comprehended the nature of reading all at once; no other learning has been as glorious or as liberating. I believe that most people probably do not learn to read in that fashion because more of them would remember the emotional impact of the experience.

Naturally enough, there is some controversy over just exactly how reading is learned, which seems to center around whether the medium or the message is more important. Some experts insist that children need to be taught the relationships between spoken language and written language, and other experts are equally insistent that there are so many exceptions in every language to "phonics rules" that children teach themselves how to find meaning in what they read (Smith, 1982). In her book, *Stages of Reading Development,* Chall (1983) suggested that decoding and meaning-making are both important, but at different times as the individual learns to read.

Chall calls her work a model or a scheme rather than a theory because she believes it to be preliminary to the development of a theory of how reading is learned. Chall hypothesizes that people who learn to read in adulthood go through the same stages as children; however, we refer only to children in the following summary of her model. The scheme consists of six stages. The first of these is Stage 0, the prereading stage, which lasts until approximately age 6. During this stage children are learning to speak and become acquainted with books and reading through the reading that is done by the adults around them. Children see adults reading, and in many cases children are read to by family members. There is agreement among experts that having books read aloud to them before they are able to read is extremely important to children's later reading development (R.C. Anderson, Hiebert, Scott, & Wilkinson, 1985; Chall, 1983; Smith, 1982). Children in Stage 0 memorize favorite stories adults have read to them, and they "read" by telling the stories in their own words as they turn the books' pages. Many children also learn the names of letters and the sequence of the alphabet, but at Stage 0, the message and its meaning are more important than decoding the medium.

Chall's view of the learning-to-read process corresponds to the notion of *emergent literacy,* a concept that has come to replace *reading readiness.* The emergent literacy perspective suggests that children learn continually about reading through experience and observation from birth. They do not have to wait until they have reached a particular state of maturity to become interested in books and reading (Dixon & Dowd, 1993). Conceptually, emergent literacy corresponds to a view of infants as active participants in life, interested in their surroundings, and not purely egocentric.

Although a few children learn to read before entering the first grade, this is when most children begin learning to read. They become Stage 1 readers. This stage continues until about the middle of the second grade, according to Chall. She characterizes Stage 1 as a time of decoding, of learning the sounds associated with letters. Children become "glued to the print" in order to learn what it is about, and meaning is less important. However, if they stay at this stage, concentrating on the surface of the print, children will not become fluent readers able to make meaning out of print.

It is during Stage 2, from the middle of the second grade through the end of the third grade, that children confirm what they have learned about reading and build fluency, that is, the ability to read quickly without having to stop to decode each word. They continue to learn some decoding skills, but they are able to use their knowledge of context and the redundancies of printed English to make meaning out of what they read. However, children are not reading for new information. They can read books that were read aloud to them in Stage 0 instead of telling the stories from memory, for example. They can also read folktales because the story structures resemble those of familiar picturebooks. Chall recommends immersing children in books at this stage as they move away from medium and decoding toward message and meaning.

Stage 3 marks a major shift in reading development. This stage starts with the fourth grade and lasts through the eighth grade. Readers at this stage are expected to read for new information, and much of what is taught in the classroom begins to be available in textbooks as well as in the form of oral instruction from the teacher. Chall characterizes this stage as "reading to learn instead of learning to read." Cognitive abilities and background knowledge, both important to reading, are still developing in the Stage 3 reader so Chall recommends that printed materials for the beginning of this period be clearly written, untechnical, and have a single point of view. She also recommends a greater emphasis on reading nonfiction trade books for academic and recreational purposes. Some reading skills are still being taught during this stage, such as increased vocabulary and how to find information efficiently. Reading for the message or information rather than figuring out the medium has become the focus of reading, and silent reading is faster than oral reading.

For young people in high school, the target stage is Stage 4, the ability to deal with multiple viewpoints, increased depth of treatment of various topics, and many layers of facts, concepts, opinions, values, and beliefs. Readers become increasingly critical and evaluative of what they read. This is the stage that Chall believes is desirable for the majority of American students to reach in order to meet society's needs for workers. Chall's final stage, Stage 5, she calls "construction and reconstruction." She cites research evidence suggesting that at least some college students move from a conceptualization of knowledge as a quantitative accretion of data to a realization that knowledge is qualitative assessment of relationships and observations in context. These students read selectively and know what not to read as well as what to read. The Stage

5 reader constructs knowledge for himself or herself through analysis, synthesis, and judgment, using past experience and background knowledge (of the world, reading, and text construction) as guides. This is the stage required for reading abstract subjects such as philosophy but also for some literature—Chall's example is *Moby Dick*.

Although Chall supports her suggested stages with research findings, they also have some support from an intuitive "pretty good fit" standpoint. She is quick to point out that everyone does not reach the same stage and that individuals may be at different stages at the same time in regards to the types of materials read. One person might be a Stage 3 reader of mathematics but a Stage 5 reader of literature. It is interesting to note that Chall's stages coincide to a certain degree with the stages of reading development posited by Donelson and Nilsen (1989), young adult literature scholars and authors of a valued textbook on young adult literature, although their stages deal with the development of reading for literary purposes, rather than the more global point of view that Chall takes. The comparison is shown in Table 3.1.

Donelson and Nilsen propose the following stages. Reading readiness is the first stage, during which the prereading child enjoys being read to. This coincides with Chall's Stage 0. Learning to read (decode) is Donelson and Nilsen's second stage, which they point out goes on all through one's life to some degree (Chall's Stage 1). Children are not very demanding about what they read when they are learning to read, but by Donelson and Nilsen's third stage they become more critical, at least in the sense that they want books with certain characteristics that meet their needs.

Table 3.1. Comparison of Stages of Learning to Read

Chall	*Donelson and Nilsen*
Stage 0 - Pre-reading Preschool through Kindergarten	1. Reading readiness
Stage 1 - Learning to read (decode) Grades 1 and 2	2. Learning to read (decode)
Stage 2 - Beginning to make meaning Grades 2 and 3	3. Awareness of books' potential to meet needs and interests
Stage 3 - Reading to learn Grades 4 through 8	4. Reading to understand self and society
Stage 4 - Reading for under- standing Grades 9 through 12	
Stage 5 - Construction and reconstruction College and beyond	5. Reading for appreciation

Children at this stage can be completely absorbed in books, and the stage seems to coincide with Chall's Stage 2 and the first part of Stage 3.

Larger issues relating to society as well as oneself characterize Donelson and Nilsen's fourth stage: "conformity, social pressures, justice, and all the other aspects of human frailties as well as strengths" (1989, p. 41). This would seem to tally well with the end of Chall's Stage 3 and all of Stage 4, and Donelson and Nilsen's final stage also seems to fit her last stage. This is reading for literary or aesthetic appreciation during which one reads at all levels simultaneously: for enjoyment, skills improvement, losing and finding oneself, discovering one's relationship to society, as well as the conscious analysis of literary techniques.

Both of these schemes emphasize the reader's growing independence from the text, that is, the ability to step back from the print, analyze it, evaluate it, and use it for the reader's own purposes. We do not know how many people are capable of attaining the highest stage of reading, though Chall (1983) presented research findings suggesting that not all college students have reached Stage 5 by the time they graduate. Reading ability appears to be related to general cognitive and language ability, and like these abilities, reading is susceptible to environmental influence to some extent.

It is completely accepted by reading researchers that children's parents are their first teachers and continue to play a vital role in the development of reading at least through Stage 2 (R.C. Anderson, Hiebert, Scott, & Wilkinson, 1985; Chall, 1983). Parents are advised to read to their children and discuss what is read and to provide books in the home. Indeed, providing many kinds of listening and speaking experiences helps children develop their vocabularies and assists the understanding of the sound-alphabet correspondences that are the foundation of reading. Children need experience with various kinds of texts in order to learn how to alter their approaches to the demands of different kinds of reading. However, not all parents know that they can help their children learn these things.

Chall (1983) also believes that the community, which she distinguishes from the home and the school, plays a role in the development of children's reading skills, particularly in making books available. She stated: "Probably the most important factor in reading development is the wide reading that depends upon the easy accessibility of books" (Chall, 1983, p. 107). Whereas some homes and schools provide the quantity and quality of books needed, many others do not. Chall noted that communities furnish opportunities for increased availability of books when supermarkets and bookstores sell children's books, but not all parents can afford to buy the wide range of children's books that is most helpful to children. Prices for children's and young adult books range from less than $1 for a mass market book such as those published by Little Golden Books to an average of $14.17 for hardcover books from trade publishers (Gerhardt, 1992a). The hardcover list price for Maurice Sendak's classic picturebook *Where the Wild Things Are* (Harper, new edition, 1988) is $12.89 and for Jack Prelutzky's *Random House Book of Poetry for Children* (Random House, 1983) is $15.95. Prices for children's trade paperbacks are about one third to one half of trade hardcover, averaging $6.80 in 1990 (Grannis, 1991b).

At these prices, most parents will be selective, even in purchasing paperbacks. Children, who in the early picturebook years should have at least one book read to them a day, can easily "go through" two or three hundred books in a year, allowing for favorites to be reread. It is not surprising, then, that Chall lists the public library as the first community resource that can assist the development of reading at all of her five stages. Like many people, however, Chall thinks of the public library only as a source of books. She seems unaware that activity programs and the services of knowledgeable staff also may make contributions to the development of literacy.

Librarians contribute indirectly to the development of reading when they help parents and children select books to use at home; when they compile lists of books recommended for reading aloud; and when they teach parents how to choose books, how to read to their children, and how to provide other kinds of language experience. When librarians read to preschoolers, help school-age children with materials for homework, and discuss books with adolescents, they contribute directly to young people's reading development. When parents observe librarians doing these things, the librarians are providing behavioral models that may fulfill some of the conditions needed for social learning to take place. That is, librarians are encouraging parents to read, discuss, and listen to their children.

As noted in the section on social cognitive theory, books are not the only medium of communication from which human beings can learn. The use of computers and video is becoming common in homes, schools, and libraries. The next section presents research findings relating to the educational value of these newer technologies.

LEARNING FROM TELEVISION, VIDEO, AND COMPUTERS

Television, Video, and Film

If reading is the process of making meaning out of written symbols, then viewing is the process of making meaning out of visual symbols and listening is making meaning out of sound symbols. Just as children arrive at their own understandings of their reading by using their personal experience, knowledge of the world, and knowledge of how printed texts operate, so they use experience, knowledge of the world, and knowledge of visual and sound conventions to make meaning of other forms of communication. Further, children frequently teach themselves to decode visual and aural symbols as there is little direct teaching of these codes in school. Thus, researchers disagree with critics such as Marie Winn (1985) and Neil Postman (1982)—children are *not* passive zombies unable to resist the siren song of television. Children exercise choice and selectivity, preferring some programs over others, attending only to the parts of TV shows that interest them, and voluntarily ceasing to watch when other activities are more attractive to them (D.R. Anderson & Collins, 1988; P. Palmer, 1986).

No one has ever doubted that children learn from television, film, and other audiovisual materials. It would be surprising if any medium as pervasive as these did not have any impact on observers. However, it is generally assumed that what is learned from television and similar media is either of little value or actually detrimental, particularly in regards to social, emotional, and behavioral learning. For example, public opinion and many commentators hold that children learn sex role stereotypes, ethnic stereotypes, and violent behavior from commercial television. Greenfield (1984), in her summary of research on television, film, and computers, cited research studies that confirm these views. But she also described studies that indicate that television programs and films specifically designed to teach what has been called *prosocial behavior* are effective in reducing gender and racial prejudice in child viewers, especially with preadolescent viewers. Furthermore, when parents or teachers discuss programs and commercials with children, positive effects increase and negative ones decrease in intensity.

When we talk about education, we are also concerned about children's and teenagers' knowledge base. What do young people learn relative to their school curricula or general knowledge? Research findings and interpretations seem to vary considerably. D.R. Anderson and Collins (1988) noted that there have been no content analyses of commercial television programs watched by children that relate the shows to the information base of academic subjects such as history, chemistry, social studies, and so forth. Although some studies have tried to show that the formal characteristics of the medium of television aid in the learning of some kinds of material, other commentators are skeptical of the claims made. Greenfield (1984), for instance, reported that Salomon's studies of the development of spatial reasoning skills had positive results: Children who watched televised films of tasks involving moving objects in space performed the tasks better than students who had seen still pictures. D.R. Anderson and Collins (1988) were more circumspect in their interpretation of this research, noting that it cannot be generalized to all spatial reasoning skills.

Other educational outcomes that have some support in the television research literature include learning dynamic processes and activities in which movement is a major aspect. Greenfield described a study in which 7-year-olds who viewed an animated film about plant growth retained more information about the subject than those who had viewed a film of stills with the same information. She also cited research that found that young children who watch film versions of stories remember the action of the story better than those who listen to the story being read. Other studies suggest that children who watch tasks being performed on television learn to do those tasks more easily. Adults find much utility in how-to videos describing such activities as automobile repair and home remodeling; it is a common-sense proposition that children could also learn sports, crafts, and other process-oriented subjects via video. In terms of verbal knowledge, D.R. Anderson and Collins (1988) noted that there is some evidence that watching commercial television improves vocabulary, though not greatly.

Television has been used to deliver education to people of various ages in situations where distance or lack of qualified teachers made regular classroom instruction impossible. Researchers evaluating *Sesame Street* and *The Electric Company* have found those programs to be effective learning devices. Studies of educational television in developing countries have shown it to meet educational goals (Greenfield, 1984). At several schools of library and information studies, educational television has been used successfully for years. As this is being written, American library educators are developing the Library and Information Science Distance Education Consortium to provide professional level coursework over a telecommunications network.

A major concern with research regarding children and television is the nature of the research itself. Most studies have been conducted in laboratory settings very unlike the "natural" viewing conditions of home, school, or library. Few of the studies have tried to ascertain how children perceive television or its place in their lives. Many of the studies that find positive learning outcomes for television are based either on educational TV products or films made particularly for the experiment, rather than on commercial television, which is what young people watch predominantly. An exception to this is the work of Patricia Palmer of Australia (1986). Her study involved interviews, home observation of television use, and a questionnaire, with three different groups of 8- to 11-year-old children. Describing these children as "a lively audience" that interacted with television programs, Palmer recorded their tastes and their perceptions.

For these children, television was not a monolithic phenomenon; it was particular programs that they liked or disliked. The shows they liked they defined as "exciting and fun," although the adult researchers sometimes found that the children's meanings for these terms did not always coincide with their own. Children were very critical of programs they did not like and wished there were more programs that catered to their interests. The children believed that they learned from watching television; what they wanted to learn from television was to understand themselves and the world around them (P. Palmer, 1986). Certainly, we should take this study as suggestive rather than generalizable, but it is hard to believe that American children would differ greatly from their Australian counterparts.

Although the impact of television on children and adolescents has been studied more than the effects of reading, as with so much social science research, the results have not always been consistent or conclusive. The three researchers reported here would agree that the focus of attention for adults living and working with children should be on the content and presentation of shows, rather than on the medium itself. Greenfield, for example, in describing the increased racism of preadolescents and adolescents after viewing the film *Birth of a Nation*, which is sympathetic to the Ku Klux Klan, commented that programs or films that are dramatic, emotionally involving, and produced with high artistic and technical skill may have a greater impact on viewers.

Computers and Learning

As noted in Chapter 1, computers are increasingly common features of homes, schools, and virtually all other aspects of life. Like broadcast television and video, they offer many opportunities for instruction and entertainment, and possibly, abuse. A search of the Education Index on CD-ROM for 1983 through 1991 yielded over 1,300 items under the topic of "Computer-assisted instruction." Perusal of the abstracts disclosed articles on computer learning in a range of subject areas and for all ages, including senior citizens. Clearly it is impossible to do justice to this body of literature in a short space, but a few points may yield helpful information.

In their overview of research on the use of computers in education, Tolman and Allred (1991) found that microcomputer software applications are available in virtually all academic subject fields, but they are used most often in mathematics and language arts classes. Where computers were initially used to provide enrichment and variety, they are now used for practice of basic academic skills in elementary schools and for spreadsheets and databases in high schools. Word processing and other software for creative expression are becoming more common at all grade levels. However, not all teachers make use of computers in their classrooms, and not all of those who do use them take full advantage of computers' capabilities.

Research on the effectiveness of computers has found that they have positive results in computer-assisted instruction, in helping teachers manage individual learning programs, and in giving tests and keeping records of student progress (Tolman & Allred, 1991). Kulik and Kulik (1991) performed a meta-analysis on 248 studies of computer-based instruction (meta-analysis is a statistical technique that combines quantitative data for central tendencies from several studies) and concluded that "the average student from the CBI class would out perform 62% of the students from the conventional classes" (p. 80). Other generalized positive results include findings that students learn more when computer-assisted instruction supplements conventional instruction, using computers increases student motivation, and students learn faster (saving 20% to 40% of the time required by conventional teaching; Kinnaman, 1990; Tolman & Allred, 1991).

Several studies have found that both gifted and low-ability children benefit greatly from using computer programs geared to their instructional needs. Students and teachers appreciate the individualization of instruction that the computer permits. Students are able to proceed at their own paces and the identification of weaknesses is nonjudgmental (Tolman & Allred, 1991). Public librarians are unlikely to purchase tutorial or drill and practice software that are the frequent subjects of research; however, instructional games are popular purchases for public libraries. Librarians will be pleased to know that a few studies have found that children learn more factual information from the games than from textbooks. One researcher identified the motivating characteristics of games: curiosity, challenge, and fantasy (Tolman & Allred, 1991). This is not news to anyone who has observed children playing computer games!

The fascination that children have for computer games may be disappointing to those who expected that children would use home computers to increase academic involvement. Giacquinta and Lane (1990) conducted qualitative research with 51 families that owned home computers and found that only in 8 of them did the children sporadically use the computer for activities that could be described as academic or school-related. None of the children used a home microcomputer for regular or continual study of subjects that are part of the school curriculum, despite the fact that their parents may have purchased the computer with the expectation that children would benefit academically. Giacquinta and Lane hypothesized that lack of encouragement from parents and teachers might be the cause of the low academic involvement, but perhaps human nature plays a part as well. For children, going to school is the equivalent of going to work for adults, and everyone needs a break from work.

It is very likely that children's use of computers in public libraries is similar to their home use—more for entertainment than for learning. Because recreation is a legitimate part of the public library mission, librarians need not be concerned to present only purely educational gameware but will exercise judgment in selecting materials in this area as in all other formats. As noted earlier, and as social cognitive theory suggests, children do learn from activities that are not intended for educational purposes, including computer software.

Some researchers and commentators find that computers may not fulfill the early enthusiasm for them. Becker (1989) cautioned that many of the studies used in the meta-analyses have methodological flaws, such as inadequate numbers of subjects, inadequate randomization, possible bias introduced by having different teachers for the control and treatment groups, and so forth. His own analysis of studies that met more stringent requirements found smaller effect sizes than those reported in the large meta-analyses. He remained optimistic that better designed studies will be more informative for educators. Williams and Brown, quoted in Kinnaman (1990), also criticized the research on instructional computer use for focusing on the medium instead of on the content and context of instruction. This complaint is one that applies to television, as we have seen. Becker (1989) added that instructional goals, instructional design, and understanding how people learn may be more important than the technology in which they are embodied. In his review of the claims that computer use enhances cognition itself, Sewell (1990) noted that research has thus far not shown that the facts support the theory.

The Marriage of Computers and Television

When we think of the combination of computers and television, the first thing that comes to mind is video games, both the home consumer electronics such as Nintendo and the arcade games available in every shopping mall in the country. The initial hostility to video games has died away, and the most recent research on them appears to have been published in 1989. Initial concerns about video games had to do with the violent nature of many of them and their reliance on fast reaction times rather than reflection. Researchers have found positive correlations between playing violent video games and aggressive behavior among children (Dominick, 1984; Graybill, 1987; Greenfield, 1984; Schutte, Malouff, Post-Gorden, & Rodasta, 1988). C.R. Anderson and Ford (1986) found that a highly aggressive video game left players feeling more anxious than a mildly aggressive game, but both games increased feelings of hostility.

Unfortunately, only a few researchers have tried to find positive aspects to the games for children or teenagers. Redd et al. (1987) found that playing video games while undergoing chemotherapy significantly reduced children's nausea and anxiety. A survey of high school students showed that frequent game players were young, intelligent males who liked competition, challenges, and science fiction movies (R.F. McClure & Mears, 1984). Greenfield (1984), an experienced media researcher, hypothesized from her own attempts to play video games that they require and stimulate complex spatial perception skills, the ability to remember multiple dimensions of a problem, and the ability to estimate quickly, using several kinds of information. She also reflected on the possibility that their interactive nature permits children to exercise creativity, and both she and Selnow (1984) found that children enjoyed video games because they could control the action.

In fact, the chief attraction of video games is likely to be the combination of television's dynamic action with the computer's capacity for user control (Greenfield, 1984). The negative aspects of video games—violence and little time for reflection—are not inherent in the technology but in particular uses of it. Nonviolent games are available, as are games (such as the fantasy adventure games) that allow for reflection. In the future, the ability to direct and manipulate interactive technology may be very important, as the prospects of virtual reality and interactive laser disc technologies open before us. Familiarity with video games today may allow tomorrow's adults to prepare for the world they will live in.

SUMMARY

In this chapter, we have looked at social cognitive theory, which suggests that people learn from observation and modeling as well as "doing," a theory that allows for the educational efficacy of library collections and services. Jean Chall's model of reading development suggests that the community participates in the process of learning to read, though her view of the public library's contribution is limited. Finally, we have discussed the contributions that audiovisual media and computers make to learning, tempering early enthusiasm with realistic appraisals of voluntary use and the limitations of classroom use.

The discussion proposed several ways in which public librarians serving children and young adults could be supporting child development and educational goals. These discussions leave us with a number of questions about whether librarians and libraries are providing services relevant to these child development and educational goals and to what extent library services are effective in their contributions. The following three chapters present the evidence available to help answer these questions. Chapter 4 describes public library youth services based on two national studies and research from several states. Chapter 5 tells the history of youth services with special attention to the goals and values of the services. Chapter 6 summarizes the available research regarding the effectiveness and penetration of youth services in public libraries.

CHAPTER 4

Youth Services in Public Libraries

INTRODUCTION

One of the tasks of policy analysis is to suggest what services should be provided by government and how those services might be offered in a way that is both efficient and effective. When considering the policy implications of a service that already exists, a comparison between the real and the ideal is implied; therefore, it is necessary to understand how the service functions currently and to consider how it fits the criteria set for it. In the case of public library services to children and young people, services can be thought of as having four major components: the collections of materials available for the public's use, the staff that provide access to the collections, the activities that the staff engage in to carry out the goals and objectives of the library, and the physical space that houses both collections and activities. This section examines what is known of the current situation of youth services in United States public libraries vis à vis collections, staff, services, and facilities. In essence, the data in this chapter represent the heart of the policy of providing library services to young people.

A DESCRIPTION OF YOUTH SERVICES IN PUBLIC LIBRARIES

From the adult user's point of view, areas designated for youth services in libraries can seem either placid or frenetic, depending on the number of young people present and what they are doing. Much of what library staff does is not apparent to patrons, nor can patrons easily distinguish the librarians from the support staff. With the exception of children whose parents require them to use the library as an after-school refuge, most young library patrons come voluntarily for specific purposes and brief periods of time. Patrons' contact with staff can be quite personal, as in the occasional case of a child with a problem who confides in a staff member, but contact is usually courteous and friendly without becoming intimate. It is part of the public library's peculiar nature that its contact with most of its clients is limited but, ideally, caring.

The policies and practices of individual libraries are set by the library director and the library board of trustees, often with input from library staff and other advisory groups, within the constraints of local ordinances and politics. Neither the federal constitution nor the state constitutions require local governments to provide public libraries. State and federal library policies are advisory and permissive, not mandatory. (Hawaii is the only state in which the state government operates all public libraries. Public libraries may be provided by cities, counties, school districts, special districts, or combinations of these entities.) Professional associations at the state and national levels, such as the American Library Association, may make an impact if individual librarians implement recommendations. The associations, in general, have no legal force. For these and probably other reasons, public libraries vary a great deal among themselves. Nevertheless, the available research shows some patterns along the broad dimensions of collections, services, personnel, and facilities in youth services.

At least five studies of children's services have been conducted at the national level. The earliest study was published in 1927 as part of a large survey of public, academic, and school libraries; the data were collected in 1924 (*A Survey of Libraries in the United States*, 1927). It seemed more pertinent to include the information from this report in Chapter 5, which covers the history of youth services. Two other studies, Gross and Namovicz (1963) and Benne (1977), studied the organizational patterns and administrative relationships of children's services in ways that have limited value for the current investigation. A national survey of public library services for children was completed during 1989 (Lewis & Farris, 1990), and the analysis and findings provide current, useful information for the discussion at hand. A book by Riechel (1991) reported a national study of reference service that collected data in other areas of service, as well.

In addition, the Public Library Association's Public Library Data Sevice (PLDS) requested some information about children's services on the 1991 questionnaire, and aggregate information is available (Zweizig, 1993). The information in PLDS does not result from a random sampling; rather, the library directors volunteer to report it. Even though some bias may inhere in this data, which would prevent its being generalizable, it is worth reporting for the benchmark information it provides us.

Statewide surveys of children's services sometimes provide more detail regarding services and collections. Since 1975, studies have been carried out in Florida (Terrie & Summers, 1987) Illinois (Erdahl, 1975; Richardson, 1978), Indiana (Fitzgibbons & Pungitore, 1989), Ohio (Ohio Library Association, 1979), Wisconsin (Wisconsin Department of Public Instruction, 1981), and California (Grover & Moore, ca. 1981; Willett, 1987). Another study was carried out in New Jersey (Lesser, LiBrizzi, & Stephenson, 1985; Razzano, 1986a). These seven states may not be representative of the United States as a whole, because four of them are located in the midwest. Further, because the studies used different variables, methodologies, and techniques of analysis, they cannot be compared directly with each other through meta-analysis. However, certain patterns emerge from the studies when their findings are viewed together.

Useful studies of young adult services are few in number. One study is available for the state of New York (P. Boylan, Fifer, Gellert, & Rubinstein, 1983) and the New Jersey State Library surveyed young adult services and reported the findings of that study with those of the survey of children's services (Razzano, 1986a, 1986b). In 1987, the Westat Research Corporation completed the first national survey of public library services to young adults for the U.S. Department of Education, using the Fast Response Survey System. Findings were released in July 1988 (National Center for Education Statistics, 1988). In addition, Riechel's reference survey included young adult services. Findings of the available studies of children's and young adult public library services are presented in the following.

Readers are referred to several tables in the pages that follow. Data in the tables are arranged in chronological order of the study's year of publication; each study is identified by the authors' names and the place of origin, if necessary. Some of the tables concern both children's and young adult services; these tables give children's services information first (in chronological order), then studies that report both age levels, and finally, young-adult-only studies last. Other tables cover one age level or the other. Some data given in the text are not included in the tables, particularly if they were not available in the form of percentages or could not be translated into percentages.

COLLECTIONS

Virtually all public libraries provide a collection of books and other items selected expressly for children. As previously noted, most selectors devote the major portion of their materials expenditures to books and other print materials. The discussion of television and computers in Chapter 1 described the nature of most library collections for young people and their access to audiovisuals, personal computers, and software. Table 4.1 presents this information in tabular form as percentages of public libraries that purchase, own, or circulate various materials for children. The more recent studies indicate that microcomputer software and videocassettes are becoming more common. Richardson (1978) found that children's staff ranked audio recordings a first priority for purchase along with books and periodicals, but films, filmstrips, and toys were ranked second, with artworks, realia, and slides ranked third. Statistics from the other studies make very clear the preference for print materials. The problems identified in regards to nonprint media should not be taken to mean that libraries should give up books. Rather, the recommendation is to take a broader view of what constitutes meaningful graphic records.

Limited information is available about the nature of young adult collections. Table 4.2 summarizes this data; the preference for print materials is clear, particularly in the study by the National Center for Education Statistics, which found that 91% of the materials in young adult collections were books. The reader will note that Fitzgibbons and Pungitore (1989) asked their research questions in a manner distinctly different from most studies. They took the view that the *topics* available to young adults were of more importance to an understanding of young adult collections than merely counting the number of items in different formats. Given the range of adult opinion regarding the rights of the young to information about sex, it is perhaps not surprising that 13% of Indiana libraries did not provide materials on sex in their young adult collections. It is less clear why college selection, careers, personal needs, and health are not represented in 100% of the libraries. The NCES study of 1988 also found that nationally only 92% of public libraries provided college and career information in young adult collections.

The NCES data in Table 4.2 indicate that book collections were predominantly fiction, hardcover, juvenile/young adult books. The study noted that in libraries with a young adult librarian in charge, the book collections were 48% paperback books versus 38% paperbacks in collections without the oversight of a young adult librarian. Experience suggests that teens prefer paperbacks, so it is desirable to have a large percentage of the book collection in softcover. The presence of a young

Table 4.1. Percentage of Libraries Owning/Circulating/Buying
Various Materials for Children

Study	n	%	Type of Material
Ohio Library Ass'n 1979	92–100*	88–77%	Purchase records
		48–29	Purchase cassettes
		47–60	Purchase pamphlets
		40–27	Purchase filmstrips
		29–29	Purchase pictures
		25–12	Purchase films
		21–23	Purchase games
Grover & Moore ca. 1981 (California)	310	99.0%	Own hardcover books
		98.2	Own paperback books
		82.9	Own records
		53.6	Own audiocassettes
		55.8	Own games
		36.5	Own films
		9.6	Own videocassettes
Wisconsin Dept. of Public Instruction, 1981	363	68%	Of budget spent on books
		9	Of budget spent on audiovisuals
		100	Circulate books
		93	Circulate paperbacks
		81	Circulate disc recordings
		46	Circulate audiocassettes
		14	Circulate games
		11	Circulate toys
Razzano, 1986a (New Jersey)	116	100%	Own records
		70	Own cassettes
		70	Own filmstrips
		50	Own toys
		40	Own computer software
Lewis & Farris, 1990 (National)	773	24.6%**	Personal computers available to all or some children
		22.9	Software available to all or some children
		40.0	Videocassettes available to all or some children
		77.4	Audio recordings available to all or some children
		73.5	Foreign language materials available to all or some children

Note. *For Ohio study, left-hand number of each pair refers to independent libraries; branch libraries' figures are the right-hand numbers in the n and % columns.

**Author calculated percentages based on data given in the report.

Table 4.2.   Percentage of Libraries Owning Various Materials for Young Adults

Study	n	%	Type of Material
Boylan, Fifer, Gellert & Rubinstein, 1983 (New York)	378	61%	Periodicals
		45	Pamphlets
		35	Phonorecords
		34	Audiocassettes
		4	Computer software
Razzano, 1986a, 1986b (New Jersey)	214	60%	Records
		50	Cassettes
		10	Computer software
		5	Filmstrips
		5	Films
NCES, 1988 (National)	794	91%*	Books
		6*	Other print materials
		3*	Audiovisuals
		60	Of books are hardcover
		73	Of books are fiction
		85	Of books are juvenile/young adult
		68	Have audio recordings
		34	Have videocassettes
		26	Have personal computers
		92	Offer college & career information
Fitzgibbons & Pungitore, 1989 (Indiana)	283	92%	Health information
		90	Career information
		89	"Personal needs" information
		87	Sex information
		84	College selection information

Note.   *These figures refer to the *proportion* of the collections devoted to each type of material.

adult librarian increased slightly the percentages of nonbooks in the collection. Clearly, some librarians view their young adult collections as purely recreational and do not attempt to purchase materials on a full range of subjects, intending young adults to use instead the general adult collection for "serious" reading.

The study by Fitzgibbon and Pungitore is the only one that comes close to discussing the real issue of collection adequacy. We know very little about the size of the collections relative to use, about the currency and physical condition of the materials, or about their quality and usefulness to young library users. Lewis and Farris's (1990) national study found that libraries that devoted the largest proportions of the book budget to children's books had the largest proportions of children as users. The study did not attempt tests of statistical significance or correlations, so we have no information about the nature of the relationship. It is a chicken-and-egg problem—did the children come first, creating demand, or did the budget come first, leading to a more attractive collection?

Zweizig's (1993) analysis of the Public Library Data Service information showed that children's materials had consistently higher median per capita circulation and turnover rates (turnover is the annual circulation divided by the number of items in the collection) than the general collections, across all sizes of libraries. A pair of hypotheses might be advanced about this situation. One is that librarians selecting children's materials may be more efficient and effective than their counterparts in adult services in choosing items desired by patrons. Or, the children's collections may not have enough items to meet demand, so that those items that are available are used frequently.

In fact, both hypotheses might be true if children's services materials budgets were inadequate to meet demand. That would force children's selectors to choose popular items and be cautious about purchasing items that appeal to only a few patrons, requiring them to be efficient purchasers. This might have a negative impact on the scope of collections, not only in terms of formats available but also in terms of the scope of subject areas covered and the depth of coverage. Inadequate budgets would affect the size of collections as well. Zweizig offered some data for cogitation when he noted that median children's materials budgets ranged from 15% to 17.5% of total materials budgets, but median children's circulation ranged from 32.7% to 35% of total circulation, a fact complained of frequently in the literature of youth librarianship. It should be noted that Lewis and Farris (1990) found in their national stratified random sample that children's services received a mean of 35% of materials budgets. The mean may be more subject than the median to influence from the smaller libraries, which devote larger proportions of their materials budgets to children's services than larger libraries do.

Although the studies of children's collections do not provide us with the kind of information that would be most desirable, studies of young adult services are even less informative. According the the NCES study, the 84% of public libraries that have a young adult section spend 15% of their materials budget for young adult collections. No records are kept of young adult circulation distinct from loans to children or adults, so we cannot make a comparison between circulation and budget. The libraries in the NCES study found that an average of 25% of people coming to the library were between the ages of 12 and 18, so by that measure of use, budgets may be inadequate. Young adults do have access to general adult collections and services as well as specialized materials collections. This is entirely appropriate when the materials are intellectually accessible to the user who is on the verge of adulthood. That said, it does not entirely mitigate the concern about adequate funding for young adult collections.

SERVICES OFFERED TO CHILDREN AND YOUTH

In addition to the collections, public librarians offer a variety of services to their patrons. The availability of specific services varies among libraries, but some are particularly common. It would be helpful if one could categorize the services under the goals of the public library—information, education, recreation, and culture—but the same service could fall under more than one category, according to the place the user assigned to it. For instance, a Punch and Judy puppet show is certainly entertaining. It is also a cultural experience because it is an art form with a long history. Nevertheless, one expects services to be somehow related to the institution's goals, and this portion of the analysis examines the services offered under the broad headings of the goals.

The two goals that public librarians like to focus on the most are information and education. Today it is hard to imagine a library that does not offer assistance in retrieving information and finding desired materials, although librarians did not always help patrons in this way. Examples of this kind of service for young people would include assistance in finding answers for personal or school needs, instruction in using catalogs and indexes and finding materials on the shelves, and tours of the library. Youth librarians also engage in activities that bring the library to the attention of other agencies in the community, such as schools, scouting organizations, day-care councils, and relevant government agencies, such as parks and recreation departments. These public relations or marketing strategies can be viewed as directly informational for the outside agencies and as indirectly fulfilling all of the library's goals by presumably widening the audience for the library's services. Because librarians desire to promote leisure reading and library use, activities such as preschool story hours, summer reading programs, visiting schools, and individual reading guidance are also services offered by many youth librarians. Librarians view these activities as both recreational and educational for the recipients. National and statewide studies give some indication of the extent to which youth services librarians engage in these activities.

Reference and Reader's Advisory

Tables 4.3 and 4.4 report the findings of several studies of reference and reader's advisory services for children and teenagers. The NCES,

Indiana, New York, and New Jersey surveys were general studies that asked respondents about reference or other kinds of assistance in retrieving information. In New Jersey, nearly all libraries offered reference service for children and young adults, and librarians at most of the libraries helped individual children and young adults find books for leisure reading. Additionally, assistance with homework was available for young people at most of the libraries (Razzano, 1986a, 1986b). The New York survey of young adult services found that more than 50% of the responding librarians reported that the library staff emphasized homework assistance, research and instruction, and telephone reference "a great deal" or "a fair amount" (P. Boylan, Fifer, Gellert, & Rubinstein, 1983). Fitzgibbons and Pungitore (1989) took a different approach and asked about services at four different levels. The reference level (use of catalogs, indexes, bibliographies, and staff) was the penultimate level, with personal guidance as the highest level of provision. Not surprisingly, reference level service is more widely available than personal guidance. Three quarters of the libraries in the NCES (1988) study reported moderate to heavy use of adult reference collections by teenagers.

These results support an earlier study of the use of the central library by teens in Rochester, New York. Junior and senior high school youth surveyed by Gratch (1978) reported that they used the library primarily for school, although 30% said that they used the library for both school and recreational reading. They viewed the library as a source of print materials and did not think of it as a place to go for other kinds of needs.

Researchers in Connecticut and Canada conducted large studies of reference services for children, and a children's librarian conducted a case study of reference service in the children's department of her library in Illinois. The Connecticut State Library project documented the numbers and kinds of questions asked in children's rooms in 14 libraries from September 25, 1978 to September 24, 1979. Sample counts collected between November 1978 and June 1979 found that each children's department averaged 55 reference questions per week asked by children, young adults, and adults. This figure does not include the kind of question librarians call *directional* (i.e., questions such as "Where is the water fountain?"). The respondents estimated that 89% of the reference questions during March, April, May, and June 1979 were related to school assignments (Hektoen, 1981).

The Canadian study, conducted in the city of Calgary, found that whereas 72% of 1,635 child respondents (grades four, five, and six) used the public library in the prior year "for fun reading," 44% had used the public library "to find information" and 38% "for school assignments" (CACL Committee on Reference Materials for Children, 1984). There

Table 4.3. Reference and Readers' Advisory Services for Children

Study	n	%	Type of Service
CACL, 1984 (Calgary)	1635	72%	Of children used library for "fun" reading
		44	Used to find information
		38	Used for school assignments
Lewis & Farris, 1990 (National)	773	93%	Had readers' advisory
Razzano, 1986a (New Jersey)	116	100%	Had reference service
		86	Had readers' advisory
		81	Had homework assistance
Fitzgibbons & Pungitore, 1989 (Indiana)	283	76%	Reference support for homework
		34	Individualized homework support
		70	Reference support for reading guidance
		40	Individualized reading guidance
Riechel, 1991 (National)	138	37%*	CD-ROM database searching available to children
		12	Allowed children to search online
		41	Did online searches for children
		15	Owned CD-ROM databases in children's collection
		48	Catalog use instruction
		44	Reference tools instruction
		49	Discussion of collection

Note. *These percentages were calculated by the author from reported data.

may be some local differences between Calgary and Connecticut (i.e., school library services may be better in Calgary) that could account for some of the differences between librarians' reports and children's reports about library use. However, children's independence in selecting leisure materials most likely explains the apparent discrepancy.

Harrington (1985) reported the results of a 6-week study of reference services provided by the professional librarians in her own children's department in Urbana, Illinois. She found that most questions asked were not actually "reference" questions requiring extensive use of library materials to answer, adults asked 29% of the questions directed to children's staff, and children and young adults made more than 90% of the requests for materials. Adults asked more reference questions than children, but 64% of children's reference questions were judged to be related to school assignments. Harrington's and Hektoen's studies tally well with Garland's (1989) finding that 80% of public library circulation of children's nonfiction was related to curricular subjects (she did not correlate circulation with specific assignments).

Table 4.4. Reference and Readers' Advisory Services for Young Adults

Study	n	%	Type of Service
Razzano, 1986b (New Jersey)	214	100%	Had reference service
		81	Had readers' advisory
		71	Had homework assistance
Fitzgibbons & Pungitore, 1989 (Indiana)		77	Reference support for homework
		31	Individualized homework support
		66	Reference support for reading guidance
		26	Individualized reading guidance
Boylan, Fifer, Gellert, & Rubinstein, 1983 (New York)	378	50%	Emphasized homework, instruction, & reference
NCES, 1988 (National)	894	87	Readers' advisory for school needs
		88	Readers' advisory for independent needs
		75	Reported moderate to heavy use of adult reference section by young adults
Riechel, 1991 (National)	138	41%*	CD-ROM database searching available to young adults
		14	Allowed young adults to search online
		44	Did online searches for young adults
		14	Owned CD-ROM databases in young adult collection
		33	Catalog use instruction
		38	Reference tools instruction
		33	Discussion of collections

Note. *These percentages were calculated by the author from reported data.

Riechel's (1991) national survey of 138 libraries, directed specifically at reference services for young people, offered information on the availability of reference technology such as CD-ROM indexes and online retrieval systems, as well as conventional reference services. She found that most libraries had basic reference book collections for children, but fewer than half had reference collections for young adults. Librarians at 120 libraries indicated that children and young adults most used reader's advisory service and homework assistance, with children also wanting library skills instruction. Other services, such as reading lists, were less used.

Although one might expect that young adults would have more access than children to various services, Riechel found that this was not always the case. Nearly half of the libraries offered instruction in catalog use, reference tools, and other library resources to children, but only about a third of them did so for young adults, indicating perhaps that young adults are not presumed to need instruction. Access to library collections was slightly more restricted for young adults than for children, but 60% claimed to provide unrestricted access to telephone reference for both children and teenagers. (Many libraries limit the time spent on telephone reference regardless of the patron's age.)

As reference services have become more dependent on technology, there has been concern about young people's access to the new products and services. Microcomputers and software were not available in youth collections in more than half of the libraries surveyed; CD-ROM indexes were available in 14.5% of children's collections and 13.8% of young adult collections (figures in the tables are rounded). Fewer than 10% offered instruction in the use of computer reference technology. However, about 40% of the libraries offered CD-ROM or online database access to young people, apparently through adult or general reference services. As age-appropriate reference products are developed, these numbers will change.

Services to Education

Another aspect of the informational/educational program of the library is classes visiting the library or library staff visiting classes at school. During visits to the library, young people may be given instruction in library use or tours of the library, listen to book talks and stories, and search for and check out materials to take home. When librarians visit a classroom or make a presentation at a school assembly, they may talk about library services and materials, tell stories and do book talks, and distribute information about the library. Children's librarians frequently visit schools toward the end of the school year to inform children about their summer programs. Table 4.5 summarizes data regarding school and class visits. The New York, California, Ohio, New Jersey, Indiana, and NCES studies give some indication that such visits are fairly common for children's services.

Fitzgibbons and Pungitore (1989) estimated that 8,120 classes visited Indiana public libraries in 1987, bringing 189,397 children. Librarians visited approximately 184,851 Indiana children in their classrooms, making school and class visits the activity that reaches the most children. Terrie and Summers (1987) presented similar figures for Florida public libraries: In 1986, 245,520 young people from preschool to high school age visited public libraries and 170,623 were visited by a librarian in their classrooms. Terrie and Summers also reported that

Table 4.5. Percentage of Libraries Offering Services to Schools

Study and Age Level	n	%	Frequency & Type
Ohio Library Ass'n, 1979 (Children's services)	99	70%	Of independent libraries visited schools
	144	82	Of branch libraries visited schools
Grover & Moore, ca. 1981 (California) (Children's services)	310	95.2%	Had class visits at least occasionally
		41.6	Had class visits weekly
		87.4	Visited schools at least occasionally
Lewis & Farris, 1990 (National) (Children's services)	773	83%	Cooperated with schools serving children 14 and under
		59	Provided study space
Razzano, 1986a, 1986b (New Jersey)	116	95%	Had class visits for children
	214	50	Had class visits for young adults
Fitzgibbons & Pungitore, 1989 (Indiana) (Children's services)	283	77%	Had class visits
		23	Offered library instruction
		56	Visited schools
(Young adult services)		21%	Had class visits
		14	Visited schools
		13	Offered library instruction
		5	Offered homework help
		3	Provided group tutoring
Riechel, 1991 (National) (Children's & Young adult)	138	43%*	Visited schools for reference instruction
		67	Had class visits
		84	Coordinated activities with elementary schools
		62	Coordinated with junior and senior high schools
		10	Coordinated with school guidance counselors
Boylan, Fifer, Gellert, & Rubinstein, 1983 (New York) (Young adult services)	378	34%	Had class visits "a great deal" or "a fair amount"
		7	Visited schools "a great deal" or "a fair amount"
NCES, 1988 (National) (Young adult services)	794	20%	Cooperated with school-sponsored after-school programs
		61	Provided study space

Note. *These percentages were calculated by the author from reported data.

67

persons under 18 visited public libraries an average of 4.38 times in 1986, and 2.18 of these visits had an educational purpose.

School and class visits are less common for young adult services. For instance, Razzano's (1986a, 1986b) studies in New Jersey found that 95% of the libraries provided class visits for children, but only 50% had class visits for young adults. In comparison with the figures for Indiana class and school visits involving children, Fitzgibbons and Pungitore (1989) reported approximately 503 classes of 13- to 18-year-olds visited libraries with total attendance of 11,347, and 16,875 were visited in their classrooms, less than 10% of the figures for children's services. The NCES (1988) survey results noted, "Libraries hosted an average of 6 class visits to the library for 12- to 18-year-olds, presented book talks in schools about 3 times, and met with school staff an average of 2 times" during fiscal year 1986–1987 (p. 9). In comparison, children's services staff cooperated with schools an average of 24 times per year and 14 times with preschools (Lewis & Farris, 1990). The difference between children's services and young adult services cannot be accounted for by the smaller population of young adults. It undoubtedly has to do with the greater frequency with which a staff member is designated to serve children in public libraries in comparison with the frequency of young adult staff (see following). If we assume that each young person had only one visit, Indiana librarians reached about 27.3% of the 0 to 17 population of the state and Florida librarians reached 15.8% of their youth population. These percentages may seem relatively small, but one has to wonder if any other nonschool organization contacts as many young people as the public library does.

Public librarians connect with schools in other ways, such as volunteers to help with homework, space for tutoring, and long-term loans of books to meet curricular needs. An instance of the latter is the Brown County Library of Green Bay, Wisconsin, which provides local schools with classroom sets of children's novels (30 copies of *Charlotte's Web*, for example) for group study. These more intense involvements are relatively uncommon. Fitzgibbons and Pungitore (1989) reported that only 5% of Indiana public libraries provided homework help for young adults and 3% provided group tutoring. Riechel (1991) found that just 10% of the libraries in her survey worked cooperatively with school guidance counselors.

Two educational services that are far more common are the availability of space for study during nonschool hours and materials to support homework. The two studies conducted for the National Center for Education Statistics found that 61% of the respondents provided study space for young adults and 59% did so for children. Furnishing materials to support homework is so common that it frequently is assumed by researchers and few questions are asked. In Indiana, Fitzgibbons and Pungitore found that 80% of the libraries supplied materials for young adult homework support and 81% for children's homework. Observing these figures and those for homework reference support, it is no surprise that 52.9% of responding Indiana librarians perceived the public library serving as a school library "to a great extent" and another 42.7% said "to some extent."

For some families in the United States, the public library literally is a school library. These are families involved in home schooling. Whether for reasons of religion, distrust of the public schools, or having a child with special needs, a number of families have opted to teach their children at home instead of in a school setting. Usually the teaching parent is the mother and frequently the family is middle class and can afford to give up the mother's income. For many of these families, public library materials and services are important educational resources. A survey of home schoolers in Whatcom County, Washington, found that 93% of them used public libraries, and 54% used the library at least once per week (Madden, 1991). This constitutes intensive use. The presence of the public library may make it possible for these families to meet their specific educational goals for their children.

Services to Community Groups

Contact with youth-serving agencies other than schools is also part of the informational program of some public librarians. As Tables 4.6 and 4.7 show, children's services is not necessarily more active in this area than young adult services, despite the number of staff assigned to children's services compared to that for young adult services. However, vague terms such as *great deal, fair amount,* or even *cooperate* do not specify the level or type of involvement. One person's "great deal" may seem only a "fair amount" to someone else. Some figures in Tables 4.6 and 4.7 may represent the agencies' asking the library for services rather than library staff actively soliciting involvement. Razzano's (1986a, 1986b) more specific comparison for New Jersey libraries showed that children's services were more active than young adult services in their community contacts. It is clear from these data that public library youth services are not as active in their support of community agencies as they are with schools, though Lewis and Farris (1990) indicated a high level of cooperation with preschools and day-care centers, as did Riechel (1991).

Assistance in locating agencies to help with specific kinds of problems is called *information and referral* (I & R); sometimes social work and charitable organizations such as United Way offer the service. It is also

Table 4.6.   Percentage of Libraries Cooperating with Non-School Agencies:
Children's Services

Study	n	%	Agency
Grover & Moore, ca. 1981 (California)	310	35.8%	Involved with community agencies, parks and recreation departments
Razzano, 1986a, 1986b (New Jersey)	116	51%	Community agency visits to library
		27	Librarian visits to community agencies
		45	Have community information files
Fitzgibbons & Pungitore, 1989 (Indiana)	283	25%	Outreach to day-care agencies
		17	Outreach to scouts
		7	Outreach to community groups
		6	Outreach to hospitals
		4	Outreach to recreation organizations
Lewis & Farris, 1990 (National)	773	62%	Cooperated with preschools and day-care centers
Riechel, 1991 (National) (Children's & young adult services)	138	60%*	Coordinated activities with childcare agencies
		85	Coordinated with day-care centers
		41	Coordinated with parents or guardians
		37	Had information & referral services
		24	Coordinated with family support groups
		10	Coordinated with crisis centers

Note.   *These percentages were calculated by the author from reported data.

appropriate for the public library to provide information and referral, but the data from Razzano and Riechel in Tables 4.6 and 4.7 indicate how infrequently I & R specialized for young people is offered. Information and referral services for young people were available in only 37% of libraries in Riechel's (1991) national study and in 22% of the New Jersey libraries studied by Razzano (1986b) for young adult services.

Reading-Related Programs

Programs that foster an interest in reading are another major category of services to young people that might fall under the heading of education

Table 4.7. Percentage of Libraries Cooperating with Nonschool Agencies: Young Adult
Services

Study	n	%	Agency
Boylan, Fifer, Gellert & Rubinstein, 1983 (New York)	378	54%	"Great deal" or "fair amount" of cooperation with community agencies
		32	"Great deal" or "fair amount" of cooperation with government agencies
Razzano, 1986b (New Jersey)	214	16%	Community agency visits to library
		1	Librarian visits to community agencies
		22	Have information & referral for teens
NCES, 1988 (National)	794	51%	Scouting & other clubs/associations
		41	Volunteer/service organizations
		41	Literacy programs
		31	Tutoring programs
		33	Community recreational programs
		20	Health education groups

and information. Activity programs that involve reading differ from
readers' advisory services in that activity programs are organized to
serve groups, whereas reading guidance is usually given to individuals.
In practice, of course, many librarians would see the distinction as
artificial because whether one is working with a group or an individual,
one's aim is to convey the pleasure and importance of reading, which is
a supremely individual act.

The two most common reading activities for children are preschool
story hours and summer reading programs, as shown in Table 4.8. The
range of libraries offering preschool storytimes was 43% in Indiana to
97% in New Jersey. Some libraries in Indiana offer toddler storytimes
and others combine school-age children and preschoolers at storytime,
so that 43% does not cover the actual frequency of preschool programs.
Terrie and Summers (1987) found that Florida public libraries provided
13,359 preschool programs attended by 316,544 children in 1986. A
national study of libraries serving over 100,000 persons found that 26%
of the libraries offered storytimes for children under 18 months (accompanied by an adult, of course; Dixon & Dowd, 1993).

The percentage of libraries providing summer reading programs
ranged from 62.9% in California to 96.7% in Florida. At the time the
surveys were done, the California State Library did not make materials

Table 4.8. Percentage of Libraries Offering Reading-Related Activities for Children and Young Adults

Study and Age Level	n	%	Activity & Frequency
Richardson, 1978 (Illinois)	503	56%	Reading aloud, at least 3 times/year
(Children's services)	503	76	Storytelling, at least 3 times/year
	28	87	Summer reading program, annually
Grover & Moore, ca. 1981 (California)	310	6.4%	Preschool story hours at least irregularly
(Children's services)		58.7	Preschool story hours weekly
		72.0	Story hours for others, irregularly
		72.5	Book talks, irregularly
		62.9	Reading programs, irregularly
Wisconsin Dept. of Public Instruction, 1981	363	75%	Preschool story hours, regularly
(Children's services)		26	School-age story hours, regularly
		89	Summer reading program, annually
		3	Book discussion group, regularly
Razzano, 1986a (New Jersey)	116	97%	Preschool story hours, frequency unknown
(Children's services)		63	School-age story hours, frequency unknown
		86	Reading programs, frequency unknown
Summers & Terrie, 1987 (Florida) (Children's services)	41	97.6%	Summer reading programs
Lewis & Farris, 1990 (National)	773	95%	Summer reading programs
		89	Story hours
(Children's services)		87	Reading lists or book lists
Fitzgibbons & Pungitore, 1989 (Indiana)	283	43%	Preschool story hours
		27	School-age story hours
		36	Parent/toddler programs
(Children's services)		86	Summer reading programs
(Young adult services)		6	Summer reading programs
		9	Other reading programs
		13	Book talks

available for a statewide program, but Florida's State Library did. In Indiana, approximately 152,300 children participated in summer reading programs in 1987.

Except for the NCES and the Fitzgibbons and Pungitore (Indiana) studies, few surveys of young adult services inquired about reading-related programs for young adults. The information from Indiana is presented in Table 4.8. As noted previously, NCES found that the average library staff presented book talks in the schools three times per year, with no indication of the number of classes or young adults reached. Book lists or reading lists for young adults were available in 78% of the libraries surveyed by NCES, but only 24% reported moderate or heavy use of the lists. This does not mean that those responsible for young adult services are not "pushing the books"; it only means that the studies have not surveyed reading-related programs for young adults. In fact, Fitzgibbons and Pungitore (1989) reported that their survey did not ask for reading-related programs for teens; their data came from write-in responses to a query for "Other" programs, which may mean the programs are underreported.

Other forms of reading-related programs not listed in Table 4.8 include public library contributions to increase literacy. Many literacy programs focus on adults, but some projects specifically target families, using motivation to read to children as an incentive for parents to improve their reading skills. We know these programs exist because of descriptions in the literature, but no national data report on the extent of family literacy programs in public libraries. Davidson (1988) could find no examples of public libraries providing literacy services to adolescents.

Informational, Recreational, and Cultural Activity Programs

Again, we find that programs for recreation and culture are more commonly available for children than teens, as shown in Tables 4.9 and 4.10. For instance, film programs were offered for children at 78-89% of the libraries (Razzano, 1986a; Wisconsin Department of Public Instruction, 1981), whereas only 42% of libraries in New York offered film programs for teenagers (P. Boylan, Fifer, Gellert, & Rubinstein, 1983). This study also found that 32% of the New York libraries did *not* offer any programs for teenagers. In New Jersey, the figure was 68% not offering programs for teens (Razzano, 1986b). Fitzgibbons and Pungitore (1989) found that programs for teenagers were offered by very few libraries, but they recorded the variety of topics presented. Again, the difference between activity programming for children's and young adult services is most likely due to lower staffing levels, though librarians also perceive that teenagers have many more options for filling out-of-school time than children do and are less interested in attending programs at the library.

Films, crafts, and puppetry are among the most commonly offered activities for children, although two of the more recent studies indicate that performances by professional entertainers may have become more frequent. Librarians today may feel that children are used to technically sophisticated presentations because of the strong presence of television in their lives. It may also be the case that parents value such performances, and they provide transportation for children. Lewis and Farris (1990) noted that preschool programs predominate, with an average of

Table 4.9. Percentage of Libraries Offering Recreational/Cultural Programs to Children

Study	n	%	Type/Frequency/Notes
Grover & Moore, ca. 1981 (California)	514	81.9%	Films, at least irregularly
		64.8	Puppet shows, at least irregularly
Wisconsin Dept. of Public Instruction, 1981	363	41%	Films, regularly
		37	Films, occasionally
		15	Crafts, regularly
		20	Crafts, occasionally
		12	Puppet shows, regularly
		32	Puppet shows, occasionally
Richardson, 1978 (Illinois)	503	26%	Puppet shows at least 3 times/year
Razzano, 1986a (New Jersey)	116	89%	Film showings
		51	Family programs
		54	Professional performances
		84	Craft programs
Fitzgibbons & Pungitore, 1989 (Indiana)	283	55%	Arts & crafts
		32	Performances
		28	Puppet shows
		9	Creative dramatics
		11	Author visits
Lewis & Farris, 1990 (National)	773	29%	Group programs for infants through 2-year-olds
		83	Group programs for ages 3 to 5
		82	Group programs for school-age children
		22	Group programs for unspecified or combined ages
		29	Programs for parents and childcare workers

Table 4.10. Percentage of Libraries Offering Informational/Recreational/Cultural
Programs to Young Adults

Study	n	%	Type/Frequency/Notes
Boylan, Fifer, Gellert, & Rubinstein, 1983 (New York)	378	42%	Film programs, frequency unknown
		24	Craft programs, frequency unknown
		32	*No* programs for young adults
Razzano, 1986b (New Jersey)	214	32%	Young adult programs: films, crafts, contests, game-related
Fitzgibbons & Pungitore, 1989, (Indiana)	283	5%	Career programs
		2	College selection programs
		1	Sex education programs
		4	Health information programs
		6	Personal needs programs
		4	Summer recreation programs

43 group programs offered to 3- to 5-year-olds and 25 programs offered to school-age children. For infants and toddlers, an average of nine programs per year were offered. Children's services departments may offer programs for parents and child caregivers. Lewis and Farris reported that 29% of their respondents offered an average of two such programs per year.

Fitzgibbons and Pungitore (1989) detailed some of the activities Indiana libraries offered to children: reading aloud, computer and video workshops, writing workshops, babysitting training, holiday programs, model building, balloon launch, and zoo programs. These indicate a rich variety of opportunities for children to supplement their educational experiences. When Lewis and Farris indicated that more than 80% of American public libraries offer group programs, these are the kinds of things that generalization covers. Similarly, young adult programs offered in Indiana included computer and writing workshops, bicycle repair, karate, music, stamp collecting, and babysitting.

STAFF

The services and collections described here are designed and implemented by library staff members. The issues that concern librarians regarding staff are the availability of a specific person designated to serve children or young adults, the educational level of youth services staff, the specific courses taken before service, and the continuing education of youth services staff. The studies summarized in Tables 4.11 and 4.12 variously report the numbers of personnel assigned to work with children and young adults in public libraries and some of the characteristics of the staff. Again, the data indicate that children's services fare somewhat better than young adult services in the availability of specialized personnel designated to provide services. Libraries that have someone designated to serve young adults as their primary responsibility are in the minority. Most libraries give young adult responsibility to someone who has other client groups to attend. It should be pointed out that about one third of the public libraries in the United States are so small as to have only one librarian on staff (Lewis & Farris, 1990).

Table 4.11.   Characteristics of Personnel Serving Children

Study	n	%	Staffing variable
Grover & Moore, ca. 1981 (California)	310	73.0%	Had master's degree
		67.7	Librarian had taken children's literature
		58.7	Had taken storytelling
		46.5	Had taken evaluation of nonbook materials
		29.1	Had taken management
		20.3	Had taken developmental psychology
		14.8	Had taken learning theory
Wisconsin Dept. of Public Instruction, 1981	363	31%	No children's staff
		18	Children served by general staff
		14	Had a person whose title indicates service to children or youth
		21	Had master's degree
		75	Had taken one form of continuing education
Razzano, 1986a (New Jersey)	116	72	Had children's librarians (no definition)
Willett, 1987 (California)	108	98.2%	Had staff and/or programs for children
	44	54.5	Had children's coordinator
Lewis & Farris, 1990 (National)	773	42%	Had a children's librarian
		49	Of children's librarians had an MLS
		32	Of children's librarians had a 4-year college degree
		67	Had children's coordinator

Table 4.12. Characteristics of Personnel Serving Young Adults

Study	n	%	Staffing Variable
Boylan, Fifer, Gellert & Rubinstein, 1983 (New York)	378	32%	Had staff member designated to serve young adults
		27.2	Had master's degree librarian for young adults
Razzano, 1986b (New Jersey)	214	40%	Had staff member designated to serve young adults, majority spend less than 25% of their time serving young adults
NCES, 1988 (National)	794	11%	Had a young adult librarian
		45	Young adults served by generalist
		22	Young adults served by adult services staff
		12	Young adults served by children's services staff
		5	Young adults served by reference librarians
		3	Young adults served by adult/young adult librarians
		51	Had young adult coordinator
		45	Had neither a young adult librarian nor a YA coordinator
Willett, 1987 (California)	108	46.3%	Had staff and/or programs for young adults
	44	18.2	Had young adult coordinator, most were part-time

The availability of someone designated to serve children ranged among the studies from a low of 42% of libraries in the national survey (Lewis & Farris, 1990) to a high of 98.2% of California libraries providing staff and/or programs (Willett, 1987), although a previous study found that only 73% of California libraries had a children's librarian with a master's degree (Grover & Moore, ca. 1981). Young adult staff availability varied from 11% found by the Westat survey (NCES, 1988) to 46.3% of libraries providing some form of staff or programs for young adults in California (Willett, 1987). Lewis and Farris correlated the presence of youth services librarians with the level of patronage, which is a measure of the size of a library. Busier libraries were more likely to have youth services librarians and libraries with six or more public services librarians were more likely to have a children's librarian than smaller libraries.

Grover and Moore (ca. 1981) found that although children's librarians in California were relatively well prepared with children's literature and storytelling, fewer of them had an academic background in the evaluation of nonprint media, management, or child development. Lewis and Farris (1990) found that less than half of the persons designated "children's librarian" had a master's degree in library science (M.L.S.), and another 32% had only a 4-year college degree. (The remaining 19% are described as having other educational backgrounds, which could mean anything from a high school diploma to a PhD.) Compared to public services librarians in general, children's librarians seem to be better educated (Lewis & Farris, 1990).

If the persons serving children and teenagers in public libraries have the assistance or supervision of others who are experienced and educationally qualified in youth services, then the situation might not be as negative as these figures seem to indicate. These senior staff are generally called consultants or coordinators, and they might be part of the local library staff or members of regional cooperative staffs. The figures for youth services coordinators from the writer's dissertation represent the situation in California in 1982–1983. The two recent national studies queried librarians about the availability of youth services coordinators or consultants; 67% of the libraries had a children's coordinator available and 51% had the services of a young adult coordinator. However, 45% of public libraries had neither a young adult librarian nor a young adult coordinator or consultant to help librarians meet the needs of teenagers.

FACILITIES

The fourth component of service to children and teenagers is facilities — separate rooms or areas of the library set aside for their use. As noted before, the variables collected differed among the surveys, but general tendencies can be noted in Table 4.13. And, as we have seen before, areas set aside for young adults are not as common as areas for children. Razzano (1986a, 1986b) reported that 94% of New Jersey libraries had separate areas for children and 79% had separate areas for young adults, though only 25% of the respondents considered their areas attractive to young adults. All Wisconsin libraries made some kind of separate provision for children's materials, even though 61% of them had the children's materials in a room that also housed other kinds of materials. This undoubtedly reflects the large number of small rural libraries found in Wisconsin. Of these libraries, 25% had a separate young adult area, but 30% of the libraries did not provide even a separate young adult collection (Wisconsin Department of Public Instruction, 1981). A similar pattern was found in New York State, where 8% of the libraries had a young adult room and 20% had a separate area for young adult materials (P. Boylan, Fifer, Gellert, & Rubinstein, 1983).

Table 4.13. Facilities for Children and Young Adults

Study & Age Level	n	%	Description
Boylan, Fifer, Gellert, & Rubinstein, 1983 (New Jersey) (Young adult services)	378	92%	No young adult room
		20	Separate area for young adult materials
		23	Interfile with adult or children's
Wisconsin Dept. of Public Instruction, 1981 (Children's & young adult services)	363	61%	Separate area for children in a room with other materials
		39	Separate room for children's materials
		43	Young adult materials housed with adult or children's materials
		25	Separate area for young adult materials
		30	No separate young adult collection
Razzano, 1986a, ACLN, 1985 (New Jersey) (Children's services)	116	94%	Separate area for children
Razzano, 1986a, 1986b (Young adult services)	214	79%	Separate area for young adults, 25% of these consider it attractive to young adults
NCES, 1988 (National)	794	84%	Section or collection for young adults
		74	Consider it moderately to heavily used

The NCES (1988) study found that 84% of the responding libraries provided either a separate section or a separate collection of young adult materials. The corresponding national study of children's services (Lewis & Farris, 1990) uncovered only a single library among the 773 respondents that had no children's collection and also a single library that had only a children's collection. This latter library was located in an elementary school.

The study of California libraries by Grover and Moore (ca. 1981) reported in some detail the characteristics of facilities for children, noting such aspects as easily identifiable service desks and collections, appropriately sized furniture and shelving, adequate floor space, provisions for handicapped users, bulletin boards and display space, restrooms, and audiovisual capabilities. The 310 respondents rated their facilities for children as generally average, with no item being rated above average by a majority of respondents. The two weakest areas were restrooms and facilities for audiovisual equipment and materials.

The researchers attempted to correlate the educations of the children's personnel with the facilities measures. Only two variables exhibited significant chi-square relationships: Audiovisual capabilities and availability of facilities for other agencies correlated with the presence of a children's librarian with a master's degree.

SUMMARY

Using the available data, it is possible to create a general picture of youth services in public libraries. In most public libraries we would find at least a separate area of shelves and seating for children (if not a separate room), with a collection of varied materials, although books would consitute the most abundant format provided. We would expect to find someone designated to serve children, although that person might not have a professional education. Reference, reader's advisory, preschool storytimes, and summer reading programs would be the services we would be most likely to find, along with programs for school-age children on a variety of topics. For young adults, however, a designated staff person could not be expected, although we would be likely to find some materials identified for teenagers, though it would be unusual to find a separate room set aside for them. Again, most of the materials would be books. Reference services would be available for young adults but not the range of programs and activities offered to children, due to the lack of staff and the perception on the part of librarians and young adults that the library's purpose is to provide school-related information.

We have examined the potential theoretical bases for library services to young people and the reality of what is available for young people in libraries in terms of collections, services, staff, and facilities. It is now necessary to connect the theoretical and the actual to discuss why we have public library services for youth in the condition in which we find them and how well these services meet the purposes for which they were designed. The next chapter offers a historical perspective on how the services developed, and Chapter 6 presents the research that evaluates the services' effectiveness.

CHAPTER 5

History of Public Library Youth Services

INTRODUCTION

A student of mine once wrote a paper titled "Ashurbanipal: Ancient King, Modern Librarian," which attempted to demonstrate the continuity of library principles through two and a half millenia of changing technological, social, and political life. For all the time that libraries have existed, however, young people have only had staff, services, and facilities expressly and systematically designated for them for the last 100 years, with a century of forerunners. The thesis of this chapter is that the development of children's and young adult services has been a response to social values of particular times and places. As with any institution, youth services' continued existence relies on society's continuing to value them.

The history of public library youth services is not only part of the history of public libraries in the United States; it is also part of the history of childhood, education, and the socialization of young people in this country (Wayne Wiegand, personal communication, June 2, 1992). As such, it reflects both changing and constant social conditions and changing and constant beliefs about children and teenagers held by adults in the general society and by librarians. The collections, services, staffing patterns, and facilities described in the last chapter are not recent developments, but products of the public library's relationship with children and teenagers over the past century or more. That century witnessed the movement from an agrarian society to a postindustrial age, from the horse to the Concorde, from letters delivered by coach to electronic mail, from penny-dreadfuls to Saturday morning cartoons, from handwritten catalog cards to online catalogs manipulated by touching a screen. The century also witnessed the development of a new understanding of the nature of childhood and youth, from children as small adults to developing human beings with needs and interests different from those of adults. Let us examine how the development of youth services represents the intersection of public library history with the history of young people in American society. For a capsule view of the history of youth services, readers should consult Table 5.1, which presents a chronology.

PUBLIC LIBRARY PRECURSORS

What makes the public library "public" is financial support through regular contributions of tax revenue, but before the value of public support was seen, private libraries existed to provide cooperative access to books, which were expensive and difficult to come by in the United States in the 18th and early 19th centuries. The American public library is considered by most library historians to have its beginning in New England. Social and subscription libraries began appearing in the 1730s with the rising interest in education (Long, 1969; Shera, 1949). One paid either a lump sum or an annual subscription to belong to one of these libraries, and most of them catered to men only. Shera (1949) identified 1,085 social libraries founded between 1733 and 1850; of these, only 21 were "juvenile and youth" libraries, although the 48 libraries designated as "young men's," "mechanics'," and "mercantile" libraries likely served males of the age we now call young adults. (McMullen [1985] enumerated more social and subscription libraries than Shera but he did not categorize them by audience.)

Like the social and subscription libraries, the Sunday school libraries were supported by voluntary private funds. The Sunday schools were engaged in teaching reading and basic education as well as Protestant evangelical religion and secular middle-class values appropriate to an industrializing society. Their clients were working-class poor children in New England and the midwestern frontier (A.M. Boylan, 1988). Loaning books extended the educational effort, although today we might find the books exceedingly didactic, sentimental, and full of evangelizing zeal. "[T]he stories in Sunday school books and magazines reinforced the schools' teachings on the importance of cleanliness, order, self-control, and delayed gratification" (A.M. Boylan, 1988, p. 52). Long said of the Sunday school libraries, "There is no doubt but that they reached more children with freely loaned books than any other

Table 5.1.   Selected Chronology of the History of Public Library Youth Services

Dates	Events
1733–1850	Era of social and subscription libraries
1803	Founding of Bingham Library for Youth, Salisbury, CT
1810	Municipal support for Bingham Library for Youth
1825–1890	Era of Sunday school libraries
late 1830s	Legislation permitting school district libraries
1854	Opening of Boston Public Library
1875	Caroline M. Hewins becomes librarian of the Young Men's Institute, Hartford, CT
1876	Publication of *Public Libraries in the United States*
1876	Establishment of the American Library Association
1876 or 1877	Minerva Sanders opens the Pawtucket (RI) Public Library to children
1882	Caroline Hewins's first report to the Conference of Librarians
1888	First children's reading rooms opened
1893	Caroline Hewins's survey
1896	First new libraries with reading rooms designed for children: Pratt Institute and Providence, RI
1897	First general discussion of children's library work at an ALA conference
1898	First children's department staffed, Carnegie Library of Pittsburgh
1899 or 1900	First training course for children's librarians, Pratt Institute Library School
1900	Section for Children's Librarians formed in ALA (now the Association for Library Service to Children)
1906	Anne Carroll Moore appointed head of Children's Department, New York Public Library
1919	Children's Book Week inaugurated by Frederic Melcher and Franklyn Mathiews
1922	First presentation of the Newbery Award
1925	Stevenson Room for teenagers opened in the Cleveland Public Library
1927	Publication of *A Survey of Libraries in the United States*
1930	Young People's Reading Round Table formed in ALA (now Young Adult Library Services Association)
1930s	Introduction of preschool story hours
1938	First presentation of the Caldecott Award
1941	ALA organizations serving children, young adults, and schools combined to form the Division of Libraries for Children and Young People (DLCYP)
1942	First publication of *Top of the News* (now *Journal of Youth Services in Libraries*)
1951	Separation of DLCYPL into three divisions (AASL, ALSC, and YALSA)
1950s–1960s	Baby boomers use the public libraries
1956	Library Services Act
1958	National Defense Education Act
1960s–1970s	Civil rights movement and the Great Society
1963	Lowell Martin's study of Enoch Pratt Free Library
1963	Specialist in children's literature hired by the Library of Congress
1965	Elementary and Secondary Education Act
1970	Proposal to turn all children's services over to public schools, New York Commissioner of Education
1978	Passage of Proposition 13 in California

(continued)

Table 5.1.   *(continued)*

Dates	Events
1979	First White House Conference on Libraries and Information Services
1980	Passage of Proposition 2 1/2 in Massachusetts
1988	Publication of NCES young adult services study
1989	First presentation of the *School Library Journal*/Young Adult Services Division Author Award (now the Margaret Edwards Award)
1990	Publication of NCES children's services study
1991	Public Library Data Service collects data about children's services for the first time
1991	First presentation of the Andrew Carnegie Medal for Excellence in Children's Video
1991	Second White House Conference on Libraries and Information Services
1992	Publication of *Output Measures for Public Library Service to Children*

agency between 1825 and 1890" (1969, p. 49). Toward the end of their existence, the Sunday school libraries became more secular in their collections and many were absorbed into public libraries as these developed children's services (Long, 1969).

In the early 19th century a few instances of private philanthropy inspired town fathers to contribute to libraries for young people. In fact, the earliest known instance of municipal support for a library was the Bingham Library for Youth, established in Salisbury, Connecticut, in 1803 by Caleb Bingham, which was granted $100 by the town meeting in 1810 for the purchase of additional books (Shera, 1949). Municipal support was also given for juvenile libraries in Lexington (1827) and Arlington (1837), Massachusetts. The men who made the initial donations remembered their own longing for reading in childhood. Others allowed young people access to their personal books. A generous man who opened his private library to local young men in Allegheny, Pennsylvania, was partly responsible for the library philanthropy of one of them—Andrew Carnegie.

The didactic intentions of those who founded social and philanthropic libraries for young people might best be enunciated by a quote from the 1856 report of the Apprentice's Library Company in Philadelphia. The anonymous author noted that 48,000 volumes had been borrowed by 3,637 readers in the previous year:

> diffusing far and wide, at the home fireside and happy family circles, blessings, and benefits untold and inestimable, to an interesting and useful class of youth of both sexes; many of whom, but for the attractions afforded by our Library, we believe, would have spent much of their time thus happily employed, in a manner less advantageously to themselves, or profitably to the community. (Rhees, 1859/1967, p. 379)

Disentangling the torturous syntax, one perceives the emphasis on youths' spending their time to their own advantage and the community's profit through reading books. Of course, the library's supporters did not spend much time considering young people's reading that did not come from a library—such as the sensational *Police Gazette!*

School district libraries were another forerunner of public support. Beginning in the late 1830s, several states passed legislation allowing school districts to tax residents for the purpose of setting up libraries in schools for the use of the local population, adults as well as children. Eventually 22 states had such legislation (Long, 1969). One of the plan's supporters was educational reformer Horace Mann, who believed that the school was a convenient location for all citizens to find materials that would educate and improve their tastes. By the 1870s, these libraries had begun to fail because of lack of adequate funds to purchase new books, maintain the collections in good repair, and support staff to undertake maintenance and circulation duties (Long, 1969). They also lacked proper physical facilities (Shera, 1949). These problems were typical of many social and subscription libraries, as well, although social libraries continued to be founded until the end of the 19th century when they were finally superseded by tax-supported public libraries, although a very few continue to exist (McMullen, 1985).

Such was the situation in the mid-19th century when educated professional men—teachers, clergy, lawyers, and businessmen—began lobbying state legislatures to pass laws permitting municipalities to tax citizens for the purpose of supporting a public library (Shera, 1949). The legislatures of New Hampshire and Massachusetts were the first to do so, in 1849 and 1851, respectively. A few public libraries had been founded previously, but they operated without legislative blessing. The legislation was permissive rather than mandatory—cities and towns were not required to provide libraries—and to this day legislation supporting public libraries generally remains permissive. The opening of the Boston Public Library in 1854 is credited with creating a great deal of interest in public libraries nationally because it was the first major city with a public library.

EARLY PUBLIC LIBRARY SERVICES TO YOUNG PEOPLE

The founders of the public library in New England were well-educated professional men who believed a public library would encourage self-education by the less fortunate and assimilation of the immigrant, but children were not part of the clientele they envisioned (Harris, 1984). William I. Fletcher's essay in the landmark study Public Libraries in the

United States, published during the United States' Centennial, urged public librarians to open their doors to youngsters, saying, "The lack of appreciation of youthful demands for culture is one of the saddest chapters in the history of the world's comprehending not the light that comes into it" (Fletcher, 1876, p. 413).

Minerva Sanders opened the Pawtucket (RI) Public Library to children that same year, but other librarians heeded Fletcher's advice slowly. A national survey of 146 public libraries in 1893 found that 74 of them would not serve children under 12 or 14 and another 16 would not serve young people under 15 or 16. Only 36 libraries (25%) had no age limit (Hewins, 1893). However, the movement to provide services for children had begun. Many libraries started their service to children by providing books for the use of the public schools, rather than service in the public library building. Books were loaned to teachers who then loaned them to their students, the assumption being that teachers could best guide youngsters' reading.

As public libraries began to do this, the inadequacies of publishing for children became apparent. Although the quality of children's books had been improving after the Civil War (Darling, 1968), few books were available for children below the seventh grade. Librarians such as Caroline Hewins began lobbying publishers for better children's books, beginning a relationship that continues today. Although serving children through the schools was successful in some places, it was not successful everywhere, and there was concern to reach the students of teachers who did not participate in the plan.

There was also the insistence of young people themselves. They wanted access to the books housed in libraries. Because adult patrons were disturbed by youthful exuberance, a way was sought to segregate them from adult readers. Public libraries began to make not only space but separate rooms for children. Before the turn of the century, children were finding the doors open at public libraries in Brookline (MA), Minneapolis, Milwaukee, Hartford, Cleveland, Denver, Seattle, San Francisco, and many other places (Long, 1969; Thomas, 1990). Thomas (1990) reported that the first libraries to be built with reading rooms designed for children were those of the Pratt Institute in Brooklyn and the Providence (RI) Public Library, both in 1896. Many of the ideas that guide the design of contemporary children's rooms were developed in the 1890s: natural light, cheerful colors, child-sized furniture, and room for display of materials, exhibits, and pictures of interest to children (Thomas, 1990).

Note that most of the libraries with children's rooms were in urban centers. Urbanization is one of the factors that historians believe plays a role in the development of public libraries. Other factors include a strong economy, the proportion of children enrolled in school, and industrialization (Williams, 1986). In areas other than New England, women and women's clubs played a major role in the founding of public libraries and schools, but this aspect of library history is as yet little studied (Carmichael, 1986; A.F. Scott, 1986), as the relationship of women and women's clubs to youth services is not understood. By 1900, preparation for working in libraries was established as a university course, and some of the graduates were inspired with missionizing zeal to bring libraries to the untamed West, and, evidently, children were part of the audience they sought (Joanne Passet, personal communication, January 20, 1993). It seems unlikely to this writer that libraries founded by women would have neglected the interests of young people.

For the purposes of this policy analysis, it is important to note the social context in which the development of public library services to children took place. The years between 1870 and 1914 were marked by increased interest in the welfare of children in the United States and Europe. Immigration and industrialization made the miserable living conditions of urban children very visible. Young people's lives were especially obvious because they were a much larger proportion of the population than they are now. Persons aged 19 and under accounted for 50% of the population in 1870 and 46% in 1890, whereas children aged 17 and under were estimated to be 25.57% of the 1990 population (U.S. Bureau of the Census, 1975, 1992).

Many children attended school for only 4 or 5 years before joining the labor force because their families needed the income from their work; high school graduation was relatively unusual. Immigrant children needed help learning to read, write, and speak English. "Americanization" of the immigrant from Eastern and Southern Europe was also a concern of the established Anglo-American culture (Bodnar, 1985; Harris, 1976). Compulsory school attendance laws were used to ensure that immigrant children became "good citizens and good workers" (Bodnar, 1985, p. 191)

White, middle-class, Protestant women were especially interested in alleviating the situation, which coincided with increasing college education for women. The years between the Civil War and World War II were a period of reform in and widening availability of education for white children as well, including the kindergarten movement, increased numbers of public high schools, and compulsory school attendance laws. The juvenile justice system and the parks and recreation system were founded in the large cities, and laws restricting child labor were strengthened. The profession of social work was established, as were the major scouting organizations. The psychology and development of children and adolescents became legitimate topics of scholarly inquiry through the work of William James, G. Stanley Hall, and John Dewey. The federal government expressed its concern when President Theodore Roosevelt called the White House Conference on the Care of Dependent Children in 1909 and established the federal Children's Bureau in 1912 (Long, 1969).

The founding of public library services for children formed part of the widespread interest in the welfare of children, and there is some evidence of connections between librarians and social reformers, particularly social workers and settlement workers. For instance, Boston librarians assisted settlement workers to set up a children's library in a settlement house 2 years before the first public library children's room was opened in 1888, and the general secretary of the Children's Aid Society in Boston attended the American Library Association conference in 1891, 1894, and 1902 (Garrison, 1979). Librarians worked with juvenile courts, YMCAs, and other organizations (Long, 1969). Historian Dee Garrison went so far as to say that "the activity of settlement workers. . .influenced the activity of the public librarian to a marked degree" (1979, p. 205). One of the great pioneers of children's services, Caroline Hewins, lived in a settlement house in Hartford, Connecticut, for 12 years (Gambee, 1978). Many of the activities that she introduced at the Hartford Public Library—reading aloud, storytelling, nature walks—bear a family resemblance to settlement house activities and contemporary children's public library programs alike.

Nearly all of the people involved in the first public library services for children were women. Although they were sometimes encouraged by male library directors like William Fletcher, women library directors such as Caroline Hewins, Minerva Sanders, and Mary Wright Plummer of the Pratt Institute in Brooklyn, frequently initiated youth services. Librarianship, like teaching and social work, was one of the few professions open to college-educated women. Work with children was viewed as especially appropriate for women, and the pioneering aspect of a new service most likely gave scope to individuals such as Anne Carroll Moore, whose leadership abilities might have been unrecognized in other fields. Moore's implementation of children's services at the Pratt Institute and the New York Public Library established many of the services now provided.

Reading journal articles written during this period gives one a sense that the founders of children's services had very clear goals; they knew what they wanted to do and why. They were appalled by the reading available for children in and out of the public library. These librarians believed Oliver Optic, Horatio Alger, and other authors now all but forgotten taught children profanity, vulgarity, brutality, and reliance on luck, which could affect their entire lives. Children were thought to need the guidance of a sympathetic adult to select good books for educational and moral reasons, books of high quality in terms of both content and style. These librarians believed in the efficacy of literature and art to build the personality and spiritual life (Braverman, 1979).

In this, the children's librarians were not alone. Virtually all librarians believed in the ideology of reading or the *library faith*, defined as the belief that reading is good for you and reading good books is better, a belief in which most white, educated 19th-century elites would have concurred. The emphasis on "quality" books is emblematic of "the traditional high culture bias of librarians and library collections," partly stemming from "a 19th-century WASP•definition of 'character' which is still with us" (Wayne Wiegand, personal communication, June 2, 1992). Over time, librarians' reactions to comic books, formula series fiction, and television programming have been influenced by this 19th-century tendency to believe that white middle-class values were right for everyone (West, 1988). The founders of children's services were genteel crusaders, sisters under the skin to other social reformers, and the term missionaries is still used to describe children's librarians' view of themselves (see D.J. Anderson, 1987, and Edmonds, 1989).

Within a selected collection of books, children were allowed to choose freely what they wished to read; thus, librarians believed, they would come to love good reading. Age restrictions on borrowing books were lowered so that children could enjoy books at home. Teaching children to care for books was a first lesson in citizenship, and children were thought to learn how to behave in public by being made to feel both at home in the library and responsible members of it. The motto of the children's Library League at the Cleveland Public Library is a fair sample of the attitude: "Clean hearts, clean hands, clean books." At Milwaukee Public a sign in the children's reading room proclaimed, "This room is under the protection of the boys and girls of Milwaukee" (Long, 1969). The evidence librarians used to substantiate their point of view was the memory of reading's importance in their own childhoods and the belief that reading is a powerful influence on behavior, for good or ill, reinforced by the social climate of the times.

In these years before radio and television, children had few options for entertaining themselves or satisfying their curiosity, and their working lives left many children little time for personal pursuits. When public libraries opened their doors to children, the children came in droves. "In the first decade of the new century, service to 300 or even 600 children a day was typical in branch work, especially in the poorer sections of large cities" (Garrison, 1979, pp. 209–210). It was not unusual to have more than 100 school-age children at a story hour. Perhaps the old-fashioned image of the librarian as a grim-faced enforcer of silence originated in these days when librarians had to deal with so many children at once, especially when good citizenship was one of their goals!

By 1924 when the American Library Association undertook a survey of public libraries, service to children was well-established. Many services would be recognizable to today's children's librarians. Children were being given help in locating materials that were freely available on open stacks, and story hours for school-age children were being held in most of the libraries with more than 50,000 volumes. Many librarians organized activities for children as clubs or contests around themes such as reading, nature, and travel. Librarians reported various schemes to encourage children to read, including summer reading programs, book lists, displays, and book talks, and some librarians visited schools and invited classes to visit the library for instruction in library use. Several of the largest libraries maintained a "school department" with services and collections for teachers. Out of the 1,243 institutions that replied to the survey, 51 reported having at least one branch library located in a school. These activities represent an enormous change from the public libraries of 50 years previous. Nevertheless, the survey found that children had more restrictions on their borrowing than adults and that many libraries still put children to the test of being able to write their names before being allowed borrowing privileges (*A Survey of Libraries in the United States*, 1927).

Over the next 30 years, children's librarians used the techniques developed during this early period: reading guidance, individual and group activities, library instruction, cooperation with schools and community agencies. Their goals were "to maintain, extend and modify" these techniques (Fenwick, 1976). All of these techniques are still in use, as shown in the description of youth services in Chapter 4. Gradually the popularity of story hours for school-age children waned as family lives and schooling patterns changed. During the 1930s and 1940s the newest technique was the preschool story hour where the librarian read aloud picturebooks and told stories to children between the ages of 3 and 5 (Carlson, 1991; Fenwick, 1976). The child study movement and the founding of preschool education programs such as the Montessori schools seem to have encouraged the admittance of younger children, and the development of picturebooks for younger "readers" furnished material for programs (Carlson, 1991). As the baby boom generation came along in the 1950s and 1960s, preschool story hours became very popular.

THE APPEARANCE OF YOUNG ADULT SERVICES

A significant development of the period after World War I was the introduction of library services for young adults. A number of librarians in the largest cities observed that a transitional service was needed between the guidance provided in the children's room and the complete freedom of the adult stacks. The 1924 survey disclosed a variety of practices regarding "certain books which are close to the indefinite border line between juvenile and adult" (*Survey of Libraries in the United States*, 1927, p. 29). Some libraries shelved "intermediate" books in either the children's or adult general collection but marked the spines in some fashion to indicate the age interest, and 40% of the libraries with collections over 100,000 volumes and 20% of the libraries with 50,000 to 100,000 volumes maintained "intermediate" or "young people's" collections. The collections varied in size from one shelf to an alcove. A few libraries had separate reference departments for high school students.

Braverman (1979) analyzed the post-World War I situation from which she believed the new services arose. Technological changes had shrunk the labor needs of industry, and the school-leaving age was raised to keep young people economically dependent. Librarians had set the age for transition to adult status at 12 or 14, ages at which many children in the 1890s left school and started to work (these ages remain the most usual ones at which public libraries transfer children to adult status for borrowing purposes). In the first two decades of the 20th century, more young people went to high school, making demands on adult reference departments for homework assignments at a time when adult services librarians were trying to expand their services: "All four coordinators of the young people's services studied here mentioned on many occasions the irritation with young people of the librarians who served adults" (Braverman, 1979, p. xiii).

Public libraries in New York City, Cleveland, and Baltimore were among the first to provide materials, space, and personnel especially designated for teenagers. Each library had its pioneering woman founder of young adult services: Jean Roos at the Cleveland Public Library, Mabel Williams at the New York Public Library, and Margaret Edwards at the Enoch Pratt Library in Baltimore, the counterparts of Anne Carroll Moore (who hired Mabel Williams). However, without the support of library directors such as Charles Rush of Indianapolis and Cleveland, Linda Eastman of Cleveland, and Joseph Wheeler of Baltimore, young adult services would not have developed. (Nevertheless, the proportion of young adult staff did not match the proportion of young adults as patrons.) As Braverman told it, each of these women had the gifts of liking teenagers as individuals and understanding the difficult position of teens in society. They had strong personalities that challenged their staffs to keep up with their ideas. Their philosophy was to work with young adults as they found them, to respond to the needs and interests that young adults had, rather than to impose an ideology of the library's making on them (Braverman, 1979; Edwards, 1974).

And yet, one has to wonder at this self-description. It is true that young adult librarians have always welcomed teenagers and have genuinely liked them. Many have earnestly sought to make their libraries attractive and interesting to teens. However, they, too, have been influenced by the ideology of reading. Witness this passage from Margaret Edwards's memoirs:

> We need young-adult librarians dedicated to establishing rapport with the city kid and convincing him that the public library can furnish him not only with the informational material he needs, but also with the wonder and joy of reading. The book is our message. (Edwards, 1974, p. 106)

The classic statement of the reading ideology of young adult librarians is Munson's *An Ample Field* (1950), which is almost entirely about books and dedicated "To all those who have helped me learn to read."

Enthusiasm and the positive attitude toward teens led to a good deal of experimentation. Very close cooperation with the schools was maintained in all three libraries, including New York's continuation and vocational high schools. Separate young adult rooms were opened in the central libraries, and some branches catered to high-school-age young people with special programs and materials. Some of these experimental branches were successful, but others were not, especially in areas with changing populations where the branch staff seems not to have been able to adjust to non-white, non-middle-class clienteles. The successful branches included equipment for playing popular music and space for socializing with peers, as well as sympathetic staff to locate the "right" books and materials. Some librarians looked on this as social work — not appropriate for libraries.

Thus, the cultural concern for promoting literature and the social concern for the conditions of young adult life did not always interact smoothly with each other (Braverman, 1979). Braverman noted instances where materials and programs about sex, race, and violence were proscribed by librarians working with young adults, reminding us about public librarians' view of themselves as agents of moral uplift as well as belles lettres, located in an institution founded in the Victorian era. It is to Margaret Edwards's credit that she attempted to serve African-American teens in Baltimore at a time when library services along with all other social institutions were racially segregated (Braverman, 1979; Edwards, 1974).

THE "STUDENT PROBLEM"

The years of the Great Depression and World War II saw major development in young adult services, and children's services was strengthening and expanding the techniques librarians had evolved. The 1950s brought both a tremendous increase in the numbers of young children – the baby boom generation born between 1946 and 1964 – and the conformist climate of the McCarthy era and the Cold War. Youth services "turned inward" in Braverman's phrase (1979, p. 247), concentrating on middle-class users or poor people who wanted to become middle class, which Braverman and others attributed to the emphasis on services to adult cultural elites favored in the Public Library Inquiry, the classic study of the 1950s that virtually ignored youth services. Both children's and young adult services became strongly book-oriented, as can be seen in the professional journals during the 1950s, even though films were well-established as library materials and television was rapidly developing into a major popular culture force.

Although librarian awareness of young adult needs was not universal, teenagers in the late 1950s and 1960s flocked to the public library. The baby boom generation coincided with a period of educational reform, just as the 1920s had, and materials beyond textbooks were needed for more students to do independent and individualized projects in more subject areas. Only 50% of schools had libraries in 1958 and only 42% had school librarians (Watts & Simpson, 1962). Federal funding in the form of the National Defense Education Act (NDEA) in 1958 and the Elementary and Secondary Education Act (ESEA) aided school library collections. However, NDEA monies were for a few selected subject areas only, and the ESEA funds did not arrive until 1965, when the need had been in existence for several years.

Students, in the meantime, were using the public library as they had since World War I: "Surveys of public library users in these years showed that often more than one-half of the users in the majority of libraries were high school students" (Fenwick, 1976, p. 3). One survey's respondents reported that teenagers used reference services more than adults at 77% of the libraries.

Lowell A. Martin, who spent his career studying many of the major urban libraries, completed two studies during the 1960s. In his study of the Enoch Pratt Library, just over half of Pratt's users were high school students doing school-related reading, and the public library supplied two thirds of all library service used by high school students, the school libraries contributing the other third (L.A. Martin, 1963). His study of the Chicago Public Library revealed that children and young adults constituted 62% of users. In comparison to adults, a higher proportion of young people used the public library: 42% of children aged 5 to 14, 58% of 15- to 19-year-olds, 19% of 20- to 39-year-olds, 10% of 40- to 59-year-olds and 6% of adults 60 and over (Martin, 1969). What is striking about these figures is that nationally, young people under 18 represented 36% of the population in 1960 and 34% in 1970. They were using libraries to a far greater extent than their numbers in the population would lead one to expect.

Their use was so great, in fact, that some librarians began putting restrictions on use by teenagers. A 1962 survey of 1,800 libraries in the United States and Canada found that 97% of the respondents welcomed student use, but, "we don't have enough space or staff or money. But the adult readers are suffering. But we can't give the students what they need" (Watts & Simpson, 1962, p. 246). The librarians also reported discipline problems, theft, and mutilation of materials. They blamed the problems on the inadequacy of school libraries and a lack of understanding from teachers and school administrators, although less than 40% were involved in cooperative planning with schools. A small percentage (13%-20%) of libraries placed restrictions on student use: limiting the number of items borrowed, refusing reference service and space in reading rooms, requiring permits from teachers and parents. High school and elementary students were the prime targets of these restrictions, but undergraduate and graduate students at the college level were also limited in a few libraries (International Research Associates, 1963; Moon, 1963; Watts & Simpson, 1962).

Emotions ran high. Historians have not yet studied the impact of this period on present library services. A lingering residuum is the occasional limitation on student use at some public libraries, such as refusing telephone reference service for homework assignments. Cooperation and communication with schools was hurt also, although Lewis and Farris (1990) reported that 83% of public libraries cooperated with the local schools. The nature and effectiveness of the cooperation were not reported, however. As the echoes of the baby boom move through the school system, librarians must be aware of the past in order to be prepared for future fluctuations in student use and to respond in ways that support the educational enterprise and avoid turf battles with schools.

MOVING FORWARD

A major development in public library services came in 1956, when the federal government first began providing some financial support for public libraries through the Library Services Act. Originally intended to ensure that public library service was available in the rural areas of the United States, the Act was later expanded to include construction projects (the name was changed to the Library Services and Construction Act, or LSCA) and demonstration projects of so-called outreach services to ethnic and language minorities and other groups. Currently the LSCA includes separate titles for service demonstration projects, construction, services to Native Americans, foreign language materials, cooperation, and literacy, although not all titles are funded every year. Public libraries were also eligible for other federal programs of the Great Society, and librarians look fondly back on the 1960s as years of relative affluence.

Librarians have designed and implemented a great many projects for or including children and young adults since the implementation of LSCA. The 1960s and 1970s were the years of the War on Poverty and the civil rights movement; librarians' consciousness was raised. Projects were intended to "serve the unserved" and reach new groups of patrons through new kinds of materials and new services. Librarians placed special emphasis on outreach – services provided outside a public library building. Thus many projects had a mobile component, a bus or van stocked with materials of special interest to African-American or Hispanic citizens, for example.

The impact of federal aid on services to children and young adults has never been measured. Many projects are funded for up to 3 years with federal money, but local jurisdictions frequently fail to support them when federal funding stops. Thus, many, but not all, of the programs disappear, and it is difficult to assess the impact on users when programs have such limited duration. The legacy of the 1960s and 1970s is a number of creative and innovative ideas for service and awareness and sensitivity to the needs of minority populations, including the handicapped. Although the sense of ferment and optimism is gone, the ideas are sometimes utilized by librarians in current situations requiring a less conventional or less institution-bound response. As librarians once again respond to renewed interest in serving ethnic, racial, and language minorities, some of the innovative services of the 1960s and 1970s are being revived, such as the Hispanic bookmobile service of the Santa Ana (CA) Public Library ("Library reaches out," 1988). Current interests in literacy and education have sparked reading readiness and family literacy programs that are sometimes targeted for populations that use the library less than the middle class. The ability to experiment has been the feature of LSCA most prized by youth librarians (Willett, 1987).

Youth services programs have always responded to the currents of fashion in public discourse, as the LSCA projects show. In keeping with the publicity surrounding research into the importance and efficacy of stimulating the intellects of very young children, librarians introduced the toddler storytime for children as young as 18 months in the 1970s. A parent or other adult stays with the child during the programs, so parent education is one of the objectives of such an activity. Although relatively few libraries offer such programs (see Table 4.8), they represent one development on the way to the current emphasis on work with parents and caregivers.

The 1970s were not only a decade of creativity. They were also a decade of threats to the existence of youth services from economic recessions and well-intentioned bureaucrats. A 1970 proposal by a committee appointed by the New York Commissioner of Education recommended entirely disbanding public library service to children. Under the recommendation, children preschool through sixth grade would have been able to use school libraries only. Neither school nor public librarians were in favor of the plan, and a proposed experiment was never funded because of the financial crisis in New York later in the 1970s.

To add to youth librarians' alarm, the economic downturns of the 1970s and early 1980s affected public library youth services along with the rest of the library. The taxpayer revolts in California, Massachusetts, and elsewhere resulted in reductions in support for public libraries as noted previously. Although a number of writers claimed that youth services were disproportionately affected, the limited research evidence does not support that claim for children's services, though there were marked decreases in support for young adult services, notably in California (Willett, 1987). Unfortunately, the number of young adult staff and coordinators were so few before Proposition 13, statistical tests for significant differences afterwards were not very meaningful. As I write this, the country is very slowly recovering from a recession that continues to affect public libraries. The economic signs do not point to long-term prosperity for the United States when one considers the national debt and the foreign trade deficit.

Planning, evaluation, goal setting, and other techniques for measuring accountability continue to interest public librarians; witness the number of documents the Public Library Association has published to assist librarians in this process, beginning with *Performance Measures for Public Libraries* (DeProspo, Altman, & Beasley, 1973), and continuing with *The Public Library Mission Statement and Its Imperatives for Service* (Goals, Guidelines, and Standards Committee, 1979), *A Planning Process for Public Libraries* (Palmour, Bellassai, & DeWath, 1980), *Output Measures for Public Libraries* (Van House, Lynch, McClure, Zweizig, & Rodger, 2nd ed., 1987; Zweizig & Rodger, 1982;), and *Planning and Role-Setting for Public Libraries* (C.R. McClure, Owen, Zweizig, Lynch, & Van House, 1987). Youth services is included in each of these documents, at least implicitly. With the publication of *Output Measures for Public Library Service to Children* (Walter, 1992), children's services has its own tools for measuring productivity. Some of the measures may be adaptable to young adult services.

In 1988, the Public Library Association began the Public Library Data Service (PLDS), which collects the results of output measures studies at individual libraries and makes them available through a national database. Although participation in the program is voluntary, it is hoped the PLDS will be a reliable source of national public library statistics. In 1991, some information about children's services was collected, as summarized by Zweizig (1993). Unfortunately, PLDS does not yet collect any data about young adult services, although an effort is being made to add them.

SUMMARY

Over the course of the last hundred years, the goals and techniques of youth services have maintained a remarkable consistency. Youth librarians have concentrated on supplementing formal education and promoting self-development through leisure reading and activities. As understanding about education and development have grown, public library services to young adults and children have changed with the addition of new materials and services. Although historically not all youth services librarians have been willing to acknowledge the legitimacy of working-class and lower-class values, they have perceived themselves as advocates for young people always. Thus far there has been very little structural change; despite youth librarians' willingness to provide services outside the library building, they always return to the institutional library and its bureaucratic structure. Whether public librarians will be able to continue their historic attachment to a physical collection for much longer is a question now being debated in the profession (Robinson, 1992). Longevity is one factor that aids an institution's survival, but change is also a necessity.

Despite the long tradition of serving children and young adults at the public library, history also records that not all librarians in other areas of the library have welcomed children and teenagers. The fact that the public library was founded for the use of adults seems to have colored the acceptance of young people as legitimate clients. D.J. Anderson (1987) delineated the negative views of library directors, who, over time, described children's librarians as sentimental, insular, and petty. The attitudes and events of the past have left youth librarians sometimes feeling defensive. Anderson fortunately documented that current attitudes of library directors are more positive, viewing children's services as a focus of good public relations and future library supporters, although the member survey completed by the Young Adult Library Association in 1992 revealed that young adult librarians still believe their services are not appreciated by administrators or the public.

If the reader has understood from this chapter and the previous one that young adult services have not become as firmly fixed in the minds of public librarians and the public as services to children, then the reader has grasped one of my messages. The fact that PLDS does not collect data about young adult services reinforces young adults' invisibility to the library community. It will be argued that few libraries collect data about young adult services, and that is undoubtedly the case, but surely having whatever data is available will be an aid to the profession and to those who fund the public library. Except for a few years at the begining of young adult services in the very largest public libraries, public library administrators have failed to provide an adequate number of young adult librarians.

Like services to children, young adult services call for charismatic, flexible, and imaginative staff; despite the popular image of librarians, there is truly no reason to think that librarians lack these characteristics. Fenwick (1976) described what happens when staff is lacking:

> The interest in the physical location and the characteristics of the facilities for young people's services often took precedence over the concern for adequately trained personnel in the planning of library buildings. As a result, buildings were equipped with special rooms and attractive furnishings but lacked staff and a range of books-not only adult literature, but also reference and nonfiction titles related to schools [sic] assignments. Inevitably, many rooms were given up as failures, while the need for an informed, sympathetic librarian who was trained to recognize and respond to the needs of adolescents persisted in every department of the library. (p. 349)

Why has service to teenagers failed to catch the imagination of public librarians generally? It is often said in the library press that the reasons for young adult services not being available everywhere are (a) the lack of a nationally accepted age definition of a young adult, (b) the lack of agreement that young adults require different kinds of services than children and adults do, and (c) the wide variation in maturation among adolescents, which makes them an unpredictable challenge. Adolescence is a biological state as well as a social status, which further complicates the definitional problem.

However, at least two of these arguments can be advanced to show that services to adults are problematic. Adulthood is not all that well defined, for example. Legally, one must be 18 to vote, 21 to drink alcohol, and 25 to rent an automobile (in some localities). Furthermore, adults exhibit a wide range of intellectual abilities and levels of maturation, and their physiology is also constantly changing. Despite the enormous range of adult interests and capacities, public libraries have adapted to serving them, and, in fact, are constantly looking for new ways of doing so.

At the national level, the divisions of the American Library Association that promote children's services and young adult services have agreed to overlap the ages that "belong" to each association, as exemplified by the ages covered in the two national surveys described in Chapter 4. The survey of children's services covers ages 0 to 14 and the young adult survey covers ages 12 to 18. The overlap creates a number of difficulties when one tries to articulate these two surveys or discuss the two services.

Braverman (1979) offered another explanation for the lack of acceptance of young adult services; she pointed to the status of young adults generally in society, reminding us that many adults are hostile to teenagers. The hostility may arise out of envy for the energy and vitality of the young or fearfulness of the physical strength and sexuality of teenagers. The general public sometimes conceives of adolescence as "not normal," although all adults have passed through it. As repositories of graphic information, libraries are about vicarious experience; the presence of exuberant teens ever hungry for real-life experiences may seem foreign or inappropriate to library-using adults, librarians and patrons alike. Today, we also see a certain amount of blaming teenagers for the social problems that beset them: drug abuse, unemployment, illiteracy, crime, and unmarried parenthood. The "just say no" campaigns suggest that if teenagers would just control themselves, all would be well. In comparison, children are seen as cute, dependent, and easily controlled by adults.

Perhaps adults are trying to avoid responsibility; to provide young adult services in public libraries requires accepting at least some responsibility to the present and the future. It requires a realistic assessment of the public library's contribution to society and not just a theoretical, flag-waving statement about the public library as the foundation of American democracy. As Braverman pointed out, librarians have not always felt comfortable considering all the social ramifications of their work, though they subscribe to the ideal that their work is meaningful to individuals and through them the larger society.

In light of the foregoing history, it is reasonable to ask: What are the impacts and effects of the services described here? Are they achieving the potential educational and developmental benefits proposed in previous chapters? To answer these questions in the most desirable way would require experimental research of the sort that would be extremely difficult, if not actually impossible, to implement. Long-term effects are likely to be confounded with many other influences in young people's lives: family, school, religion, television, peers, hobbies and avocations, and even genetic makeup. All may play more dramatic and observable roles in a young person's life than the public library, and yet, the public library may be part of the background in which all of these activities take place.

Ethically, it is not acceptable to provide publicly supported services to an experimental group and withhold them from a control group for purposes of a longitudinal study. In addition, testing young people in a public library setting violates the professional norms of many youth librarians, who value highly the voluntary attendance nature of the public library and think testing children is too much like school, where attendance is required. For these reasons, only a limited amount of experimental and correlational research is available regarding children's and youth services. This evidence is examined in Chapter 6. While reading Chapter 6, the reader should keep in mind the testimonies of library users that we have already seen in Chapter 3, which presented anecdotal evidence of library use effects.

The Effectiveness of Youth Services

INTRODUCTION

The previous sections have described public library services to children and young adults and two main criteria against which the effectiveness of the services are to be measured: enhancing development and providing education. In this section, we look at the research that attempts to find relationships between the criteria and public library youth services. There are few true experiments and a relatively small number of correlational studies. Some of the most interesting studies we consider are actually evaluations of libraries rather than research. Evaluation studies might be distinguished from pure research by the fact that they generally deal with a single library or a group of specific libraries, rather than a random sample, and the purpose of evaluation is to suggest to librarians how they might improve services, rather than to test hypotheses or answer research questions. Because librarianship is a practical endeavor and not an academic discipline, these kinds of studies should not be derogated. Though their results cannot be generalized, they generate information that suggests areas for research and speculation.

Not all services have been investigated, and as we found with the descriptive research, there is a decided lack of studies about young adult services. In addition to studies conducted in the United States, we also look at Canadian studies because public libraries there resemble American libraries more than libraries in any other country. The available research and evaluations cover some discernible categories: user studies, preschool programs, summer reading programs, reference and information programs, childhood use related to adult use, and public preferences.

USER STUDIES

User studies attempt to find out how many people use the public library, who uses it and who does not, what materials and services people use, and how, when, and why they use them. There have been national studies as well as local ones. In their review of major user studies from the 1930s to the mid-1970s, Zweizig and Dervin (1977) concluded that 20% of the adult population uses the public library once a month. Examining their data, one could also estimate that about 50% of adults use the public library once a year. Studies that try to describe who uses the public library have looked at a variety of demographic and other variables. The major demographic variable seems to be education—the more educated use the library. Other socioeconomic variables such as income and occupation appear to be redundant with education. Sex, marital status, and race have little or no significant predictive power, and findings regarding age and library use are mixed (Zweizig & Dervin, 1977).

Zweizig and Dervin (1977) noted that other, nondemographic variables may be more important and more useful to librarians. Researchers have found that amount of reading, especially book reading, relates very strongly to library use, as do community involvement variables. Information use, distance from the library, and other contextual variables (plans for adult education, plans to send children to private colleges) and personality traits (open-mindedness, achievement motivation) have also been found to relate positively to adult library use. Zweizig and Dervin also noted that the importance of library use is what people get out of using the library, not the use per se, and this is little studied. Multivariate studies have not been able to account for more than 20% of the variance in adult public library use; clearly there is a good deal more to learn.

Of all library investigations, user studies are the most numerous. If we include all the studies of individual libraries, there are hundreds if not thousands of user studies, but few of them focus primarily or even tangentially on youth services. As we look at the studies of use by children and young adults, it will be helpful to compare their findings with the findings regarding use by adults.

One of the earliest studies of young library users was conducted by librarians from the Racine (WI) Public Library. Hunt and Davitt (1937) administered questionnaires in the public schools to 7,073 children in grades four through nine. Of this number, 77.7% reported that they used the library. Slightly over 60% of the nonusers were boys. Children in grades four through eight were asked about attendance at story hours; 66% attended at least occasionally. When asked about hindrances to library use, the largest difficulties from the children's point of view were distance from the library (for 15.6%), other activities (19.6%), and a preference for listening to the radio over reading (24.3%). The children participated in a number of activities outside school; the most popular were clubs, going to the movies, and going to the playground in summer.

Two later studies of public library use by young people were done as part of larger evaluations of major public libraries by Lowell Martin. Some of his findings were mentioned in the previous chapter; they are repeated here for convenience. Martin used a variety of methods (statistics, interviews, documentary evidence) to evaluate the Chicago Public Library (1969) and the Enoch Pratt Free Library (1963) in Baltimore. In the Baltimore study, Martin found that two thirds of high school students read an average of four books (other than textbooks) per month for personal and educational reasons. These students spent 8 to 9 hours per month in school or public libraries; public libraries supplied almost two thirds of the hours and books used by students, and school libraries only one third. The majority of the high school students preferred the public library over their school libraries because of better collections, longer open hours, and fewer restrictions. Secondary school students used the library more intensively than other users, needing more staff assistance and borrowing more books. Martin estimated that between 60% and 67% of Enoch Pratt's service effort went to high school students (L.A. Martin, 1963).

The Chicago study (L.A. Martin, 1969) found that 57.8% of young adults (15- to 19-year-olds) and 41.7% of 5- to 14-year-olds were library users, although the frequency of use was not defined. Children made up 38.7% of library patrons and young adults represented 22.9% of users; the 5-to-20 population made up 61.6% of the Chicago Public Library users at the time of the study. Because children under the age of 5 were not included in the study, the percentage of child use should be higher. Martin also found that over one half of all users were using the library for schoolwork, and only 12.5% of library users were out-of-school adults.

In his study of *Library Usage by Students and Young Adults*, Wilder (1970) found that in the four Indiana libraries he examined, 39% of users were under 20 and in the two small towns, 57% were under 20. Help with schoolwork accounted for 43% of the motivations for coming to the library, with 52% coming for self-improvement and 56% for entertainment (respondents could choose more than one answer and college students were included). The under-20 group was more likely to have come to the library to use the reading rooms and reference collections than the over 20s. Wilder also found that at all ages there was a group of users who used the library frequently (i.e., several times per month or more) augmented by a small group of irregular and infrequent users (Wilder, 1970).

It should be noted that the Martin and Wilder studies were conducted during the time that the baby boom generation were teenagers and a larger proportion of the U.S. population was under 20 than currently is. It was also a time when teaching methods emphasized independent projects and reading beyond textbooks. At the time, school libraries were not as numerous or as well equipped and staffed as they are now. Because current educational methods also employ trade books and the whole language approach, we might find that formal education today makes demands similar to those of the 1960s, but we might also find that some potential public library use by young people is handled by school libraries. I have located no studies that compare public library use by young people in cities with strong school libraries to use in localities with poor school libraries.

A study that attempted to compare school-age children who were library users with non-library users was conducted in Regina, Saskatchewan (Fasick & England, 1977), although it was discovered that the majority of children who were nonusers had visited a public library at least once. The children were grouped by age, the 6- to 9-year-olds in one group and the 10- to 12-year-olds in another, with girls and boys separated. The researchers found that more than 90% of the children who used the library do so for the books, not surprisingly, and the library users read more books and newspapers than nonusers, although the differences were small. As one might expect, the younger children (6 to 9) used the library for personal interests more than for schoolwork. Younger children are given less "research" type homework than older children. Among the older children, 48.3% of the boys used the public library for schoolwork, whereas only 24.2% of the girls did so (Fasick & England, 1977).

One of the more interesting findings of this study was that the library users among the 10- to 12-year-olds had more ambitious educational and career goals than did nonusers. The differences between the two groups of boys are particularly striking. Library-using boys planned to finish 4 years of college at the rate of 67.2% to 29.6% of boys who did not use the public library, and 41% of library-using boys planned to become professionals, against 14.8% of the non-library-using boys. The n is fairly small here; the groups contain 61 male users and 54 male nonusers. Socioeconomic data were not available for the nonusers because they were interviewed at school and the school authorities would not allow the researchers to collect SES information. The children interviewed at the public library did provide such data, and only 15% of the older library-using boys had fathers who were professionals, which was about the proportion of professionals in the general Regina population. No information about mothers' occupations is given (Fasick & England, 1977). This particular finding coordinates well with the finding that adult library users are achievement oriented, as noted in Zweizig and Dervin (1977).

This should not be taken to mean that the public library was somehow responsible for the boys' ambition. Because library use is voluntary—no one is required to use it—those who use the public library do so because they perceive some advantage to themselves in library use. Ambitious boys perhaps saw the public library as a place to develop themselves in ways that their schools or families did not provide. Remembering that this is only one small study in a single community, one should be very cautious in generalizing this finding. The question is worthy of replication, however. We should also note the gender differences in library use as being worthy of more study.

Librarians are concerned about making libraries accessible to children; Fasick and England found that younger children most often came with parents and friends, whereas older children came on their own or with friends. Fasick and England also asked children who were nonusers why they did not use the library. For the 6- to 9-year-olds, the most important reasons for their infrequent use of the public library were lack of time to go, difficulty in obtaining permission or transportation, and distance to the library. Distance and lack of time were the main reasons given by the 10- to 12-year olds (Fasick & England, 1977). From the answers given by both users and nonusers, it is clear that parents restricted girls more than boys in going to the library on their own or in permitting them to go.

In the late 1970s a group of investigators at the University of California at Berkeley conducted a study of 764 sixth graders living in Oakland (Medrich, Roizen, Rubin, & Buckley, 1982). The purpose of the study was to find out how children spent their time when they were not in school. Although the public library was the least frequented place (the researchers also asked about attendance at restaurants, movies, parks, and church), 55% of the children said they went to the library at least a few times per year. Only 6% of them went to the library with their parents, the least of all the activities studied. This, along with Fasick and England's (1977) findings, indicates the importance of voluntary use and location of libraries near children's homes.

The Regina Public Library was also the site of a survey of young adult library use in 1981 (Murray, 1985). The researchers not only approached young people in grades 7 to 12 at school and at the public library, but at shopping malls, a pinball arcade, and a community swimming pool as well, obtaining 1,871 usable questionnaires. Although this study was reported in a narrative form without any tables, which makes it difficult to extract specific figures, some of the reported findings are appropriate to our endeavor. All but 10% of the respondents said they used the library at least occasionally, but the infrequent users (less than once per month) were the largest group of users. Nonusers said they did not need the library or did not have time for it (many students reported having part-time jobs or being involved in sports). More students preferred the public library to their school libraries (61% to 39%), but convenience of location was more important than available materials in choosing which public library branch to go to.

The most frequent reason selected for using the public library was to borrow books; the second most frequent reason was to do homework. The researcher was surprised that over 20% of those who responded that they read for recreation did not use the public library as the source for their reading materials. Less than 20% of the students said that they used the nontraditional services of the library, but these services were undefined in the the report. Respondents reported having an overall positive view of the library, but there were lots of "don't know" answers to the attitude questions, leading the researcher to conclude that the library's image was only weakly positive (Murray, 1985). From these and other findings, Murray concluded that the library needed to make various changes in policies, collections, and public relations activities.

A more recent study conducted in Calgary, Alberta (CACL Committee on Reference Materials for Children, 1984) surveyed 1,635 children in fourth, fifth, and sixth grades. Only 18% of the children said they had *not* used the library in the previous year. (Compare this to 50% of adults.) Most users (72%) said they went for "fun" reading, 44% used the library for personal information, and 38% for school assignments, rather similar to the results in the Regina study (Fasick & England, 1977).

A telephone interview study conducted in Rock County, Wisconsin, contacted a random sample of homes (Center for Survey and Marketing Research, 1989). Unusually high library use was reported by these respondents—67.7% reported having visited a public library in the past year. A group of 121 young people between the ages of 12 and 17 were also interviewed, and their library use was even higher than the general use in the county; 86.5% claimed to have visited a public library in the past year and 55.5% of those had visited at least 10 times. The most frequent reasons for 12- to 17-year-olds to visit the public library were: information for school (95.5%), leisure use (74.2%), to study a subject of personal interest (67.6%), and to get materials for others (46.6%).

Without trying to sum across these studies, each conducted in different ways with different purposes in mind, a number of patterns seem to appear. Although one has to use caution in accepting self-reports of behavior, children and young adults, particularly young adults, are more frequent library users than the general adult population, although the numbers and percentages vary from one community to another and from one time to another. This remains the case despite improved school libraries and a smaller proportion of young people in the population. Teenagers' main use is for school assignments, although leisure reading is a close second, whereas for younger children, recreational reading is a stronger reason than school assignments. For both groups, school assignment use is a major portion of total motivation to use the library, and it is clear that the public library continues to play a role in supporting formal education. Distance and lack of transportation may create barriers to library access for children under the age of 12.

Although the studies cited above delineate some of the broader outlines of public library use by young people, the outcomes for users have not been studied. A few studies have found relationships between the availability of well-staffed and well-stocked school libraries and measures of academic achievement (Lance, Welborn, & Hamilton-Pennell, 1992). No similar studies have attempted to correlate public library youth services with reading scores.

PRESCHOOL PROGRAMS

The descriptive surveys discussed in Chapter 4 revealed that preschool programs are among the most commonly available activities for children at public libraries. The recent national survey found that 89% of the libraries offered story hours, and most of these are likely to be for preschool children. In 1975, the children's librarian at the Wilmette (IL) Public Library wrote about the evaluation of the library's preschool program (Wayland, 1975). Eighty mothers responded to a questionnaire about their child's growth. Sixty-five said that their child's interest in books had increased, 64 said they noticed social growth in their child, and 62 saw some learning of songs and finger plays over the 6-week period of story hours. Although mothers of preschoolers do tend to observe their children closely, the lack of a control group is a methodological problem with this evaluation. Young children develop quickly, and even within 6 weeks one could expect maturation to have an impact on a number of cognitive variables. The results of this survey must have been gratifying for the Wilmette Public Library staff but they do not help us very much.

A far better study was designed and executed by Smardo and Curry (1982) at the Dallas Public Library. The study compared receptive language skills (listening skills) in children aged 3 to 5, across three treatments and a control group using the basic pretest–posttest design. The weekly treatments were: (a) "live" story hours using selected picturebooks read by the librarian-researcher (Smardo), (b) commercially produced films based on the same books, and (c) videotapes of the stories as they were read to the first group. All of the treatments were given at a branch of the Dallas Public Library. The control group received no trips to the library or any story hours. The 327 children were recruited from two private day-care centers (considered the higher SES group, they were mainly white) and two Head Start centers (considered the lower SES group, they were mainly African American). Before and after the 6-month experimental period the children were tested using the *Test of Basic Experiences* (TOBE).

The researchers found that the "live" and the film story hours were significantly more effective than no story hours in increasing receptive language skills with "live" story hours having larger effects, and "live" story hours were significantly more effective than video story hours. However, watching story hours on video was not significantly more effective than having no story hours (Smardo & Curry, 1982). Examining the differences between the Head Start (lower SES) and non-Head Start (higher SES) groups, the researchers found that the higher SES children started and ended with higher TOBE scores, and the higher SES controls had *significantly* higher posttest TOBE scores than the lower SES controls. That is, the lower SES children in the control group fell further behind the higher SES controls. For the treatment groups, the gain for both higher and lower SES children was the same, so that, although the lower SES children did not catch up with their higher SES peers, they did not fall further behind.

This is an important result, and it is unfortunate that the experiment has not been replicated. It would be useful to know if the important factor is having carefully selected picturebooks read aloud by a trained librarian in a library or whether reading aloud any books by any reader in any location would have the same effect. More information about the day-care programs would be useful, as well. One reason for the differences between the private centers and the Head Start programs could be the amount of reading aloud incorporated into their regular curricula or in children's homes.

Some librarians now offer story hours for infants and toddlers as well as 3- to 5-year-olds, a result of the publicity that early childhood research has received in recent years. In order to find out if the methods librarians use with toddlers were appropriate, Carlson (1985) devised a schema for toddler storytimes after an extensive review of the child development literature. Five experts in early childhood education reviewed the schema and suggested revisions. The revised schema was turned into a questionnaire that was sent to librarians who had been identified as providing toddler programs. Responses from 235 librarians indicated that they offered storytimes for toddlers. Carlson found that most of their practices and attitudes were appropriate for toddlers. For example, 91% reported that parents and caregivers stayed with their children during programs and 99.6% believed that children under 3 have book preferences (Carlson, 1985).

This result was very encouraging, especially as research by Smardo (1980) and Greene and Cullinan (1988) suggested that librarians were ill equipped to serve young children because they had inadequate academic preparation in child development. Carlson (1985) did find that those librarians with a background in child development either through coursework or reading followed appropriate practices for toddlers to a greater degree than librarians without the background.

These two studies represent the most substantial research in the area of services to preschoolers at public libraries. The paucity of research suggests that librarians have been content to operate at the level of belief without reliance on facts when it comes to preschool programs. A study of programs for 3- to 5-year-olds similar to Carlson's study of toddler storytimes would enhance our knowledge of the appropriateness of program content.

SUMMER READING PROGRAMS

The descriptive research reported in Chapter 4 noted that one of the most universal activities for school-age children is the summer reading program; Lewis and Farris (1990) found that 95% of libraries offered this service and 89% of the libraries reported that children made "moderate" or "heavy" use of the service. The typical summer reading program consists of some kind of form on which children write down the names of the books they read and a series of activities, usually one a week for most of the summer, that relate to the theme. Much staff energy is expended in selecting a theme that appeals to children, designing materials for children to use and programs to offer them, and visiting schools before vacation begins to advertise the entire package. Some state library agencies make centrally designed materials available, which is an efficiency for libraries with small, generalist staffs. In the past, children who read the most or read a stipulated amount received prizes or certificates. Recently librarians have adopted less competitive formats, using a lottery or drawing for the awarding of prizes, and some have devised ways of involving parents and "prereaders."

Perhaps because the finite nature of the program offers the possibility of pretest–posttest designs, research on summer reading programs is more numerous than on any other activity of children's services. The first question, of course, is whether the premise on which these programs are based is correct: Do children lose reading skills over the 3 months that they are not in school during the summer? Much of the research on summer retention was done in the 1920s and 1930s. Locke (1988) noted that some researchers found that skills diminished, others found that skills increased, and still others reported insignificant changes in learning over the summer. In her review of the literature on summer retention of learning, Heyns (1978) said, "The majority of studies find that reading, vocabulary, and language skills show insignificant change during the summer, whereas skill in arithmetic, problem solving, and spelling generally declines" (p. 15). Her own findings suggested that children of lower socioeconomic status tend to show less growth in learning over summers than children of higher SES.

Summer reading programs at public libraries might then adopt a new premise: to encourage *continued growth* in reading, rather than to focus on maintaining reading skills. Because reading is a major skill on which academic success relies, programs that aid in increasing reading ability during the times that children are not in school deserve our attention. Locke reviewed the research on public library summer reading programs in her 1988 dissertation. All of the studies found that children who participated in public library summer reading programs improved their reading skills more than those who did not. The skill most often tested was vocabulary, and the improvements were most often noticed in the youngest students, those in grades one, two, and three. As these students are still learning to read (Chall's [1983] Stages One and Two), the practice at reading may be most beneficial and the learning curve steepest for these youngest participants.

The studies of summer reading programs tend to have the same weaknesses that Heyns (1978) found in the summer retention research. That is, they tend to overlook the socioeconomic status of the children tested. The results of some of them are worth noting, however. Cook (1952) reported on 12 summers of research involving different approaches to summer learning among second graders. Some summers children were given books to read with assigned pages for each day and various kinds of worksheets to complete. For two summers, children were simply encouraged to participate in the local public library's summer reading program. In terms of intelligence and reading ability, the children who participated were similar to those who did not. Cook found that children who participated in some reading program during the summer gained significantly more on a standardized reading test than those who did not, but the children who participated in public library reading programs gained most of all, and the gains persisted for several months. The following January, the reading skills of those who had used the library were still half a year above nonparticipants. Cook concluded:

> No summer program for any individual child is superior to one which includes a relaxed child, a good library, a trained librarian, and at least one parent who takes time to listen, to discuss, to supply information, and occasionally to visit the library with the child. (1952, p. 417)

This positive evaluation is offset somewhat by the realization that fewer children chose to use the library than chose the other reading plans in previous years and that self-selection played a part in who participated. Children cannot be forced to use the public library, whether for research or in real life, and intelligence and the ability to read are not the only determinants of actual reading. Other researchers have studied the possible impact of self-selection on summer reading programs. In 1945, Fair raised the issue of who were the readers who joined summer reading programs. Looking at the 107 members of the Summer Reading Club in Maplewood, New Jersey in 1944 in grades four through nine, she found that participation dropped off sharply after grade seven. The average reading grade of participants was C+, and most of the participants were average or above-average readers. The findings disturbed the researcher, who asked which children libraries fail to reach and what could be done about it (Fair, 1945).

A larger study was published by Goldhor and McCrossan (1966). Using all children enrolled in the fourth grade in Spring 1962 in Evansville, Indiana, the children who completed the requirements of the summer reading program were compared with all those who did not. Those who completed the program differed from nonparticipants in that they had higher IQs (by 4.7 points), higher socioeconomic backgrounds, higher spring reading grades, and were 5 months ahead of nonparticipants on the reading test in the spring and 7 months ahead on the fall test. The researchers found that fall reading test scores correlated most highly with test scores and reading grades for the previous spring. The effect of summer reading program membership was small but measurable and significant at the .01 level. These results are quite different from Cook's

(1952). The differences may be due to more sophisticated statistical techniques or to the fact that Goldhor and McCrossan tested fourth graders whose reading skills and interests might have been more confirmed than Cook's second graders who would have been beginning readers.

In 1978, Heyns published her study of the effects of summer learning on Atlanta sixth graders. The factor that made the most impact on summer learning was whether or not the child had read during the summer, and the major determinant of that reading was public library use (Heyns, 1978). Library use was especially important for black children because it had a direct impact on the number of books read during the summer, regardless of family income. Heyns concluded, "like schools, libraries effectively increase the achievement of children" (1978, p. 183). It should be noted that Heyns was talking about reading during the summer, not whether a child joins a formal summer reading program.

The final study we examine is Locke's dissertation (1988). Locke estimated the effectiveness of public library summer reading programs by determining their penetration rate; that is, the proportion of the local children aged 13 and younger who participated in the program. She selected the figure of 8% penetration as indicating a successful program because earlier research had indicate the national average was a 7% participation rate. She found a median percentage of 5% participation and a mean rate of 6.6%. Of the 200 libraries (out of 376 respondents) that could supply both child population and the number of summer reading participants, only 31% were deemed successful, and they reached a median of 11% of their child population. The unsuccessful libraries reached just 3% of children in their communities. Locke looked only at libraries serving 25,000 people or more; she believed that higher participation rates might be found among libraries in smaller communities where presumably children have fewer options for how they will spend leisure time.

Considering the amount of effort that librarians put into designing and implementing summer reading programs, the percentage of children who participate in the programs is rather low. If over 50% of children use public libraries, why do so few of them join the summer reading program? Do summer reading programs encourage children to read more than they would without the program? If the programs only reach children with above-average reading skills, should librarians attempt to find a technique that will appeal to children who need the reading practice more? What should be the public library's response to the finding that the skills most endangered by 3 months of summer vacation are arithmetic, problem solving, and spelling? Summer reading effectively improves reading skills; however, a reassessment of summer reading programs seems to be in order.

REFERENCE AND INFORMATION SERVICES

Librarians stress the provision of information as one of the most important services offered at the public library, yet less than 5% of the adult American public will spontaneously list the public library when asked for sources of information (Zweizig & Dervin, 1977). Fasick and England (1977) found that 18% of the non-public library using children mentioned the public library as a source of information, though the responses might have been biased because the children were interviewed in their school libraries. The accuracy of reference services has also been questioned. Unobtrusive studies have found that only 55% of questions are answered accurately (Crowley & Childers, 1971), although Murfin and Bunge (1988) found that trained reference librarians with master's degrees completely satisfied their patrons' requests 60.4% of the time, whereas paraprofessionals did so 50% of the time.

No studies of youth librarians as reference librarians have asked whether their accuracy is any greater, but we have no reason to expect that it would be, given that all librarians receive fairly similar education in the basic required skills. In fact, although research in adult reference is a well-traveled path, very few studies of information and reference use by child and teenage patrons of public libraries have been published. Three studies first considered in Chapter 4 are mentioned here in more detail, along with some research into the information search process of library users.

The first is a study of 14 public libraries in Connecticut that sampled data from September 1978 to September 1979 (Hektoen, 1981). Findings included the following: About 44% of all reference questions asked in children's rooms were asked by adults, many of whom wanted information about other community agencies and organizations that serve children; 63.6% of questions asked were school related (librarians' estimate) and requests for reader's advisory were about 25%, a proportion that the researcher found surprisingly low. Many poor and incorrect answers were noted, leading Hektoen to conclude that staff needed more training in reference techniques and children's materials, and as the project proceeded, staff became more aware of the need to offer interlibrary loans and reserves to children (Hektoen, 1981).

The Calgary study mentioned previously (CACL Committee, 1984), included a questionnaire given to librarians at the 13 Calgary Public Library branches during April 1982. During that period 1,423 questions were asked in children's departments and 791 of them were followed. Of these questions, 77.6% were answered, we do not know how correctly. The most common reason for not finding an answer was that all the books on the subject were out. Of the 177 persons whose questions went unanswered, only 35 were referred to the Central Library or given a reserve. The committee doing the research speculated that children's information needs are too immediate for them to be willing to wait for a book to be returned. Transportation was also assumed to be too difficult for children so they were not referred to another library (CACL Committee, 1984). There is nothing to indicate whether children were asked if they wanted a reserve or were able to travel.

The third study was a case study of the Urbana (IL) Public Library's children's department reference services. Harrington (1985) found that adults asked 29% of questions and children and young adults asked 71% of questions. Young people were more likely to ask questions regarding audiovisual equipment, games, and other materials, whereas adults asked more frequently about locations of materials and library policies. In fact, 46% of the questions asked by young people were for help with audiovisuals or games. The differences between the kinds of questions asked by adults and young people were statistically significant at .01. When children or young adults asked a true reference question, 64% of the time they were most likely asking a school-related question (Harrington, 1985).

The results of these three studies again reinforce the notion that a good deal of the use of the public library by young people is for school-related purposes. The large number of questions about use of audiovisuals asked by children and young adults at Urbana suggests the degree to which the current generation prefers these materials, which are probably used for recreation. The results also suggest how much we do not know about children's and young adults' information needs or preferences, because they do not seem to be asking the kind of personal interest questions that public librarians feel most equipped to answer. On the other hand, of course, frequently we have only the librarians' perception that all these questions are school generated. It is quite possible for children to develop personal interests in subjects introduced at school; thus it may be quite difficult in practice to be sure what the motivation is for any particular question, and many librarians are loath to inquire about a patron's motivation or intended use of information.

It should be noted that all these studies were conducted from the librarians' standpoint, rather than from the user's view of the quest for information. A series of studies by Kuhlthau (1991) began to elucidate not only the behaviors involved in the information search process, but also searchers' feelings and cognitive processes. Although most of her subjects have been college students and adults, some of them were high school students. The feelings, thought processes, and behaviors were similar among all groups, with subjects expressing confusion, uncertainty, and little confidence in their searches at the beginning, and greater confidence as they moved toward completion of their searches. The high school students, however, were not as confident as the older subjects. Kuhlthau found that information search was an iterative, recursive process-it did not happen in a straight line. She concluded that current methods of reference service and bibliographic organization emphasize the middle and end stages of information search, in which people are able to clearly state their needs, and do not help users in the confusing early stages of search formulation.

If this is the case for high school students, who may be presumed to be well launched on the road to adult logical abilities (Piaget's formal operations stage), we can only speculate about the difficulties of younger people attempting to negotiate an information system designed and prepared by adults. Librarians know that patrons of all ages frequently are unable to clearly state their questions, and the librarian must assist the question-asking process. Librarians experienced in reference services for children are very aware of the intricacies of communication with them, in which the only guides seem to be patience, goodwill, persistence, and intuition. This important aspect of reference service has not been addressed in the research.

DO CHILDHOOD LIBRARY USERS BECOME ADULT LIBRARY USERS?

Librarians who work with children and young adults often say that they are building up the adult audience for the public library, that today's young people are tomorrow's adult library users and taxpayers. Leaving aside the obviously self-serving character of such blatant appeals to institutional survival instincts, we can say that, in general, society seems to feel that there is some value to library use. If youth services are the developmental ground for continued use in adulthood, then they can be said to have fulfilled one of their major purposes. There are three studies that produced information relevant to this point. Two of them are dealt with in some detail.

Powell, Taylor, and McMillen (1984) were guided by Bandura's theory of social learning, the notion that behavioral models can influence later behavior in the observer, as discussed in Chapter 3. The research was conducted via telephone interviews with a national random sample of 342 adults (18 or over), by the Survey Research Center at the University of Michigan. The level of current public library use reported was similar to that in the studies mentioned by Zweizig and Dervin (1977)–48% had visited a public library at least once during the past year. The researchers asked a variety of questions about childhood use of libraries: ease in getting to a library, parental reading habits, parental encouragement of child's reading, frequency of childhood reading and library attendance, age at first use of public or school libraries, and who went with the respondent to the library. Several demographic questions were asked as well.

Multiple classification analysis was used to analyze the data regarding adult reading habits and adult public library use. Adult reading of magazines was most strongly linked to frequent library use as a child, and adult book reading was most strongly correlated with the frequency of reading in childhood. Those persons who had used a public library at least once during the preceding year were likely to have started using libraries when in grade school, had been accompanied by a parent, had used the library at least 10 times per year at some period of their childhood, and had read often as children. Those persons who had used a public library at least 10 times during the past 12 months were characterized by having been heavy library users as children (10 or more times per year), began using libraries with parents during their pre-school years, and most likely read frequently as children. The authors noted that "frequent childhood use of libraries is more important to the frequency of adult use than it is to the mere existence or absence of use" (Powell, Taylor, & McMillen, 1984, p. 261). This finding was corroborated by Lange (1987–1988).

Overall, the most important factors in current public library use for these respondents were, in order: (a) having been taken to the library by a parent during childhood, (b) having persons under 18 in one's current household, and (c) having a college education. The researchers noted that 80% of those who began using libraries with their parents had visited a library in the previous year, which they believed indicated the importance of parental influence. Looking at their data tables, however, one sees that people more often began using libraries on their own (34.9%), with friends (21.1%), or with teachers (16.9%), whereas only 13.6% first went with their parents (Powell, Taylor, & McMillen, 1984). Parents seem to be stronger but less frequent models than friends or teachers when it comes to library use.

A somewhat different approach with less statistical sophistication was undertaken by Razzano (1985). Interviewers at 28 small libraries in New York State conducted 1,240 in-library interviews in the spring of 1982. The interviewees were all adults aged 21 or over. The findings indicated that 85% of adult library users began using the library during their youth, and 75% of them began before the age of 12. More than a third of those under the age of 50 began their public library use as preschoolers. Powell, Taylor, and McMillen (1984) found that 98.4% began using school or public libraries before leaving high school. Razzano also asked respondents about bringing their own children to the library. Parents represented 73% of the total sample, and 82% of them said that all their children were regular library users, even those whose children were now adults: "Only 6% of the children of parents who were young library users are now nonusers" (Razzano, 1985, p. 114). Again, parental behavior appears to be a strong factor in public library use by young people.

Although the socialization studies are few in number, the direction of their findings is quite clear: Childhood library use has an impact on adult library use. Although some reservations about the reliability of interviews *about* library use conducted *in* libraries are warranted, Razzano's findings do not contradict the national random sample of the earlier study.

WHAT PEOPLE SAY THEY WANT FROM PUBLIC LIBRARY SERVICES TO YOUNG PEOPLE

Librarians clearly have some ideas about what makes good public library service for children, even if they do not test these ideas very often. Library users also have expectations and criteria about library services, but they are infrequently asked to comment on children's or young adult services. Three studies that examined the preferences of library users and other constituents are discussed. The earliest study that compared the interests of users with librarians was conducted by Fasick (1978) at the South Central Regional Library System in the province of Ontario. Four groups were identified and administered questionnaires: library trustees, librarians, elementary and nursery school personnel, and parents.

Fasick found that librarians rated the availability of Canadian-origin materials and French language materials higher than users, that parents and teachers valued audiovisual materials higher than librarians, and that users and librarians agreed that such popular materials as comic books and TV spinoffs were not very important (would children have agreed?). Queries about traditional services such as story hours, reading guidance, provision of books, and information services found that the services were considered less important to the public than to the librarians, but still valued by all. Newer services for young children, such as programs for under threes and the provision of circulating toys were more controversial. Parents and nursery school personnel rated these higher than elementary teachers and librarians. In the matter of information for school assignments, Fasick found that librarians were more satisfied with the service than users or school personnel (Fasick, 1978).

Another rather controversial area was the notion of providing for socializing, such as places for children to meet with friends, programs for parents and children together, and meeting rooms for community groups; opinion was divided. Fasick reported that more users than librarians thought these aspects of library use were important. On a number of issues, Fasick noted that there seemed to be a communication gap between the librarians and the patrons. She urged librarians to market their services so that more users would be aware of the availability of Canadian materials, interlibrary loan and reserves, and reference services.

Childers and Van House (1989) conducted research into library effectiveness variables important to seven groups: library directors, library public service staff, members of library friends groups, library users, trustees, local officials, and community leaders. After an extensive analysis of the library effectiveness literature, the researchers identified a manageable set of 61 potential indicators and administered questionnaires to a nationally stratified sample of libraries. Library directors were charged with selecting local officials, community leaders, and library users to receive the questionnaires; this undoubtedly biased the responses positively toward public libraries and toward those who share the library directors' views. The researchers did not consider this a random sample.

Usable responses were received from 2,418 persons, and the data were subjected to factor analysis that identified eight dimensions among the 61 indicators. Respondents also ranked the importance of the indicators in responding to the question, "In describing a public library, how important would it be for you to know each of the following about that library?" Six indicators appeared among the top ten choices of all seven constituent groups: convenience of hours, range of materials, range of services, staff helpfulness, services suited to the community, and quality of materials (Childers & Van House, 1989).

Although Childers and Van House were not asking about youth services but general public library services, there is no reason to think these indicators would not be important to all age levels. Looking again at Fasick's (1978) findings we see that most of these six indicators appear there; the exception seems to be convenience of hours, which Fasick perhaps did not ask about. Childers and Van House anticipated further research to validate their findings; let us hope youth services will be included.

Estabrook and Horak (1992) reported the results of a telephone survey of a representative national sample of the public which, was compared with a mail survey of librarians. Some of the questions asked involved services and materials for young people. On most of these questions, there was a divergence of opinion between the public and the professionals. A striking difference was registered around the question of after-school care for children; 39% of the public felt all libraries should offer such a service, whereas 60% of librarians felt libraries should *not* offer it. The public was also more prepared to limit access to offensive materials than librarians were, except for material on AIDS. On that subject, 85% of the public and 96% of the librarians thought anyone, regardless of age, should have access to materials. Making birth control information available to anyone was acceptable to 56% of the public, but only 10% said books on suicide should be available to anyone and 71% would keep such books out of the library. Recordings with offensive language and *Penthouse* and *Playboy* magazines were even less acceptable to the public, with 13% and 3% being willing to allow anyone to use them. For all these materials, librarians were far more willing to permit general access than the public was, though the professionals were not unanimous. Considerable opportunity for educating the public about the purposes of the public library would seem to exist.

A related point of view, though not a formal research study by any means, comes from Catherine Sleezer, mother of two boys, who wrote about how she found the "perfect public library." Sleezer wanted her boys to discover "the magic that happens when people connect to other people and events through books" (1987, p. 333). She and her sons were not successful, until they encountered an inner-city Minneapolis library branch where the staff had enthusiasm for sharing books with children, respected clients regardless of age, and worked as a team to serve the public and maintain the library. One of the areas little studied is the actual behavior of librarians vis à vis patrons, yet it is a crucial part of whether people use libraries and whether they find what they want.

SUMMARY

Although the evidence is not available in such quantity as would give us complete certainty in our assertions, what research has been done tends to confirm the notion that public library services to young people are perceived to provide certain benefits to their users. The studies particularly show a measurable impact on language and reading skills. The sheer volume of library use in support of formal schooling suggests that the public library makes an important contribution to the educational achievement of young people. It is not entirely rhetorical to wonder what would happen to K–12 education if the public library were not there to back it up. Finally, the public library seems to have a self-perpetuating quality in terms of childhood users becoming adult library users, but there are disagreements of more or less substance between users and librarians about the services desired.

We are left with many questions. Most of the studies look at what are called *outputs*—how many people used a particular service—rather than the *outcome* of the use for the user. For instance, do those young people who use the public library for school use do better on their homework than those who do not? The important exceptions to this are the studies of preschool story hours and summer reading programs where the most recent studies have given us valuable data from well-designed and well-executed research. These studies are as yet too few in number to give us the kind of confidence that is desirable. The literature hints here and there that use by children and teenagers may differ greatly from adult use, but we do not know who our young users are in terms of socioeconomic status or other nondemographic variables. No one has studied why it is that such a large proportion of adults do not use the library when such a large proportion of young people are library users. If people stop using the public library after high school graduation because they see the role of the library as only connected to formal education rather than personal fulfillment, then youth librarians have failed in one of their main goals. On the other hand, some research indicates that current adult library users were childhood library users.

Other large gaps in the research involve reference services and activity programs. We have some data about how much reference work is done and what kinds of questions are asked. We do not know very much about the accuracy or efficiency of youth librarians as question answerers. From the chapter on descriptive research, we noted that many libraries offer programs on various topics. No one has done much research into the impact of these programs. Of course, a single activity of an hour or two could not be expected to yield easily quantifiable sociological or educational results, yet librarians plan and implement the programs believing that they do have a positive impact on patrons and the library. We need some way of assessing what the impacts are, even as we are aware of the difficulties of designing meaningful research in an area where effects may be short term (e.g., for a specific library activity) or cumulative over a long term and confounded with many other influences (e.g., borrowing books for 18 years).

This consideration of the effectiveness of public library services to young people is important to the next step of the policy analysis. In order for a service to be a legitimate claimant on the public exchequer, it must meet the tests of economists' public goods theory. Naturally, one criterion has to be that the service performs as stipulated. A description of public goods theory and the criteria for judging a service's appropriateness for public support are taken up in the next section. The benefits of public library services play a role in the discussion.

CHAPTER 7

The Economic Value of Youth Services

INTRODUCTION

In a free market economy such as ours, individuals generally expect to pay for the goods and services they consume. Ideally, governments, whether local, state, or national, avoid interfering in the process of exchange. But even in the United States, some commodities are not available on the free market or reliance on the free market would create problems with the use of certain services and goods. Therefore, government intervenes, whether through full financial support, partial subsidy, or regulation. In addition, there are other factors that economists look for to determine if a service is worthy of public funding (Hare, 1988; Heilbroner & Thurow, 1982; Musgrave, 1969/1986b). In this section we examine that portion of microeconomics called *public goods theory*. (Microeconomics looks at the market activity of buyers and sellers; macroeconomics deals with large flows of economic productivity such as the gross domestic product. Heilbroner and Thurow [1982] call the macroeconomic perspective a bird's-eye view compared to the worm's-eye view of microeconomics.) We also discuss market failure, merit wants, externalities, income distribution, value added, and option value as they pertain to public funding of library services for young people. We attempt to answer the question, from the point of view of economics, should the public pay for children's and young adult services at the public library? Before we do that, a brief review of economics and the theory of the free market sets the stage for the complementary notion of public goods theory.

ECONOMICS AND THE FREE MARKET

When it comes to the material goods of this world, most of us probably want more than we can have. The resources of individuals, corporations, governments, and the earth itself are limited. Economics "is concerned with the production, allocation, valuation, and consumption of goods and services" (Schauer, 1986, p. 6). It is also the study of human behavior around the allocation of resources. As such, capitalist economics subscribes to some basic assumptions about the nature of reality (McKenzie, 1979). First, there is the assumption that human beings have free will, an ability to make choices and seek out whatever makes them happiest or "maximizes their preferences." Constraints on behavior are not complete, and individuals and groups have an effect on their environments. Second, economists believe that people by and large are rational and act out of self-interest. Those of us who choose an occupation, such as librarianship, that does not pay as much as brain surgery have reasons for doing so, and we are acting in our own behalf.

A third important assumption is the notion of personal property: Individuals can own things. This is not as self-evident as it may seem. In medieval Europe, only a few privileged persons had the legal right to own land, houses, livestock, tools, and so on. Serfs did not have the right to the products of their own labor. In our own day, some American Indians do not believe human beings can possess land or other natural resources. Property ownership leads to the fourth assumption of economics: Individuals can assign economic values to things and make trades based on their evaluations. The value of an object is whatever someone is willing to pay for it. Finally, although individuals evaluate, make choices, buy, and sell, each is one of a large number of players, and under most circumstances, individuals cannot affect prices in the market.

If we operate under the given assumptions and allow people to go about the business of producing goods and exchanging them among themselves without interference, we have a free market. As Adam Smith realized over two hundred years ago, permitting exchange in this way is both self-regulating and dynamic because of the complementary operation of supply and demand. On the demand side, buyers try to purchase at the lowest price possible, and suppliers try to sell at the highest price possible. Because there are numerous buyers and sellers, competition exists, and neither buyers or sellers are able to have things entirely their own way. When goods and services are offered on the free market, sellers soon learn how much will be purchased at particular prices and regulate their production accordingly, as buyers indicate their preferences. Prices and quantities of goods will reach an equilibrium point at which both sellers and buyers are satisfied. In this way the market regulates itself.

A change in either supply or demand will cause the market to reach equilibrium at a different price-to-quantity ratio. For example, more profit can be had if the costs of production are lowered, so there is an incentive to introduce cost-effective production techniques and technology. Lower costs may lead to lower prices, which increase demand. Such a change has occurred in the production of computers. The personal computer that I used to write this book is much more powerful and much less expensive than the UNIVAC of the 1950s. Consequently, there are a lot more PCs than there ever were UNIVACs. Thus we have economic dynamism and technological and social change as well (Heilbroner & Thurow, 1982).

Life from an economist's point of view is a series of cost–benefit analyses. Buyers and sellers evaluate alternatives and make a choice based on the perceived benefits. Therefore, the cost of a good or service is the value of the alternative not chosen. If I buy a ticket to the ballet on Saturday night, I may have to take lunches to work all next week instead of eating out. I have to decide if one night of cultural enrichment is worth more than a week of tuna sandwiches. A corporation may choose to lay off American workers in order to move the operation to Singapore where wages are lower. A library director may hire 1.5 full-time equivalent clerical workers instead of a professional librarian.

Librarians make decisions based on supply and demand and cost–benefit every day, particularly if we view costs in terms of staff time as well as the library's funds and the services supplied as responses to the public's demand (Schauer, 1986). Decisions about allocating budgets among different media formats, for example, are attempts to negotiate the supply of books, magazines, videos, and so on, with public demand for these items. Knowing that young adults prefer their books in paperback, young adult librarians concentrate their book purchases in that format, adjusting the number of copies purchased to the popularity of each title. Staff time must be divided to supply activities in the library, outreach to schools and agencies, and staff for the public service desk, as well as all the "backstage" work that is necessary to support these activities. Demand for story hours can push out class visits.

Economists recognize that the market does not always work, that some desirable goods and services are not available, and furthermore, we do not always like the effects of the market when it does work. Essentially, the free market rations the world's resources, but it does not ensure equal portions or even any portion for everybody. Those who have resources to begin with are able to stay in the market, but would-be buyers and sellers who do not have job skills or capital (for instance) are closed out. In order to deal with the need for collective purchases and inequities in the way the market functions, economists have developed public goods theory.

PUBLIC GOODS

American economist Paul Samuelson is credited with describing the criteria for determining if goods and services warrant public sector support, although he developed ideas discussed by European economists such as Erik Lindahl (Hare, 1988; Heilbroner & Thurow, 1982; Musgrave, 1983/1986c; Musgrave & Musgrave, 1976). *Public commodities* are goods and services that are not available on the open market because they cannot be divided up into individually consumable pieces, must be provided by collective decision because they would not otherwise be available, are nonrival and nonexcludable, and have no extra cost (called *marginal cost*) for adding another person to the service (Heilbroner & Thurow, 1982; Loehr & Sandler, 1978).

The term *good* should not be confused with *benefit*; here, it is closer in meaning to the word *commodity*. A service or product is considered an economic public good *by its nature*, not just because it has positive consequences. Because something is currently being paid for from the public exchequer does not mean that economists would agree that it should be. In order to emphasize this point, consider smog as an example of a public good. Smog is not available on the open market and can only be provided by collective activity. No one can be denied their portion of smog, nor does one's use of it prevent someone else from experiencing smog. There will be plenty of smog to go around for every new citizen, too. In fact, each additional person may increase the supply of smog available to us all.

The classic example of a public good is national defense. Battleships and armies are not available on the free market and few could afford to purchase them if they were. Collectively, we can protect ourselves from foreign threat; individually we cannot. Defense is also nonrival; that is, your being protected by national defense does not consume the product and leave me undefended. Further, it is not physically possible to exclude people individually from national defense—everyone within the borders of the United States is protected at all times. Finally, the costs of national defense are not figured per user; every additional resident does not require additional expenditure (Heilbroner & Thurow, 1982).

When matching these characteristics with the characteristics of the public library, it is clear that the public library, and youth services along with the rest of it, does not entirely fit the pattern. Just like the private sector, the public library serves individuals; all patrons do not receive the same amount or kind of services. In fact, librarians like to market their services on the basis of providing for individual preferences. Further, individuals can and do purchase on the open market most if not all of the materials and the services offered at the public library through bookstores, video stores, newsstands, freelance information specialists, computerized database services, even professional storytellers. Willingness to purchase indicates that individuals receive the benefits of their expenditures. However, one can only purchase what is currently in print, in stock in a publisher's warehouse or other facility, or whatever is available on databases or in a storyteller's repertoire. It can be very difficult to purchase a copy of a book published last year or acquire information a few years old. At the public library, items are available for years after their initial publication date. We would not have the older materials available without the collective decision to purchase now for future use.

Although public librarians pride themselves on the idea that the library is available for all, in fact it is an excludable service. The notion of nonexcludability rests on whether it is physically possible to keep people from using the facility or inexpensive to do so (Loehr & Sandler, 1978). Again, the concept of exclusion is based on the *nature* of the thing, not on institutional policy. Unlike the national defense, which is available 24 hours a day, 365 days per year, the public library is closed every night and all day on Sunday in most cases. It would be physically possible and not terribly expensive to post guards at the library door to keep people out even when the library is open, especially if the library already has monitors or security guards. Even though librarians would be shocked at the notion of doing such a thing in general, some of the large urban libraries ban adults from the children's room unless they accompany children or have a specific need for the collections. The ability to exclude is important for the safety of children.

The notion of marginal cost (the cost of adding an additional user) is not entirely clear cut with public libraries. Usually, librarians would not say they are oversubscribed. They generally would be happy to see more patrons, and the current levels of staffing and acquisitions at many libraries (though not all) could support more use. But, eventually a point would be reached at which additional use would strain the library's ability to provide services. As we saw in Chapter 5, a number of libraries reached that point with the baby boomers in the early 1960s, and some librarians feel overwhelmed by the so-called "latchkey child" phenomenon described in Chapter 1.

In terms of rivalness, the public library situation is unusual. The *contents* of books, videos, and so on are not rival; one person's knowledge of a fact or a story does not prevent someone else from acquiring knowledge of the fact or the story. Facts and stories are not consumed in a way that leaves nothing for anyone else, as a steak dinner is. However, the *container* of the fact or story (a book or a video) is rival, as are the services of librarians. When someone has the book or video checked out of the library, it is not available for someone else's use. If the reference librarian is helping one person, that librarian is not available for someone else. However, the rivalness is not permanent. Eventually, the book or video will be returned and the librarian will finish helping one person and turn to another. The ease or difficulty of physical and intellectual access to the library and to library collections could also influence the extent of rivalness in the public library.

Strictly speaking, then, the public library is not a pure public good; it has some of the qualities of public goods and some qualities of private consumption goods. The public library is a mixed or semipublic good (Casper, 1980). In actuality, few of the services we pay for through the public sector are pure public goods; public and private goods should not be thought of as a dichotomy but rather as a continuum. The public library presents an example of a congestivity good because it is partially rival (Boadway, 1979, Loehr & Sandler, 1978). The particular variety of congestivity good exemplified by the library is called a *variable-use public facility* because individuals do not consume the same amount of library services; some consume a lot, some consume none at all. Where excludability is possible, such a service could be provided by the private sector. Public support of a variable-use facility where exclusion is possible is justified when the private sector will not provide the service because market factors do not allow for profitable competition. This leads us to a discussion of the public library's impact on selling and renting books and other media commonly circulated by public libraries.

THE PRIVATE MARKET AND PUBLIC LIBRARIES

Public libraries have coexisted with bookstores and news sellers for more than 125 years, and the public provision of print media has not supplanted the private sale of print. One could reasonably assume that each must occupy a distinct economic niche if it were not for the fact that both libraries and retail vendors of books, videos, and so on purchase their stock from the same producers. On closer consideration, then, libraries and retailers may be competitors, unless we look at the idea of a market niche from a psychological point of view. Studies suggest that library users are also book buyers (Zweizig & Dervin, 1977); apparently readers are selective about which books they purchase and which they borrow. Libraries provide an option to book ownership and a different selection.

Turning to another popular medium, the relationship of video rentals to public libraries is not yet known. Whereas some video store owners think the public library provides unfair competition, others do not (Pitman, 1990). In 1988, commercial establishments rented two billion videos, whereas total public library circulation, including books, was about one billion items (Handman, 1991). Because videos have become as ubiquitous as paperback books, video stores have many commercial rivals that are probably more important sources of competition than the public library. Public library video collections are selective—more selective than their book collections (Pitman, 1990)—(little or no sexually explicit material, for example), and again, occupy a different niche than video stores. Because so little is known at present about public library purchases of video and other materials for young people, the following discussion focuses on books.

From the mid-1700s until the 1950s, commercial book rental agencies called *circulating libraries* existed in this country. They were located in bookstores, train stations, drug stores, and other such places (Kaser, 1980). For a small sum, one could rent a book for a few days. Eventually, public libraries also had rental collections of best sellers, and a few still do; renting gave the consumer an alternative to buying books. Because public librarians initially were loath to provide fiction, the circulating libraries maintained themselves for a while after the appearance of the public library. When librarians began to accept novels as worthy of public purchase, they then provided publicly funded competition to the private sector circulating libraries. However, Kaser (1980) pointed out that the major causes of the disappearance of the rental book were television and paperbacks. These two institutions filled the same needs and desires for entertainment that the hardcover books of circulating libraries did, and television and paperbacks may have been more convenient. The renting of books became no longer commercially viable. Now, public library loans maintain the option of reading and viewing without having to purchase.

Children's and young adult books as commercial entities are quite different from adult trade books. Apparently, children's books were not available in the rental libraries, and far from providing competition for the sellers of children's books, for many years libraries and schools (including school libraries) were the market for children's books. Until the last 15 years or so, schools and libraries purchased 80% of children's books published (Giblin, 1981). When funding was cut back at libraries and schools at the end of the 1960s, the publishers began to develop private sector markets; by 1980, libraries and schools purchased about

60% of corporate publishers' children's books (Giblin, 1981)—still a major portion of the production.

Recent figures from the Book Industry Study Group indicate that libraries purchased just 13.8% of children's books in 1991 (and 8.8% of adult books; *Book Industry Trends*, 1991). One of the problems with this figure is, of course, the unstated definition of a children's book. Sometimes the production of "consumable" books such as workbooks and coloring books (which are not purchased by public libraries) is included in the overall total of children's books. There are a great many such items available, and their numbers would inflate the production figures greatly, reducing the percentage of books purchased by libraries. K.T. Horning, a close observer of children's publishing, noted a recent increase in nonfiction books, which are more likely to be purchased by libraries than sold in bookstores, leading her to believe that libraries and schools continue to be the major purchaser of children's trade books (personal communication, June 15, 1992).

The past 12 years, approximately, have seen the growth of bookstores specializing in children's and young adult books and catering to baby boom parents and, for the first time, young people themselves. Some of these bookstores provide story hours, visits from authors, and other activities for children, very much like public libraries. R.R. Bowker listed 363 juvenile bookstores in the United States and 51 in Canada in 1990 ("Number of book outlets," 1991). Children's books have become an especially lucrative part of the book trade, with sales doubling between 1980 and 1985 and predicted to have doubled again by 1990 (Roback, 1990). Nevertheless, there are far more public libraries (about 15,000) than children's bookstores in the United States. Many small communities could not support a bookstore, and the public library may be the only source of children's books in any quantity outside the school. Circulation of children's books at public libraries has continued to grow. An annual index of public library circulation disclosed that circulation of children's materials increased 68% between 1980 and 1990, whereas adult circulation increased only 19% in the same period (C. Palmer, 1991).

For the purposes of comparing "market shares," it would be interesting to know how many children's books are circulated by public libraries and how many are sold by bookstores in a given year. Doing so is not at all straightforward because children's book sales are reported in dollar amounts, not counts of books sold, and national library circulation figures are approximate. A rough estimation of the number of books sold may be made by dividing the average price of a children's book into the dollar value of sales (Grannis, 1991a, 1991b). Because the average book price is calculated by title, not by item sold, the answer cannot be exact. We do not know how many books are purchased at each price, but probably more copies of less expensive books are bought, so the results may understate the number of books purchased. Nevertheless, by this measure, approximately 58 million hardcover and 39 million paperback children's trade books were sold in 1990.

In the same year, public libraries' estimated circulation of children's books was 368.25 million. This figure was calculated by taking 37% of the estimated 1990 circulation (C. Palmer, 1991) and subtracting from it 25% as approximate circulation of nonbook materials.[1] Even if half as many children's trade books are sold as I estimate and circulation is only half of what I have computed, the public library would still supply more children's books than bookstores, especially if we remember that upwards of 50% of books published are sold to libraries and schools. (Because school libraries circulate about one book per pupil per week, they are the champion suppliers of books to children and young adults! [*Statistics of Public and Private School Library Media Centers*, 1987].)

The fact that children's bookstores could come into being and prosper even with the availability of public and school libraries seems to indicate that rather than being in competition for "customers," the public library and the bookstore complement each other. As Zweizig and Dervin noted in 1977, library users tend to be book buyers. My students have sometimes told me that they use public library collections to test their children's preferences before purchasing books. The public library in that case acts as an advertisement for the bookstore, but no one knows how widespread this phenomenon is. That children's circulation has grown tremendously even as children's bookstores have developed indicates that baby boom parents have created a demand for children's books that needs both the free market and the public sector to supply. The public library, along with the schools, is a major alternative to book purchasing.[2] We cannot say anything about young adult books because circulation figures and sales figures are not collected to separate teen "markets" from those for children and adults.

Youth librarians and school library media specialists wield the "power of the purse" in juvenile publishing. Without feedback in the form of

---

[1]Making similar calculations for adult trade books, one arrives at sales of hardcovers at 40.6 million volumes and 59 million paperbacks. However, "adult" books encompass many kinds of books not included here—professional, religious, and scientific, for example—so the market is much larger than these figures represent. Adult circulation in 1990 was about 628.5 million books, allowing 25% of Palmer's (1991) figures for circulation of nonbook materials.

[2]The change in demand from mostly institutional to partly private has also changed the nature of the supply of children's books. We see more reprints of classic children's titles familiar to parents, more paperback series books for adolescents, and more toybooks and paper engineered books for young children.

demand for certain kinds of books from librarians, the nature of children's and young adult's publishing would change. The emphasis on artistic and literary quality in a certain segment of publishing would be diminished. Whether and how youth librarians use their clout is a question that has not been adequately studied. Their impact on other formats of graphic media, such as magazines and video, is a mystery, as well. At the current time, the market for videos is largely in the private sector because libraries continue to spend a relatively small proportion of their materials budgets on audiovisuals. Potentially, the library impact on young people's video could be great. With the establishment of the Andrew Carnegie Medal for video and the Notable Video lists compiled by the Association for Library Service to Children, youth librarians are attempting to influence the market by creating more demand for videos that meet their quality standards, as they did for children's books 100 years ago.

What would happen to private sales and rentals of books and other informational and recreational materials if public libraries disappeared? Would publishers sell 368 million more volumes? They might sell more books, but they would not sell 368 million more volumes. Some users of children's and young adult books probably cannot afford to purchase any books; those readers would do without. An economist would say that they would be forced out of the market. Another group of people would simply consume (i.e., read) fewer books because the low indirect cost of the public library encourages them to charge out more books than they would willingly purchase even though they had the means to do so. This notion leads us to consider the justifications for providing public library youth services when they are not pure public goods and appear to offer some competition to private enterprise. Using the concepts of merit goods and externalities, we can assess the economic reasons for providing youth services in public libraries.

MERIT WANTS

A justification that is sometimes made for public expenditures is what some writers call *merit goods* (Musgrave, 1969/1986a). The term *merit wants* is more descriptive of the nature of this justification and is used here. As noted earlier, the free market may be successful to some degree in supplying a demand, yet the government may decide that it is not working well enough, that the public welfare would be improved if more books were supplied for young people than are done through private purchases from booksellers, for example. The general American belief in the efficacy of reading certainly leads to the possibility of governments coming to that conclusion. If we decide that we *want* to provide more books, videos, software, and related services to children and young adults so that the benefits of their use will extend more widely, we are justified in doing so. It appears that this is indeed the case with children's public library services and to a lesser degree with young adult services; local government sees these services as so meritorious that it wants to encourage more demand for them than the free market provides without intervention.

Hare (1988) pointed out that there is an aura of paternalism in this argument, the notion that the government or some proportion of the population knows better than another group, which has to be protected from its folly or coerced into consumption. Most economists are not happy with intervention from this perspective because it deviates from the doctrine of consumer sovereignty in which the consumer's preferences as expressed in the open market are the criteria for the production of goods. Furthermore, as library economist Van House (1983) noted, this argument implies that the public pays for a service simply because the public wants it. What the public wants today, it may not want tomorrow, and a service based solely on the notion of merit wants could easily disappear.

Musgrave (1969/1986a), however, pointed out that leadership plays a role in a democracy. Realistically, the consumer does not always know enough to make wise choices; furthermore, we are subjected to the claims of advertisements. Therefore, a few knowledgeable people may decide for all of us for our own protection or benefit. (We return later to the issue of how decisions are made in this and the situation of public goods.) Librarians make this kind of merit goods argument when they point to their expertise as selectors of materials. Though more pronounced in acquisitions for young people, it applies to selection for all age groups. The notion of a selected collection that yet appeals to a wide range of preferences is an indication of the professional gauntlet that librarians have set themselves, to row between the Scylla of elitism and the Charybdis of popular culture.

Some commodities initially viewed as merit goods turn out to have some properties of public goods; that is, they provide benefits to society as well as to the individual. For example, education is divisible and most of the benefit accrues to the individual who receives it. It could be provided on a private market basis. However, many people believe they derive some benefit from others' education, and the argument is made that the benefits to society are such that education should be provided at public expense because if left to themselves, people would not purchase enough education on the free market. Society as a whole would suffer. This is an argument based on the concept of externalities or spillovers. It is more powerful than merit wants, and in the next section we discuss the externalities and other social benefits of public library services to children and young adults.

EXTERNALITIES AND SOCIAL BENEFITS

Externalities are the impacts of economic activity on persons not directly involved in a transaction; they may arise from either public or private goods; they can be either positive or negative (Heilbroner & Thurow, 1982; Musgrave, 1969/1986b). For example, a family that empties its sewage directly into a river saves money on its sewage treatment bill, but downstream users of the river suffer the consequences. On the other hand, some externalities are beneficial as in the example of education given earlier. When society receives benefits from positive externalities, a private market system will not produce a socially desirable quantity of the good in question. The free market produces only enough of a good to suit the preferences of individual purchasers who do not necessarily have the well-being of society in mind. Those who receive indirect benefits do not pay for them. Thus, there is no incentive to produce the optimal amount of the commodity. In such a case, government is entitled to intervene if the good is judged important enough, but it is not required to intervene (Cohn & Geske, 1990; McKenzie, 1979).

Let us look at the benefits provided by education in general, because it is an important goal for youth services. Individuals receive many of the benefits, both in terms of present consumption (despite high school dropout rates, many young people enjoy going to school) and as an investment in their future earning capacity. Individuals also receive future nonmonetary benefits in the form of being able to enjoy recreational and cultural pursuits learned about during the school years. Other monetary benefits accrue to society, also in the form of consumption—the expense of providing education results in employing many people (school staff, producers of educational media, construction crews, etc.)—and as an investment that will produce benefits in the future.

Economists have proposed that the future value of education produces a skilled work force that will pay taxes, keep the economy growing, refrain from committing crimes, and avoid welfare expenses. Some economists have seen education's externalities as allowing for social class mobility and permitting the development of talent that would otherwise be undiscovered. Nonmonetary benefits in terms of health and family life have been suggested also. Finally, the ideological point of view sees education as the prerequisite to democracy, which requires an informed electorate. Most discussion of these topics centers around education as a product of schools, but public libraries are also part of the educational system of the country.

Interestingly, all economists do not agree that education has externalities, particularly higher education: "The problem with the externality arguments is that, to date, no convincing empirical evidence has been brought to bear on the existence of such externalities, much less on their magnitudes" (Cohn & Geske, 1990, p. 25). There are also questions about the assumptions of increased earnings and lower crime rates. We note that persons with more education tend to have higher incomes, ignoring other factors, such as gender, race, inherited wealth, motivation, and social class (Cohn & Geske, 1990). Media reports consistently point to the prevalence of illiteracy among the prison population as if the relationship were a causal one, when both illiteracy and prison residence may result from other conditions.

Lack of empirical evidence has never vanquished strong belief, however. Common sense demands that we observe the economic necessity of at least a basic literacy and numeracy level in order to function on an everyday basis. In the contemporary United States, the basic literacy/numeracy requirement is a high school education (Chall, 1983). The authors quoted earlier noted that filing income tax returns and the production of books and magazines are two quite specific externalities of education that are assumed to exist.

Some of education's benefits to individuals and society occur in the future, not immediately on expending funds. Education is therefore considered an investment in human capital, the skills and abilities possessed by individuals and by society in the aggregate that allow people to be productive economically. Media reports that compare the academic abilities of young people in the United States with those of other countries' youth are concerned about the quality of our human capital formation. Impacts that are to take place in the future are particularly difficult to measure because they are subject to factors completely out of the control of researchers. However, using years of schooling and income levels compared cross-sectionally and longitudinally, researchers have been able to estimate the earning potential of various levels of schooling, though every approach has its critics.

If it is difficult with education, which can at least be measured through the number of years of completed schooling, consider the difficulties of defining a meaningful measure of public library contributions to the economy. We need a measure that can be studied across time and associated with the economic well-being of individuals and society, and that also controls for intervening variables such as formal education, television viewing, and so forth. To attempt such an analysis would require collecting the kind of personal data from patrons and nonusers that librarians find intrusive. If we are forced to assume externalities for formal education, we can only assume externalities for public library use.

The research discussed in Chapter 6 on the impacts of public library services to youth showed where the externalities of such services are most likely to lie: support for formal education, enhancement of language development, and improved reading skills. These services might be supposed to have impacts similar to schooling – assisting in the creation of a more literate and productive citizenry. Note that assistance is as much as we can muster because the institutions of formal education have the primary responsibility for creating productive citizens. Public libraries enhance school efforts and may even assist those who are not comfortable in school, but we know little empirically about these effects. Van House (1983) believed that any use of a public library by a child is beneficial because the child is reinforcing the reading skills needed in the workplace, thereby contributing to the formation of human capital.

This presents us with a problem, however, simply in its assumption that any library use by a young person involves reading. What about the use of computer software and audiovisuals? What about the children who come for programs that involve no reading, such as crafts, films, and performances by magicians and the like? What about the teenagers who come to meet their friends? We can assume direct individual benefits of enjoyment in all these cases. Can we assume indirect social benefits of a monetary or nonmonetary type equal to the cost of the programs? To some extent, yes. Use of nonbook media undoubtedly has educational implications, and many libraries experience increased circulation on days during which programs are held. Programs may increase reading and so may social use by teenagers. However, I have found no studies that associate young people's attendance at the library or at programs with any particular level of increased circulation. Hence, we cannot compare benefits and costs.

In his economic analysis of the public library, White (1983) went so far as to state that services to children and young adults are the only services of public libraries that meet the stated goals of public libraries and are the only services likely to have beneficial economic consequences for society. He believed that services for adults should be provided on a fee-for-service basis, and youth services should be continued at public expense and expanded. It is likely that White's argument is too extreme, and it is not surprising that librarians have paid little attention to it. Goddard (1971) also argued that services to children and young adults are unquestionably supportable in an economic sense. He, too, said that certain public library services to adults should not be provided at public expense, specifically leisure services, because the benefit accrues only to individuals.

There is something to be said for these arguments. Although local government frequently subsidizes recreation such as swimming pools, golf courses, and parks, very often it is only a partial subsidy with the public paying a fee for use. Most of the benefit of such services is perceived to be private, and therefore the individual should pay for them. Certainly, it is tempting to suggest that adults should pay for services so that a greater contribution could be made to youth services. We have something more to say about this when we consider alternative policies in the next chapter.

White and Goddard ignored the contribution that recreation, including the availability of well-stocked fiction stacks, makes to the quality of life in attracting residents and businesses to a community. It might also be urged that society benefits when citizens have leisure opportunities to help them cope with stress. There is the further practical problem of separating leisure use from "serious" use. Even if we could agree that all fiction is leisure reading—and not everyone would subscribe to that—much nonfiction reading is also of a leisure nature. Any particular book or video or magazine might be used for several purposes. We need not worry overmuch about this. Unless public library funding becomes much more problematical than it currently is, adult leisure services will remain free of direct charge, enshrined not only by custom but also by the Public Library Association's *Mission Statement* (Goals, Guidelines, and Standards Committee, 1979).

Public libraries have goals for information and culture as well as education and recreation. I have not considered the externalities of the public library's contribution in these areas because in the case of young people, it would be difficult to separate information use from education and use for cultural purposes from education and recreation. Suffice it to say that information and culture furnished to young people by public libraries have aspects of present consumption and investment for the future for individuals and society, and that these are very similar if not congruent with aspects of education and recreation discussed here.

ADDED VALUE

From an economic point of view, exchange activities not only use and redistribute resources, they also increase the value of the resource at each step in the process of manufacturing and selling goods, thus creating wealth. Finished products are worth more than the costs of raw materials, labor, and distribution; the difference between the costs of production and the price for which the good is sold is called *added value* or *value-added*. Robert Taylor (1986) argued that information systems add value to information by the processes they employ to make the information more useful to their clients.

In terms of the public library, processes that add value include making materials available, such as physical and intellectual access via alphabetical and classified shelf arrangements, and protecting materials so that users can find desired items. Selecting materials so that needed items are included and unnecesary items are excluded, while covering topics and points of view representing a spectrum of opinion, adds value to information media. Mediating between the content of the material and the users' needs through staff assistance, cataloging, and provision of indexes are other ways of making information more useful and hence more valuable than information simply accumulated and stored without any guiding purpose or order. Signs, displays, and open shelves for browsing also add value to library materials. All of these activities help users save time and locate information and materials more accurately.

Youth services provide these value-adding services just as the rest of the library does. In addition, because of their active role in promoting intelligent media use and recognition of the library as a resource for young people, youth services add value in unique ways. Programs such as story hours, reading clubs, and bibliographic instruction for young people make the library more familiar and understandable (Taylor, 1986). Book talks and storytelling enhance young people's media choices in a world of information overload. Any assistance that library staff provide young people in how to locate, arrange, and use information for their own purposes, such as school reports and hobbies, also makes the library's collections and services more useful and hence more valuable.

Measuring an exact dollar value added by these services is not possible at this time. Some calculation of the value of time saved by working adults and teenagers might be possible if we knew how much time was saved and the average hourly salary of employed users. Even this simple cost-benefit analysis is not open to us in the case of children because they do not work, hence their time has no monetary value, even though it has economic value as the major human capital formation period of life. For any particular library, the worth of value-adding processes will be determined by evaluating the degree to which the library makes the user's search possible and fruitful. Very often, this evaluation may need to be made on subjective grounds rather than quantitative ones (Taylor, 1986).

OPTION VALUE

A final argument in favor of public sector support for services is *option value*, that is, purchasing goods and services now because later they may not be available or they may be needed in an emergency. Examples include fire departments (at the local government level) and wilderness areas (at the state and federal levels). To some extent, education has option value: If we do not educate people when they are young, it may be difficult to do it later when we need an educated work force.

The public library has option value as well, in two ways: as a repository for society's graphic records and for individual utility. As noted previously, when one relies on stores to purchase or rent books, videos, or other materials, one is limited to the stock of what is on hand. Public libraries, however, maintain collections of materials from many years back and offer a wider selection than a store. As a local institution, the public library frequently shares with the historical society the collection of local records, which can be important for community solidarity and available nowhere else. For instance, local history became intensely personal for children in New Bedford, Massachusetts, when they were introduced to the public library's Whaling Room.

The second option value of public libraries is that they are there even when you do not need them. For the individual, there is utility in knowing that the services and materials are there if you should ever have use for them. This may be more true for youth services than for adult services. Young people exercise the option value of public libraries by their very well-documented use of the public library after school, on weekends, and during the summer when they cannot use their school libraries.

PAYING FOR THE PUBLIC LIBRARY

The discussion of the operation of the free market at the beginning of this chapter noted how the "invisible hand" regulated the prices and supply of commodities. When a good is purely public, however, the market does not work. Even when we can establish the cost of a public good, it is not likely that all individuals will pay voluntarily their fair share or even state how much they really want to use. No one needs to buy as much as they really want because they can use someone else's "purchases" due to the nonexcludability of public goods. Public goods and semipublic goods are paid for through taxation, and another mechanism determines how much revenue is made available for various uses. That mechanism is voting. We substitute politics for economic forces (Heilbroner & Thurow, 1982).

Voting is not a precise method for determining the desirable amount of a commodity. Usually we elect other people who make the decisions for us, rather than directly for the goods in question. Inevitably, those whose candidates lose elections are not as powerful and their wishes do not count as much as the wishes of those whose parties win. Even when we vote directly for expenditures, we can only say "yes" or "no," not how much we would be willing to spend. We can easily undersupply or oversupply ourselves with collective commodities. "As a result, we swim in defense and starve in prison reform because defense has 'friends in Congress' and prisons do not" (Heilbroner & Thurow, p. 172). Savvy librarians are enmeshed in politics at all levels of government, making sure of their friends in Congress, the state house, county administration building, and city hall.

This broad perspective is needed because economists prefer that services be paid for by the level of government at which the services are used and constituents can evaluate their quality. Public library use, because of its focus on services to individuals, is generally local, the argument goes; therefore, local government should expect to fund the major portion of public library budgets. And so they do. Services that require cooperation and intervention at state and federal levels in order to be efficient should be paid for by those levels of government (Holcombe, 1992).

Public libraries are now facing this issue as we move further into the electronic information environment. Dubberly posited a future in which libraries of all types would share users as well as materials. In his vision, patrons of libraries that truly shared resources would have access to all materials in all of the libraries without regard to their status at any of them. A union online catalog might not even provide ownership information to patrons; it would not be necessary to know where an item was because the patron could request anything in the catalog. Extending this approach beyond the local level to provide maximum access would call for greater federal involvement in library funding because it would truly be national library service (Dubberly, 1992).

It is no longer simply cataloging and interlibrary loan that require interstate and national cooperation, but many forms of information itself. As more full-text databases and CD-ROM products become available and as public libraries gain access to the Internet, owning specific resources is becoming less and less required because these resources are purchased through subscriptions, leases, and fees. Location of information and location of user will become irrelevant as larger information networks develop. That children and young people may become eligible patrons for these kinds of services is exemplified by Vice President Albert Gore's bill to include students in grades kindergarten through high school in the National Research and Education Network (NREN) now being developed at the federal level. Dubberly (1992) suggested that both librarians and government need to rethink the paradigm under which public libraries are funded.

DISTRIBUTIONAL EFFECTS OF PUBLIC LIBRARIES

In addition to externalities and the other criteria mentioned previously, economists also look at equity issues when it comes to the expenditure of public money. One equity issue that must be faced has to do with the distribution of library service, or, who pays for the service and who benefits from it. A number of the studies cited in Chapter 6 suggested that the average adult user of the public library is likely to be middle class with a college education. The poorer, less educated members of the community seem to use the library less. Some analysts have concluded that this means that the public library redistributes resources from poor families to wealthier ones. This comes about because of the use of the property tax to fund public libraries. Weaver and Weaver (1979) and White (1983) pointed out that the property tax is usually held to be a regressive tax. That is, it is not based on one's ability to pay, but on the value of one's real property.

Because the poor use the library little, they pay a larger proportion of their income to support the library relative to their level of use than the middle class does. Van House (1983) quarreled with this model, noting that is impossible to compute tax incidence directly and claiming that theoreticians Henry Aaron and Dick Netzer believe that property taxes are more likely to be proportional or even progressive. She reworked Weaver and Weaver's data including the other taxes that go to support the public library and found that when standardized for differences in income, the middle-class taxpayer paid slightly more for library services (Van House, 1983).

She used time allocation theory to explain why the middle class uses the public library more than the poor or the wealthy. Using income as a measure of the value of one's time and one's productivity, she found that the time of poor people is not worth as much as that of wealthier citizens. They do not have the education to take efficient advantage of the library and their time is "not productive enough to justify using the library" (Van House, 1983, p. 86). The poor most likely seek information from family and friends or go without. At the other end of the income scale, the wealthy person's time is too valuable (in terms of income) to justify spending it on library use. They may pay other people to obtain information for them.

One of the things that is not well studied is the demographic composition of children and young adults who use the public library. Van House (1983) noted that young people are in the human capital forming years of their lives; their economic task is to prepare themselves to participate in the economy. Theoretically, the more education and skills children acquire, the better off both they and society will be, but most children have no present economic value because they do not work in the money economy. Therefore, their time in childhood has little current value but may have substantial value in the future. They can expect a greater return on their time for library use than adults and thus have a greater incentive to use the library. Of course, few children take an economic view of their time, although Fasick and England (1977) found that some of the older boys in their study had high occupational ambitions.

Parents, however, are aware of their children's economic futures and may be willing to invest time in library use for their children's sakes. And, indeed, studies have found that one predictor of library use is having children under age 18 living at home (Powell, Taylor, & McMillen, 1984; Zweizig & Dervin 1977). Even for poor parents, investing in children's future via library use may seem a good use of time. Chatman (1987) studied 52 janitors whose mean level of education was grade 10.7. Only 15 (28.8%) of them were current users of the public library, far below the average for the general population, but another 12 (23%) took their children to the library, mostly for school assignments.

Two of the studies mentioned in Chapter 6 (Smardo & Curry, 1982; Heyns, 1978) pointed out that library use helped less advantaged children improve their language skills, so that they did not fall further behind their more advantaged peers. Disadvantaged children who did *not* use the library fell further behind their advantaged peers. In her book on summer learning, Heyns (1978) commented that black people at all income levels in Atlanta used public services such as libraries more than white people, and poor black children used the library more than poor white children. Even though white children seemed to gain more from library use than black children in Atlanta, the black children were getting a significant benefit from library use and would have had the most to lose should library service be taken away or diminished.

Many young adults do work in the money economy, though often at very low wages. For working teens, it would be possible to calculate a dollar value for their time spent at the public library. Even though the current time value would be low, the future value of library use would be higher, because young adults are still preparing for their actual entrance into the economy.

Because about half of library users are under 19, and because parents may be willing to invest time in library use for their children though not for themselves, the demographics of youth library use may differ substantially from that of adult users. Poor children may use the library more than poor adults. When economists calculate tax incidence of public libraries, they forget that half of public library use is by young people, and they do not include any measure of the value of such use in their computations (admittedly, it is difficult to calculate a monetary value for use by young people). Use by poor young people may offset the lack of use by poor adults, thereby adjusting positively the distributional effects of public libraries, even if we do not accept Van House's (1983) argument that the property tax is proportional.

SUMMARY

We began this survey of economic justification for public expenditure on public library services by defining the operations of supply and demand in the free market and contrasted that with public goods. We have examined how well libraries fit the accepted criteria of public goods, market failure, merit wants, externalities, added value, option value, and distributional effects. Overall, the notions of externalities, added value, and option value offer the strongest support with public goods, market failure, and merit wants adding a little strength to the argument. Distribution effects present a challenge for researchers because of a lack of evidence. Although the public library is partially rival and wholly excludable, it meets the criteria for a type of public congestivity commodity called a variable-use public facility because it appears to fill a particular economic niche that the open market fails to satisfy, particularly in the area of children's books. It provides an alternative to buying books. The public library fits the model of the merit wants argument, but on its own this adds but a little luster to the case we are building.

The externalities of library use by children and young adults were discussed in detail in Chapter 6. Though impossible to calculate at this time, it is presumed that the same externalities claimed for public education also pertain to public library use by young people, and for two economists, youth services are the strongest argument in the library's favor. The notion that public library use by young people may influence income distribution equity has not been studied, but the possibility exists that libraries may have this effect at least in some communities. In general, public libraries add value to information by organizing materials and providing various ways of accessing it. Youth services add value through the programs and interaction of staff with young people that make the materials comfortable to use and the library an understandable environment. Finally, the option value of public libraries and youth services in particular is quite strong.

Public libraries do have one attribute of public goods: They must be provided by collective decision. The history of public libraries in Chapter 5 indicated that ongoing financial support was necessary to keep libraries useful to patrons. This support is currently based on local government's ability and willingness to pay for them and on the principle that services should be paid for at the level at which they are used. As the transfer of information, recreation, education, and culture becomes ever more electronic, local ownership will be less of a reason to insist on local funding.

The values of a capitalist economy are not the only relevant measures of worth of public services. As Cohn and Geske stated, "The historical development of the educational system in the United States is a result of social, economic, and political forces, and one need not pursue a purely economic rationale for its present state" (1990, p. 32). The same applies to public library youth services. Although there is some evidence that youth services are having an impact on child development and formal and informal learning, and that they meet or partially meet a number of economic criteria, the services are still facing several challenges, as discussed in Chapter 1. In Chapter 8, we look at a number of alternatives and some additional criteria for selecting among them.

The Alternatives for Youth Services in Public Libraries

INTRODUCTION

Thus far, we have said that any institution that does what the public library purports to do should enhance child development, provide support for formal education, foster informal education through social learning, and meet the economic tests required of agencies that receive public funding. By the available evidence, which is admittedly sketchy in some instances, the present services offered by public libraries for children and young adults meet these tests more or less well. Nevertheless, we started this enterprise by commenting on a series of problems facing youth services: funding restraints, changes in personnel structure, computerization, television, demographic changes, the condition of young people in contemporary society, and acceptance of young adult services. Any proposed changes would have to meet the criterion of addressing these problems at least tentatively.

Because library services are provided in the real world, certain practical tests have to be applied to suggested alternatives as well. These practical criteria include political and professional feasibility. Unless librarians and politicians agree to changes, changes will not be made. Political feasibility includes the fact that none of our suggested possibilities includes asking federal, state, or local governments to commit more money to youth services on a permanent basis. As economist White pointed out (1983), it is highly unlikely that more money will be forthcoming from these sources. Although fiscal status varies from place to place, as I write, a recession has cost the jobs of thousands of people and affected public libraries from coast to coast. A crowd of social programs and a large federal budget deficit are standing in line for the so-called "peace dividend," which has yet to materialize. Several times Presidents Reagan, Bush, and Clinton tried to severely cut Library Services and Construction Act funds. Congress has not supported these attempts, but we should not feel complacent about the federal political position of public libraries.

Finally, there are the criteria used by economists in judging alternative policies, including equity, efficiency, and maximizing choices. *Equity* means treating people fairly, and we can take two approaches to equity. One approach treats all people alike, regardless of their condition or situation; this is *horizontal equity*. *Vertical equity* recognizes that people are not equal; therefore, allowances are made to minimize the differences. Libraries typically employ both types of equity. For example, library users have access to materials and services regardless of income, race, or sex, yet materials are purchased and facilities modified to accommodate differences in reading ability and physical impairments. *Efficiency* means optimum use of resources, colloquially, "the most bang for the buck." In the case of the public library, efficiency often means doing as much as possible under financial restrictions to meet the library's goals. Finally, *maximizing choices* means allowing for the fullest possible expression of preferences. Even in public services, economists insist on choice as a means of judging desirability and effectiveness.

As we look at the available options, we will consider each one in the light of these criteria. The options we will examine are: abandoning youth services, keeping the status quo, establishing a new institution, going to a voucher system, turning the services over to the schools, charging for adult services, contracting youth services out, and restructuring current public library services for young people. Although some of these options may seem so undesirable as to not need discussion, each of them deserves some consideration because they have been suggested as possibilities for youth services or other types of libraries or they have been put forward as solutions to crises in other social services, particularly education.

ABANDONING YOUTH SERVICES

Because the evidence of the library's effectiveness is not clear cut or complete, it might be possible to decide that the mission of public library services to young people is not suitable for public funding, and it would be better to cut our losses. By ceasing to provide public library services to children, local government could cut expenses perhaps by as much as

$2 billion or redirect the money elsewhere. The challenges would no longer have to be faced by the public library. We could save money and effort with this plan, but we would lose the benefits that the library provides in terms of child development, education, literacy, recreation, and culture. Middle-class users could adjust by purchasing the kinds of materials libraries stock, but children in lower income families would not be able to acquire such materials and inequity would result. Many librarians would object, of course, but political feasibility is also unlikely.

Some libraries have tried to close library branches for the sake of efficiency or as a response to budget reductions. Such efforts often backfire as unhappy patrons clamor at the gates of City Hall (Willett, 1987). Cutting out service to children would likely result in similar outcry with parents, teachers, and children joining forces. Abandoning children's services would not be a politically acceptable choice. It also seems far too extreme. The evidence of growing circulation of children's materials after a period of decline indicates that the services are meeting the needs of a large number of library constituents. Children's services are not moribund; they continue to be useful in their present state.

Unfortunately, the same cannot be said of young adult services. Many libraries have abandoned young adult services without a whimper of public protest, as indicated by the fact that 89% of them do not have a young adult librarian (NCES, 1988). They do not provide the kind of personal, individualized attention paid to children's reading and media use, concentrating on reference for educational purposes and browsing collections for recreational reading but no reader's advisory. The loss to the library of young adults' goodwill and interest is incalculable, as is the loss to teenagers themselves in terms of adult attention at a time of life when they are vulnerable and still susceptible to intervention. Studies of young adults have found that many of them prefer the public library to the school library but are not completely satisfied with the way they are treated in terms of help from public library staff and rules and regulations (Fitzgibbons, 1982; Flum & Weisner, 1993). No one has studied the impact of teens' negative responses to the public library on their behavior as taxpayers and library users in adulthood, but it is unlikely that the failure to recognize the particular needs of adolescence has positive consequences.

KEEPING THE STATUS QUO

Maintaining the status quo is always an option, and it has some attractions. It requires no extra money or extra effort. The benefits of the service would be maintained, it is politically and professionally feasible, and the economic tests are adequately met. Keeping the status quo does not mean that nothing would change, however. The history of youth services demonstrates that in the past these services have taken major evolutionary steps, such as the addition of programs for young adults, preschoolers, and toddlers. Keeping the status quo means accepting the current rate, direction, and level of change in youth services. If we look at the specific kinds of programs offered, current practices, and the issues being discussed in the literature and over the Internet, it would not be unreasonable to conclude that libraries and librarians are heading in acceptable directions.

Of course, staying as we are has its flaws. Considering the many facets of the challenges facing youth services, it is unlikely that all persons providing youth services today have the education, training, or access to research to be able to meet each of the challenges at the local level. The nature of the challenges themselves suggest that a reorientation in philosophy and approach may be necessary, and although the current rate of development might eventually resolve many issues, we cannot count on that happening. Although individual youth librarians may be addressing equity, efficiency, literacy, or other challenges, others may not be aware that such issues exist. Maintaining the status quo is an inefficient way of making progress. We must consider if any of the other alternatives present a workable reorientation that will meet the challenges.

ESTABLISHING A NEW INSTITUTION

The difficulty of changing old, entrenched institutions has sometimes led to the formation of new ones, just as the public library itself supplanted circulating and social libraries in the 19th century. Instead of abandoning youth services or maintaining the status quo, one alternative could be to remove youth services from the public library and use the money currently spent on those services for a new institution dedicated to providing information, education, recreation, and culture to people under 18. A new institution could solve many of the problems of today's public library service to the age group without having to overcome the traditions or the public image of the public library. A few such institutions exist in Europe, but they are not very widespread.

We could be very creative with a new institution: use mobile and temporary facilities, hire youth-oriented administrators and staff from local communities to run the services, provide access to video and sound production facilities, and emphasize audiovisual materials, computer software, compact disc services, online databases, and Internet access on a basis equal to print. With this scenario, many of the challenges would be avoided because tradition would not hold back the service and the positive aspects of youth service would be retained. Administrative support would be assured because there would be no other age levels competing for the administrator's attention and budget. Flexible hours could be instituted to match family schedules, and nonbook materials would be given a more visible place. By hiring staff from the local community, the local cultural milieu could be matched without reliance on a system of education that does not attract people from a variety of backgrounds. Such a service could compete with the library for funding and keep the needs of young people more prominently in the eye of local government.

On the other hand, there are some disadvantages to an institution specifically for young people. Young people are already segregated from the rest of society through schooling. A separate library facility would only increase the separation of young people from adults. As a practical matter, children from at least the fifth grade and older have increasing need for "adult" materials such as reference books, and some materials intended for children also serve adults, introductory books in technical subjects, for example. Either duplication of such materials would be required by both the public library for adults and the new institution for young people, or patrons would have to become accustomed to using more than one location on a regular basis. Both options have a cost, either in money or time. Furthermore, for preschoolers and young children, library use with parents is an opportunity for families to enjoy an activity together and for parents to provide a social role model via their own use. A separate institution for young people would diminish this positive aspect of current library services. Parents would find it inconvenient to take their children to one place and themselves to another. In other words, inefficiency would result from separate services for young people.

We might take an even more radical step and deinstitutionalize youth services completely by providing dial-up access to information networks and databases over the local phone lines. For the sake of equity, we would have to give every young person a microcomputer, a modem, and access to new telecommunications technology as it develops. Individuals could communicate electronically with a librarian to search for information or browse through a virtual library for a "good read" to be delivered to their homes or picked up at a central location, or even simply downloaded to their computers, completely bypassing paper. Such access may well be the thing that eventually supplants the entire public library we know today (Caywood, 1992; Kahle, 1991; Robinson, 1992).

A change of this magnitude could happen gradually without government interference as the cost of technology decreases and more families acquire access to sophisticated hardware. Should government policy encourage the change by providing technology and access to children and teenagers? The suggestion has some attraction. In one sense, of course, it is simply a development of current services, deliberately accelerated with equitable distribution of the benefits. It might give young people in the United States a competitive intellectual advantage compared to youth in other parts of the world, a desirable economic result, particularly because microcomputers can be used for many other things besides information access. Such a policy would cultivate the evolution of developmentally appropriate hardware and software for young people in the private sector. Currently there are thousands of videos and microcomputer programs and a growing number of CD-ROMs, databases, and network services suitable for under-18s. As with books for young people, it may take government investment to demonstrate that there is a market for such things for children and young people.

What disadvantages might result from developing an electronic system? We know from child development research that young children and adolescents learn through physical contact with their environment, which includes interacting with other people and visiting places outside the home. Library services provided electronically in the home would diminish the contacts young people might have with peers and with adults other than their parents. The socialization benefits of the public library are inadequately studied, but knowing the importance of peers and unrelated adults, we can hypothesize the loss of developmentally valuable experiences if an electronic home-based library service came into existence without some compensation for the loss of social contacts. One model suggests that the public library will become a kind of centralized switching place, linking patrons to appropriate databases through library-owned hardware and software (Kahle, 1991). Still, this kind of personal, one-to-one service is much more limited in terms of social contact than public library services currently are.

Although we could expect some librarians and politicians to approve of these innovations and others to disapprove, the real problem with them is money. Whether we chose a system of mobile and temporary multimedia facilities, a home-based electronic access system, or the library as electronic access point, start-up costs would probably exceed current expenditures for youth services. These courses of action require visionary leadership and a positive attitude toward spending money on the part of government officials. Neither seems in particular abundance at this time, and it is especially unlikely that any level of government would be willing to experiment by dismantling a current program with a proven track record to entirely replace it with an unknown. However, the potential advantages of each of the proposed modifications make them worthy of experimentation.

GOING TO A VOUCHER SYSTEM

It has been found with some public services that giving people vouchers instead of commodities and allowing them to purchase according to their own preferences works rather well. The Food Stamp program is the major example, but voucher systems have been proposed for other services, notably schooling. Voucher systems are seen as stimulating the private economy and promoting healthy competition, as well. Because they can minimize administrative overhead, they may also be an efficient means of distributing services and resources.

If we went to a voucher system for library services for children and teenagers, we could eliminate the costly space and personnel now required in public libraries. Would young people get a better service? The vouchers could be used for books, videos, magazines, and so on— though we might place some restrictions regarding quality and type of material—or services of storytellers and information specialists. Young people could save the vouchers from year to year or use at will. There would be a good deal of horizontal equity in this because children who do not now use the library or own books or other resources could begin to have educational and recreational materials.

If we put into a voucher program as much money as we are now putting into public library services for young people, how much would each child get? Figures from the U.S. Bureau of the Census (1991) indicate that $4.25 billion was spent on public libraries in fiscal year 1988–1989. The two national studies of youth services (Lewis & Farris, 1990; NCES, 1988) combined suggest that public libraries spent about half of their materials budgets on youth materials. We will take 50% as a surrogate for what was spent on youth services as a whole. This is definitely overstating the case because personnel is the largest expense of public libraries and youth services staffs do not constitute half of all public library staff, but we will use this inflated proportion to make the best possible case for vouchers. This means that we have $2.12 billion to divide among an estimated 63,604,432 persons 18 and under in 1990 (U.S. Bureau of the Census, 1992), or $33.33 per child or teenager.

With $33.33, a wise shopper could purchase two hardcover books, two videos, perhaps four audiocassettes, or eight paperback books. If the vouchers were saved for 20 years, children could purchase a set of encyclopedias. Of course, they would only be eligible for library vouchers for 18 years, so they had better have siblings who want to purchase an encyclopedia. For $33.33, children might be able to purchase an hour of time with an information specialist or a storyteller. Clearly, this is not an adequate number of books or services for any child or teenager, and particularly not for a preschooler, who, as we noted before, may "read" several hundred books in a year.

One of the problems with the notion of vouchers is that local governments vary considerably in their per capita expenditure on public libraries. Children living in wealthy communities would get a far larger sum of money than children living in poor ones. We could decide that for the sake of vertical equity, only those children classed as poor are deserving of library vouchers. Wealthier families can be expected to purchase books and information services for their children. The federal government could equalize distribution among communities and provide library vouchers only to those whose families are not able to supply information materials and services through private means. The Children's Defense Fund (1988) estimates that 25% of the child population lives in poverty, about 15,901,108 young people aged 18 and younger. Dividing the $2.12 billion by that figure, we could give each young person living in poverty $133.32 per year.

This is equivalent to 9.5 books or videos or possibly 30 paperbacks, and it would only take 5 years to save up for an encyclopedia. A student could purchase 4 hours of information specialist time or about 5 hours on a computer database equivalent to *The Reader's Guide to Periodical Literature*. At this level of funds, poor children would be helped but perhaps not enough: Heyns (1978) found that children needed to read at least six books over the summer to show an improvement in reading skills; on an annual basis this is 24 books. And, once again, preschoolers need far more books than $133 can buy.

Vouchers would certainly allow for personal choice and would encourage book and educational materials purchases among many families that currently do not purchase such things. Against those advantages, we have to weigh the fact that what we can provide by vouchers would not meet the needs of the average child. Public library collections range from several hundred books for young people to many thousands, as well as containing other kinds of materials. The public library with its large collections available for sharing gives young people many more choices than vouchers could, and staff to help them make those choices. It would be more efficient and more effective to induce parents and children to use the library than to go to a voucher system.

TURNING YOUTH LIBRARY SERVICES OVER TO THE SCHOOLS

In September 1970, the Commissioner of Education's Committee on Library Development in the State of New York believed it had found a way of reaching more children with library services. It issued a report recommending that public schools be given the responsibility for all library services to children preschool through the sixth grade, including children in parochial and private schools but not those in correctional, welfare, or medical institutions. Within a few weeks, the Regents of the University of the State of New York promulgated a position paper supporting the concept and proposing a pilot project as a way of developing its implementation (Burke, 1971/1974). The proposal was discussed heatedly in the library community, especially in New York State. This option is very like that of switching services to a new institution; instead, it switches the services to another agency already in existence.

The Commissioner's Committee perceived a number of advantages to having all library services provided by the schools. The Committee reasoned that by locating all library services in the elementary schools the state could: avoid unnecessary duplication, provide access to more children because they spend so much time in school, ensure that the library met the needs of the curriculum, provide more individualized service because school staff know more about individual children than public librarians do, provide a wider range of materials and equipment and a larger number of library outlets, and free the public library to concentrate on adults and young adults. The Committee did not propose that public library budgets be reduced nor that children be barred from the public library, only that children's staff and materials be located at the school library, except for children's materials for adult study. They also recommended that school libraries be upgraded to meet the new demands.

Opposition to the plan came from public library administrators, children's librarians, and school librarians. A position paper from the directors of the libraries belonging to the Nassau Library System on Long Island (Burke, 1971/1974) stated the public library side of the opposition: Children would be restricted to one library, it would be impossible to have children's materials for adult use and not for children's use, education is lifelong and not an activity that takes place only at school, schools would not be able to have as broad a range of materials for different interests and levels as public libraries do, and more school staff would be required to work weekends, evenings, and summers. The directors also pointed out that a variety of facilities might mean a greater choice of materials for students, students spend more time out of school than in it, education is the responsibility of parents and the community as well as the schools, all members of a family can use the public library at the same time, very little was known about how children use school libraries, and the public library is responsible for serving the "whole" person all through his life.

Sattley (1971/1974), a school library media specialist in New York City at the time of the report, commented that not all school librarians were pleased with the idea of assuming responsibility for all library services for young children. Those whose schools were located in New York City had many concerns, particularly for the security of school buildings and the personal safety of users and staff during times that the rest of the school building was closed. She pointed out that school librarians in New York City had had to work with poor facilities and low budgets for a long time: "Frankly, we are staggered by the dubious honor thrust upon us by a committee on which there was no one familiar with the daily work load we carry and the dreams we have had blighted year after year" (Sattley, 1971/1974, p. 41). A single school librarian with no clerical help could not add services to preschoolers, parents, and children from private and parochial schools without further diluting the services to the public school student (Sattley, 1971/1974). As I write, school library media services in elementary schools are being eroded once again by the educational budget crisis; very few localities can afford to place all library services to children in schools (Gerhardt, 1992b).

Broderick (1974), a noted commentator on library service to children and young adults in both school and public libraries, said that school libraries, because they were not given adequate facilities and staffs, were not doing a good job, universally, although public library children's services were superior to public library services for adults. She also pointed out that the plan assumed that all school libraries were alike and all public libraries were alike. Because both are locally adapted institutions, they differ among themselves as much as between the two types. One area where schools are known to differ from public libraries is in their collection policies: Public libraries are much more likely to purchase controversial materials for young people. Broderick criticized the New York plan for looking at structure without first considering goals (Broderick, 1974).

The pilot project was proposed for the 1972–1973 school year. Unfortunately, it was never carried out. It is likely that the major flaw in the plan was the expense of it, because it did not include cutting the public library budget when it added to the school library budgets. The energy crisis and recession of the mid-1970s may have intervened. It is interesting that the Committee members felt that having school libraries serve all young children would eliminate duplication when it would actually have increased it. As Sattley (1971/1974) concluded, a branch library may serve the same area as six or eight schools. To keep the six or eight school libraries open longer and serving a more varied clientele would require more staff and more materials than were currently available at the branch library. In effect, public library service to young people is actually a means of rationing library services for them by having those services relatively centralized rather than dispersed throughout smaller neighborhoods. Indeed, if it were possible to fund evening, weekend, and summer hours in neighborhood school libraries, they might well be more convenient for children to get to on their own, their preferred method of going to the library (Fasick & England, 1977). School libraries that did not include materials for adults would, however, diminish family library use.

Although librarians perceive school libraries to have a curricular purpose and public libraries to have a recreational purpose, research shows that school library collections are very similar to children's public library collections (Doll, 1985; Garland, 1989; Rozek, 1990). We have also seen in previous chapters that public libraries support formal education with reference services. Because the pilot study was never done in New York, we do not know how much library service young people could potentially use nor have we tested the efficacy of one agency's program against the other. In a few communities, public libraries have been combined with school libraries with positive results where funds were not available to provide two buildings. In these cases, the entire public library, not just children's services, is joined to the school library function, and various accommodations have been made about hours and staffing (Brown & Mashinic, 1983; Kitchens & Bodart, 1980). All of these libraries are in quite small towns or in distinctive or somewhat isolated neighborhoods of larger communities where space is a consideration.

The research documenting that childhood use of the library is related to use in adulthood was done after the proposal was made, so little attention was paid to the issue of transition from school to public library (Lange, 1987–1988; Powell, Taylor, & McMillen, 1984; Razzano, 1985). People who had used only a school library as children might expect to continue to use school and academic libraries as adults, being ignorant of the public library's usefulness to them. Loss of children's services could lead to erosion of support for the public library as a whole.

When one considers the limited resources that are devoted to public library services to children and young adults, it is ironic that avoiding duplication of them is seen as a cost-saving measure. The great majority of staff and acquisitions budgets are spent on serving adults, but no one has ever suggested that adults be limited to one type of library or that colleges and universities take over serving the public library's adult clientele. Indeed, the general thrust in recent years has been "multitype cooperation" in which access to all kinds of libraries is broadened so that library patrons may borrow materials regardless of which type of library owns them. Adults are understood to have a variety of wants and needs for library materials and services, but young people are not expected to have a preference for or a right to more than one option.

CHARGING FOR ADULT SERVICES

The assumption that library services to adults deserve public support is not entirely unexamined. White (1983) and Van House (1983) studied public libraries and found that services for adults generally lack a strong theoretical foundation for public support in terms of public goods theory and externalities. Both of them found that services for children and teenagers are supportable. Both suggested that it would be possible and advisable to charge fees for some services to adults, and the merits of this proposition have been discussed frequently in the library literature. It is usually proposed that such "new" services as consulting electronic databases or interlibrary loans be the ones charged for and that "basic" services, such as book loans and reference services from print materials continue to be free of direct payment from users. Charging fees to adults could benefit children's and young adult services.

First, if some aspects of adult services, such as database consultation, were on a cost-recovery basis, the pressure on the library budget from public sources would be lessened. This might have the effect of freeing public money to support other kinds of library services, including youth services. Second, at the least, the incentive for library administrators to maintain or cut library budgets in the face of rising costs might diminish, and the threat of cutting youth services might consequently dwindle.

However, the notion of charging fees for some services is an example of a rational idea that encounters a good deal of political opposition. Many public libraries include the word "free" in their names, and librarians take it seriously. Despite the fact that the majority of the library's clientele is middle class, librarians do not want to make any service inaccessible to lower income people by charging fees. They ignore the fact that fees are always charged for photocopies and frequently charged for loans of videocassettes and best sellers. The social aspects of the issue are more salient to many librarians than the economic factors.

The practical aspects of levying fees must be considered. Although some public libraries provide online database searching for a fee charged to all users (Riechel, 1991), most librarians would want to charge only those adults who could afford to pay for services and subsidize those who could not afford to pay. Identifying those two groups might prove difficult (Getz, 1980), and even if that difficulty were surmounted, the stigma attached to having oneself identified as "poor" by a government official would be off-putting to patron and librarian alike. Libraries might not benefit from the revenue because local governments would simply decrease the library budget by whatever amount the fees brought in rather than make the same total available for expanded services in other areas. Although there is certainly precedent in charging fees for municipal recreational facilities, public opposition to a cost-recovery approach for adult services might well be strong, making fees politically unacceptable.

Budd (1989) argued that charging fees is actually diseconomic. Charging fees for interlibrary loans and electronic databases would not actually help the library budget very much because these services account for very small proportions of the budget. For example, public libraries paid only 1.38% of their materials budgets to database services in the 1989-1990 fiscal year ("Library acquisition expenditures, 1989-1990," 1991). The provision of staff is actually the library's largest expenditure, frequently 60% or more of the budget. It would make more sense (and more money) to charge for the services of a reference librarian, but the notion of charging a fee for a librarian's time would be abhorrent to the profession, although it might force librarians to be more accountable in their work (Budd, 1989). Further, charging fees limits demand (Blake & Perlmutter, 1977; Budd, 1989) and this is not a goal or necessity of most public libraries. Professionally, then, the charging of fees for adult services is not feasible.

CONTRACTING OUT

Instead of operating their own services or producing goods for their own use, governments sometimes contract with private firms. Garbage collection and janitorial services are frequently handled in this fashion by local governments. The federal government also contracts with the private sector for some activities, the two national surveys of public library youth services being examples, with defense procurement the largest and best known of federal contracting activities. The Reagan administration held the point of view that many activities of the federal government were more properly the province of the private sector. In the course of privatizing federal activities, some federal agency libraries were converted to contract services. Instead of hiring librarians and other staff through the federal civil service procedure, requests for proposals were promulgated. Independent contractors made proposals to cover salaries, services, and so forth. Contracting out was intended to avoid administrative overhead and to lower costs through competitive bidding by allowing supply and demand to determine the value of services (Levin, 1988).

In 1988, the British government, which regulates local public libraries in a way the U.S. federal government cannot, proposed, among other suggestions for privatization, that English public libraries contract out support services. The rationale given was that current funds could be used more effectively, money devoted to administrative costs could be redeployed to other services, and new profit-making services could be provided. The Minister for the Arts estimated that the recommended privatization methods together could increase library income from £22 million to £50 million, or 12% of total public library expenditure of £413 million in 1985-1986 (*Financing Our Public Library Service*, 1988). The government has proposed that acquisition, cataloging, and processing of materials be put out to bid under "compulsory competitive tendering" (CCT) by October 1994 (Daines, 1991a).

In a contract situation, the government retains responsibility for funding but pays a private organization to actually provide the services. Staff are paid by and accountable to the contractor, not the library or agency administration. Contractors may offer lower salaries and frequently offer fewer benefits to employees, thereby diminishing administrative overhead (Barbara J. Arnold, personal communication, July 1, 1992). A contractor that operates a number of similar facilities may achieve economies of scale in overall supervision. Contracts have a stipulated life (7 years in the case of U.S. federal libraries, 4 to 6 years in England). Knowing that their employment could be ended after a short time, employees would be anxious to provide good service and to keep their costs down to avoid replacement by another contractor. In principle, there is no reason why these measures would not work for youth services as well as for other areas of librarianship, presuming that the quality of services would not be lowered. Savings might result in more funds to expand youth services.

As independent contractors or as employees of personnel firms, youth librarians would have to know the hourly value of their time, be aware of how much time could be spent at various tasks, calculate the costs of materials collections and services, and in general adopt a businesslike attitude toward their work. Contracting out establishes a quite different relationship between librarians and patrons. Indeed, the British Minister for the Arts referred to library users as "customers" (*Financing Our Public Library Service*, 1988). Librarians traditionally see themselves as providing services more for altruistic reasons than for pecuniary ones. With contracting out, the exchange relationship becomes more obvious. Although librarians might perceive their affiliation with patrons differently, direct services probably would not suffer. A businesslike attitude of "the customer is always right" would prevail because patron dissatisfaction could lead to loss of the contract. Awareness of patron response and marketing of youth services might become more important than they are now.

Because the contract would be scrutinized thoroughly on a regular basis, expectations and requirements would have to be clearly stated, and evaluation of services might become even more important than it is now. Clarity of purpose assists in achieving goals. Contracting out might have the further advantage of being able to avoid some of the bureaucratic procedures and rigidity that can characterize public organizations. For instance, the challenge of providing services on Sundays and evenings might be easier to meet because contract librarians probably would not belong to labor unions.

Generally, librarians have not been favorably inclined toward contracting out, largely because of concerns over the loss of local control and input. British librarians worry that CCT will result in persons selecting library materials who are not familiar with local tastes and who are unresponsive to changes in local conditions ("ACC and AMA warning," 1992). Federal librarians in the United States have been concerned about the loss of institutional memory and commitment to particular agencies if librarians are not part of the agencies' staffs (Levin, 1988). Although several federal libraries have operated under contract for years, no study has been done of them, and even anecdotal evidence of their success or failure is limited because contract librarians are not permitted to speak or write about their work.

Barbara J. Arnold observed that some contract libraries work very well and others do not, largely based on the clarity of the specifications in the contract and the personalities involved (personal communication, July 1, 1992). In one notorious case, the Central Library of the National Oceanic and Atmospheric Administration (NOAA) was investigated by the General Accounting Office because of poor contract management. After 10 attempts, NOAA managers could not devise a precise statement of library activities for the contract solicitation and accepted a bid that relied partially on volunteers to staff the library and did not include funds to purchase materials (Levin, 1988).

As Levin pointed out, any efforts to privatize public services must be examined carefully. Unless the potential for profit exists, no private sector organization will be interested in administering public library services. As we observed in Chapter 7, the public sector very often takes on services precisely *because* they would not be profitable. Once connected to the private sector, library services are vulnerable to the ups and downs of the business cycle, the mergers, bankruptcies, and divestitures that can disrupt service (Levin, 1988), as well as the discontinuity of an entirely new staff and new technology being introduced every few years (Barbara J. Arnold, personal communication, July 1, 1992). British librarians with experience in contracting out bibliographic and video circulation services report complete failure because the vendors could not make a profit or were unable to meet the requirements of the library (Daines, 1991b). They are doubtful that businesses will come forward to bid on technical services contracts (Daines, 1991a).

Would youth services be attractive to the private sector? Probably not. Whereas sales of children's books are very profitable, and books appeal to an upscale audience, library services go beyond provision of books and are intended to reach a wider audience. The already low salaries paid to youth librarians are cited as a major disincentive to new librarians; contracting out youth services could result in a still more drastic labor shortage. Contracting out might work only in times of high unemployment among librarians; at other times, librarians would have more options for higher paying jobs. Even as it addressed the funding issues, none of the other challenges mentioned in Chapter 1 would be solved by contracting out.

Another objection that librarians have to contracting out is that it seems to devalue them and their services by insisting that private agencies that may or may not have experience in operating libraries can do so more efficiently than trained persons. Half the libraries in the country do not have a trained children's librarian and 89% do not have a young adult librarian. Cost-cutting measures that would be required to make contracting out profitable might lead to even fewer trained youth librarians. The quality of the services could deteriorate in ways that are difficult to measure in exchange for saving dollars and acquiring some managerial flexibility.

SUMMARY

We started this look at options by reminding ourselves of the challenges facing youth services and the criteria against which the options were to be evaluated. Table 8.1 summarizes the effectiveness of each of the options in meeting the challenges, and Table 8.2 does the same for the criteria. In the tables, + means that the criterion or challenge is met by the particular option, − means that the situation is made worse, 0 indicates that the option does not change the situation, and ? is used when the impact is not certain. Beginning with Table 8.1, we see that abandoning youth services could have a positive impact on funding, labor shortages, and technological ambivalence. It would do so simply by making those challenges moot; if there were no youth services we would not have to be concerned about funding, labor, or technology. On the other hand, if there were no youth services, the library would be unable to have a positive impact on the demographic shifts, the education of young people, or their status in society. Abandonment would certainly indicate that young adult services had not been accepted as a legitimate part of public library services

The status quo, although far from perfect, has been shown to make a positive contribution to the formal and informal education of young people, but we do not know enough about the young people who use the public library to assess the impact of youth services on the difficult status of children and young adults in our society. The option of turning youth services over to the schools held some initial attraction, but on further consideration was shown to increase the problems of funding and labor shortages and possibly adult use. Schools are as affected by the demographic changes as libraries and without extra funding, school libraries will have just as much difficulty meeting those challenges as public libraries.

Most of the other options are not so clearly negative as abandoning youth services, maintaining the status quo, or turning the services over to the schools. A system of vouchers could be recommended for mitigating the funding and labor problems, and by maximizing people's choices, it bypasses the demographic shifts. However, vouchers would not address the questions of television and computers for children, the acceptance of young adults, or provide the educational benefits that current library services do. Charging adults for services seems to have a positive impact only on funding, and even that is questionable because fees may replace only an insignificant portion of the library budget.

Contracting out and establishing a new institution appear to be the most positive options, yet they are not without their difficulties. Both options could have a positive impact on labor shortages because less educated, less expensive staff would likely be hired, although we should remember that youth services staff are already the lowest paid professionals in the public library. Because greater flexibility would be possible with a new institution or a contract situation, technology and demographics would likely be affected positively. The impact of the change in staff preparation on education is unknown, as the relationship between the education of staff and the educational outcomes of public library services has not been tested.

Turning to Table 8.2, rather similar patterns emerge as we evaluate the options using the criteria. The status quo has much to recommend it, despite the problems noted here and in Chapter 1. Even though we do not know as much as we would like to know about the outcomes of

Table 8.1. The Options Compared to the Challenges

Challenge	Funding	Labor	Tech	Demogs	Educ	Acceptance	Status
Abandon youth services	+	+	+	-	-	-	-
Status quo	-	-	-	-	+	-	?
New institution	-	+	+	+	?	-	+
Vouchers	+	+	-	+	-	0	-
Schools	-	-	0	-	+	-	?
Charging adults	+	?	0	0	0	-	?
Contracting out	+	+	+	+	?	0	?

Table 8.2. The Options Compare to the Criteria

Options	Develop	Educ	Econ	Vert Eq	Hor Eq	Effic	Choice	Pol Feas	Prof Feas
Abandon youth services	-	-	-	-	+	-	-	-	-
Status quo	+	+	+	-	+	-	+	+	+
New institution	+	+	+	+	+	-	+	-	-
Vouchers	-	-	0	-	+	+	-	+	-
Schools	+	+	+	+	+	-	-	-	-
Charging adults	0	0	+	+	-	-	-	0	-
Contracting out	?	?	0	+	+	+	+	+	-

youth services as presently delivered, we know more about them than the options. We have good reasons to believe that public library services to children and teenagers are positive forces in development, education, and economics. They provide a wide range of choices for all ages, and their long history makes them feasible among both politicians and professionals. The other options that come close to the status quo—establishing a new institution, contracting out, and locating all youth services in the schools—may be better at addressing the issue of vertical equity because they appear to offer opportunities to reach children who may not use public libraries now. Only contracting out and vouchers seem to offer efficiency, and this might come at the expense of effectiveness. Vouchers would actually limit young people's access to adequate resources, and contracts might result in less well-educated staff serving young people.

CONCLUSION: MODIFYING CURRENT SERVICES FOR CHILDREN AND YOUNG ADULTS

It may seem to the reader that we have set up seven straw men only to knock them down, one by one, so that the last alternative can appear stronger or more desirable than it may actually be. This has not been the case. Each of the options offers some advantages, though none of them meet all of our criteria. Two of the options have generated controversy in the library literature (charging for adult services and turning all children's services over to the public schools). The notions of abandoning youth services, leaving the services as they are, or going to a system of information vouchers help us focus on the value of library services to young people. Considering these ideas helps us realize what the services are doing for youth and at what cost on a per capita basis. Thinking about contracting out allows us to further reflect on why these services have been provided at public expense, rather than through the free market. The concept of a new institution permits some creative thinking that is useful to the recommendations in the next four chapters of the book.

Modifying youth services in public libraries is offered as the most viable alternative because a careful consideration of what ought to be done compared with what can be done leaves us little choice. We certainly want to keep those aspects of the services that have been shown to have positive benefits in terms of child development, education, and economic development. At the same time, the challenges described in Chapter 1 are real and must be faced. Lowell Martin, the library researcher and evaluator whose work was mentioned in Chapter

6 has a motto for the current status of public libraries: "concentrate and strengthen" (L.A. Martin, 1983). The recommendations that follow in Chapters 9 through 12 are offered in that spirit. Because additional funding is not likely to be forthcoming in many localities, efficiency and focus may be the only ways that public libraries can answer the challenges facing youth services.

CHAPTER 9

The Public Policy Roles of Library Associations

INTRODUCTION

After having considered how services for young people in public libraries are organized, what they do, what their effects may be, and the potential alternatives to them, it is time to consider them in regards to the political system of which they are a part. Before we can discuss the interactions of libraries with federal, state, and local governments, we need to think about who it is who speaks for libraries and librarians in the halls of government. Of course, individual librarians and library supporters do this, but individuals can represent only themselves and frequently have limited influence unless they are well known to government officials or have an organization behind them to add the weight of many similar opinions to that of the single person. Like many other occupations, librarians have organized themselves into private voluntary associations with a number of functions, including lobbying government.

Library associations differ from such professional organizations as the American Bar Association or the American Medical Association because their legal status is educational rather than professional. That is, one does not have to be a librarian to be a member of a library association. Anyone may join. Among its more than 53,000 personal members and 3,000 institutional members (American Library Association, 1993), the American Library Association (ALA) includes vendors of furnishings and equipment, publishers, friends of libraries, and library trustees among its members, for example. The reverse is also true: Librarians are not required to join a library association, and many do not. Frequently, library associations promote the interest of libraries rather than those of librarians. Further, library associations are only indirect gatekeepers for entrance to librarianship—ALA accredits library schools but does not certify or license individual librarians.

Each of the states has its own library association, organized much like ALA and involved in many of the same activities as ALA, but at a state level. Public librarians often constitute a large proportion of state association members, but other types of libraries are represented as well. In addition, there are some regional associations, such as the New England Library Association (NELA) and the Southeastern Library Association (SELA). Each organization is composed of several subgroups that may be called associations in their own right or given such titles as division, caucus, section, chapter, roundtable, or special interest group. The intention of the geographically organized library associations is to serve the interests of librarians in all specializations and all types of libraries, although librarians in some specialized types of libraries have separate groups not based on geography, such as the Special Library Association and the Medical Library Association. Within all of the geographical library organizations mentioned there are groups for children's and young adult librarians; sometimes in smaller associations the two specialties meet together as a single subgroup.

YOUTH SERVICES ASSOCIATIONS

For our purposes, the functions of library associations can be described as defining, developing, promoting, and defending libraries and librarians. The reader should bear in mind that association activities can serve more than one purpose; that is, something that helps develop librarianship may also serve to defend the profession, and so forth. These activities can be seen most easily perhaps through examples from the American Library Association and its subgroups that are relevant to youth services in public libraries: the Association for Library Service to Children (ALSC), the Young Adult Library Services Association (YALSA), and the Public Library Association (PLA). The American Association of School Librarians (AASL), also a division of ALA, shares many interests with ALSC and YALSA, and the three divisions sometimes act in concert, the most recent notable example being the work of the Youth Interdivisional Task Force that lobbied successfully for youth issues at the 1991 White House Conference on Libraries and Information Service.

In terms of defining the profession, ALA has a Code of Ethics to define and guide professional behavior; it has a Library Bill of Rights that defines the privileges that ALA members believe users (including young people) are entitled to at all libraries. The divisions produce statements from time to time that represent current definitions of librarianship in the areas of their interest.

Both ALSC and YALSA have promulgated competencies that delineate the knowledge, skills, and abilities required of youth librarians (Immroth, 1989; "Young adults deserve the best," 1982). Inherent in these competencies is a vision of excellent youth services. PLA has published several manuals to aid library administrators, such as *Planning and Role Setting for Public Libraries* (C.R. McClure, Owen, Zweizig, Lynch, & Van House, 1987) and *Output Measures for Public Libraries* (Van House, Lynch, McClure, Zweizig, & Rodger, 1987). Although not specifically intended for youth librarians, these documents provide much guidance and insight into the overall functioning of public libraries. In order to meet criticisms that *Output Measures* was inadequate for children's services, ALSC published a special set of output measures for children's services (Walter, 1992). At this writing, output measures for young adult services were being developed.

In terms of developing the profession, ALA and its various subdivisions publish journals and newsletters that not only permit communication among members but also discuss new developments and perspectives in all aspects of library services. ALSC and YALSA jointly publish *Journal of Youth Services in Libraries* and PLA publishes *Public Libraries*. Both journals are refereed and offer a balance of research and professional opinion. The ALA and PLA annual conferences and the yearly PLA workshops furnish continuing education opportunities for youth librarians. The ALA also furthers library development through supporting and disseminating research, although it is not the major source of research funds for librarianship.

Each of the divisions and ALA promotes itself and the work of the associations' members. ALA's high-quality graphics such as posters and bookmarks promote reading, libraries, and events such as National Library Week. Committees of ALSC select the Newbery, Caldecott, Batchelder, Wilder, and Andrew Carnegie Medal winners each year, promoting not only the division but also the division's understanding of the best in children's books and video. The Newbery and the Caldecott Medals are the most prestigious children's book awards in the United States. YALSA administers the Margaret Edwards Award to a young adult author in recognition of lifetime achievement (costs of the award are borne by *School Library Journal*). In addition, both ALSC and YALSA produce lists of notable children's and young adult books, sound recordings, and videos each year, and are concerned with evaluating computer software and technology. Awards and appearances on lists of notables can have substantial effects on sales to libraries, schools, and individuals, thus encouraging media producers to continue making items that meet librarians' tastes in content and production values.

Under the heading of defending and supporting librarians and libraries in general, ALA and its divisions are active in a variety of ways. ALA's Office of Intellectual Freedom monitors censorship attempts in libraries of all types, and ALA has a fund to assist librarians who have lost their jobs due to taking a strong stance on intellectual freedom, for example. However, the major way that library organizations defend libraries is through political action and attempts to influence policy.

POLITICAL ACTIVITIES OF LIBRARY ASSOCIATIONS

Because the U.S. constitution does not mention them, the establishment of public libraries is left to the states. In general, state legislation permits localities to support libraries but does not mandate their existence. It therefore behooves librarians and interested members of the public to maintain contact with elected representatives at all levels of government in order that public libraries be maintained. Generally, the American Library Association and the state library associations organize this at the state and federal levels; local librarians and residents, usually under the direction of the library director, take responsibility for relations with local government. At all levels of government, librarians and their associations provide elected officials with information about libraries and attempt to influence their opinions on matters of interest to the library community. Librarians also work with other agencies of government.

Information Gathering and Dissemination

The state and federal governments make several efforts at numerical description of public libraries (i.e., number of staff, number of items held, income and expenditures, etc.), as is described in the following chapters. However, PLA also provides various means for librarians to gather and analyze data about the quality of their libraries' performance. Ostensibly, the point of the methods espoused is "to assist public libraries in the areas of planning, measurement, and evaluation" (PLA New Standards Task Force in C.R. McClure et al., 1987, p. xi). Planning and evaluation should improve service to library users, but they also fill a political function in that they provide specific data to support the library in discussions with public officials. Historically, PLA, through its committees, developed guidelines and standards for public libraries, the most recent being *Minimum Standards for Public Library Systems, 1966* (PLA, 1967), which PLA now recommends librarians not use.

Standards provide a set of criteria against which an individual library may compare itself. They may be quantitative or qualitative; the 1966 PLA standards recommended the amounts of various things believed necessary for adequate service, such as the number of books, staff, and activities per capita, and also "gave some good advice on running a library" (Bolt, 1988, p. 106). A 1960 publication of the PLA Committee on Standards for Work with Young Adults in Public Libraries amplified the 1956 PLA standards in regards to young adult services, describing the numbers and kinds of staff, the services and activities to be provided, and so forth. Thus, it served as a manual for young adult services at that time as well as a set of standards (Committee on Standards for Work with Young Adults in Public Libraries, 1960).

The concept of standards engendered some discussion about how they were to work in practice. Were they minimum standards or were they goals to work toward? For two different libraries, the same standard might be either. Some standards implied that size of population should determine the characteristics of libraries, rather than the characteristics of communities determining library services. The rationale for deciding that some particular number of staff, books, and so on, was adequate or desirable for a particular size of population was not always clear. Because there is little evidence that size of population is a causal factor of public library services, standards flew in the face of reality, as well as raising questions of validity. Furthermore, standards were input measures; they prescribed what the community should contribute to the library, rather than what the library should or did contribute to the community.

With the movement toward accountability of all agencies of government beginning in the 1970s, a new approach, called the Public Library Development Program (PLDP), was designed, which emphasized planning, evaluation, and output measures that described how citizens made use of the public library in easily understood terms. For example, one of the output measures is annual circulation per capita, which is the number of items an average citizen charges out of a library in a year. The principal planning publications currently in use are the previously mentioned *Planning and Role Setting for Public Libraries* (C.R. McClure et al., 1987) and *Output Measures for Public Libraries* (Van House et al., 1987).

Not all librarians are satisfied with these tools—one of the directors in my case studies was forcefully exasperated with the lack of direction they provide in determining space needs, for example, remarking that her system had to refer the architect to the 1966 standards in building a branch library in 1989. At least one library staff have found that their local officials do not care about their library's output measures (Kathy Mitchell, personal communication, May 25, 1989). And, as previously noted, youth services librarians found that various aspects of their services were not allowed for, and separate sets of output measures for children's and young adult services were devised (see Walter, 1992).

Some librarians would like to return to national standards or guidelines. A recent survey of the membership of the Young Adult Library Services Association revealed that 71.4% of respondents placed "great value" on YALSA's developing guidelines for young adult services, and another 25.5% thought the idea had "some value." To a question asking what YALSA could do to improve young adult services, one respondent commented, "Develop minimum standards of service to YA's which libraries could use to convince adults (trustees, taxpayers) that YA service is important. Nonlibrarians need that yardstick to measure their library's services." (Young Adult Library Services Association, ca. 1992, Question #70, p.2). Of topics suggested for continuing education, guidelines for young adult services received the second highest number of points, behind services but ahead of programming, materials, and intellectual freedom (Young Adult Library Services Association, ca. 1992).

It is not surprising, therefore, that despite or perhaps because of PLA's move away from prescriptive standards (Bolt, 1988), some of the states continue to use and develop them, sometimes including output measures in their standards. Standards are often created through collaboration between the state library agency and the state library association, and separate standards for youth services have been fashioned in some states, such as Virginia in 1983 and New York in 1984. A subcommittee of the Virginia Library Association's Library Development Committee developed "Young Adult Services Guidelines" that were approved by both the Virginia Library Association and the Virginia State Library Board for inclusion in the *Recommended Minimum Standards for Virginia Public Libraries*. Although these guidelines were specific about staff—"Each library system should have at least one professional librarian with training in young adult services" (Cram, 1984, p. 91)—they were less specific about money, stating only that libraries should make an appropriate, formal allocation for young adult services. A survey of libraries in a 5-county region of New York State revealed that libraries met or exceeded state standards for programming for both children and young adults but were not meeting the materials budget standards, especially in the area of audiovisual purchases. The writer concluded that librarians were not well informed about the standards (Benedict, 1988).

The word *recommended* in the title of the Virginia standards indicates that libraries comply voluntarily with them; the standards do not have the force of law or official regulation, which leaves librarians, trustees, and citizens to convince local officials of the standards' value. In a few states, such as Illinois, standards are mandatory. Libraries that do not meet the criteria may lose state aid (Bolt, 1988). Whether or not this consequence is a sufficient carrot to local governments depends on the amount of state aid that may be lost (see Chapter 11). Ironically, losing state aid makes it less likely that a library will meet the standards in the future, of course.

Librarians continue to value statewide standards or guidelines because standards are specific and concrete; they easily communicate to the public, local officials, and legislators what librarians think good service is and what librarians want. Neither output measures nor roles provide that kind of information, though they supply some of the background needed to justify librarians' wants.

A survey by a committee of the Texas Library Association found that librarians were well aware of the political use of standards. Of those who had used the 1983 *Standards and Guidelines for Texas Public Libraries*, 89% did so for budget proposal justification and 58% to demonstrate the need for library improvements. A comparison of the standards with the statistics of Texas public libraries disclosed that only 13% of the libraries met all the measurable recommended minimums (Skinner, 1989). Perhaps standards are a measure of librarians' aspirations.

A further development of the PLDP has been the design and implementation of a voluntary system of statistical data collection called the *Public Library Data Service*, which allows librarians to compare their libraries with others that are similar, not only in total population but also in other variables such as the proportion of various age groups and the proportion of high school and college graduates. Some variables relating to children's services are collected but none relating to young adult services (see Zweizig, 1993). Skinner noted, "The measurement of a library's adequacy by any single approach, whether by comparison to predetermined quantitative standards or to the statistics of libraries serving communities of similar size, or by its level of success in filling community roles, does not produce satisfactory results" (1989, p. 105), thus librarians will probably continue to use a combination of standards, output measures, role setting, and comparisons with libraries in similar communities.

Lobbying

The collection of data and the setting of standards serve to provide library associations with some of the information needed to influence the state and federal governments. The ALA maintains contact with and lobbies Congress through its Washington Office (ALA headquarters are in Chicago). Each of the ALA's divisions, including ALSC and YALSA, has a legislation committee that sends a representative to the ALA Legislation Committee. The director of ALA's Washington Office serves as staff liaison to the Legislation Committee. The state library associations interact directly with state legislatures through their own lobbyists, or they may ally themselves with the state library agency (see Chapter 11). Lobbyists may be paid professionals or members of the library association who have assumed volunteer lobbying activities as part of their professional service. In at least one state, the association executive director's official duties include lobbying (Figueredo, 1990). Most of the associations have committees that work with the lobbyist or legislative representative.

As astonishing as it may seem, librarians did not always desire state or federal funding and legislation favoring libraries. Holley and Schremser (1983) reported vehement opposition in the 1920s and 1930s to ALA leaders' suggestions of the desirability of federal aid to libraries. At the time, public sentiment was that the federal government did not belong in education, and many librarians, seeing their institutions as educational in nature, shared the general view. In addition, the historical development of the local public library inculcated the view that public libraries should serve everyone, not the politically powerful few. Being nonpartisan came to mean being apolitical (Shavit, 1986b). However, the views of ALA leaders prevailed, and in 1938 the Library Services Division of the U.S. Office of Education was formed to collect statistics, perform surveys, and promote libraries, the first fruits of ALA's lobbying efforts. In 1945, ALA's Washington Office was founded to give the ALA a permanent presence in the nation's capital to observe and participate in the legislative process on behalf of libraries of all types.

The Washington Office staff monitor pertinent legislation, work with legislators to introduce legislation favoring libraries, organize lobbying and testimony, and inform ALA members of the progress of relevant bills. The director of the Washington Office reviews the year's legislative results in the *Library and Book Trade Almanac*. Information of a more immediate nature is available via the office's newsletter and an electronic bulletin board available over the Internet. These latter two sources alert librarians when to contact their representatives to support or oppose a piece of legislation and what to say when they do. Perusal of these sources indicates the enormous variety of issues that the Washington Office deals with. Funding and data collection may have been the starting point for librarians' interest in Washington and the state capitals, but many other issues affect libraries, such as copyright, public access to government publications in electronic form, the development of the National Research and Education Network (and many other issues in education), and postal subsidies for mailing library materials, to name a very few.

Just as state library associations collaborate with the state library agencies, so ALA's Washington Office works with the National Commission on Libraries and Information Science (NCLIS) and the office of Library Programs in the U.S. Department of Education, the successor to the Library Services Division. Chapter 10 discusses the roles and activities of these agencies.

The Washington Office also organizes Legislative Day, held annually since 1975 during National Library Week in April ("The 17th Annual Legislative Day," 1991). The timing is propitious because it occurs just after the President presents his budget proposal to Congress. Delegations of librarians and library supporters from all over the country—550 people in 1991—descend upon the capital to meet with their Congressional representatives and lobby for libraries. They have been prepared by the staff of the Washington Office about the President's requests for LSCA, the National Endowment for the Humanities, the Elementary and Secondary Education Act, the Higher Education Act, and any other legislation that is pertinent. When they visit legislators and their staffs, delegates are well prepared to present not only the overall issues but the impact of federal legislation on the congressperson's local district. In addition, many of the delegates know their senators and representatives personally, which can make them quite effective in swaying opinion (Mary Costabile, personal communication, January 5, 1993).

Because the ALA does not contribute to political campaigns, Legislative Day is a major opportunity to inform Capitol Hill about the needs of libraries. Libraries are in competition with all other social programs and the national budget deficit, and this competition is expected to increase (Mary Costabile, personal communication, January 5, 1993). State library associations sponsor similar events in many state capitals for the purpose of lobbying state legislators. In my case studies, the most successful directors were those who were active politically at both the state and local levels (Willett, 1992). Not only did they attend state Legislative Days, but they made sure the trustees of their libraries did, also.

Effectiveness of Association Political Activities

The ALA has a history of more than 50 years of lobbying Congress. The longevity of the inclusion of libraries in the Office of Education and ALA's Washington Office argue well for the effectiveness of lobbying. From ALA's perspective, if lobbying did not have positive results, the ALA would surely have ceased to do it many years ago; maintaining two

ical plants is expensive. However, ALA's perspective is
:levant criterion of effectiveness.

not a short-term activity. Congressman Major R. Owens
(D–New York), a professional librarian, noted, "Decades sometimes
pass between the time a legislative concept is launched and the date of
final passage" (1990, p. 23). Holley and Schremser (1983) documented
the 10-year effort (1946–1956) that was required to pass the first federal
funding for public libraries, the Library Services Act (now the Library
Services and Construction Act), including a heartbreaking defeat in the
House of Representatives in 1950. In fact, LSA became law 20 years after
ALA's Executive Board first voted to seek permanent federal aid. As
Carma Leigh said at the celebration of LSCA's 25th anniversary, those
who would make headway in the legislative arena must *"persist*, be
stubborn, and *be strong"* (1982, p. 285, emphasis in original).

She ought, perhaps, to have added, be unified and do your homework. Owens (1990) described a situation in which three library experts
representing three library associations testified before Congress on
behalf of a bill that he had introduced. The comments of the three
indicated that the organizations had not consulted with one another and
were not in agreement about the content of the bill, leading to the bill's
defeat and putting off for an even longer time any hope of passing it. In
the process, Owens's credibility was damaged. This illustrates the need
for careful strategic planning and preparation.

Part of the planning and preparation is knowing the legislative
process, how to approach your issues, whom to contact, and what they
need to hear. Since the 1970s, librarians have become increasingly
sophisticated at lobbying, particularly in areas where property tax
reform measures have had serious impacts on public libraries, such as
California. As Jenkins (1990) noted, legislators want to know how the
proposed policy will affect people in their districts. After the passage of
Proposition 13 in 1978, the California Library Association hired Michael
Dillon, a professional lobbyist, to assist the passage of direct state aid to
public libraries, a goal that was achieved in 1984. When asked if
legislators would be impressed if librarians could be specific about the
effects of library use, he answered that they were more apt to respond
to concrete examples, such as how far you would have to drive to find
a library open on Sunday if you lived in Sacramento (personal communication, July 1984).

State and national Legislative Days are efforts to bring this "home-
town" message to political representatives. Yet the longevity of ALA's
Washington Office and the appropriateness of the strategies used do not
mean that the ALA and public librarians are viewed as major political
forces by politicians or the general public. An institution that controls

only one fifth of 1% of public spending is a small dog yapping at the heels of a giant, an annoyance to be tossed an occasional dog biscuit. However, the small dog had best keep barking or even that biscuit may not be forthcoming. In the current climate of budget deficits and cutbacks, the small dog might even think of taking voice lessons to increase the likelihood of being heard in the halls of government.

Political Efforts of Youth Services Organizations

Like so many other aspects of youth services, the political activities of youth librarians have not been studied, and until the success of the Omnibus Children and Youth Literacy Through Libraries Act recommendations at the 1991 White House Conference (see Chapter 10), politics has been little written about in the youth services press. ALSC usually sends a representative to Legislative Day in Washington, DC, but YALSA does not (Susan Roman, personal communication, January 5, 1993; Linda Waddle, personal communication, January 6, 1993). The Washington Office reports that children's and young adult librarians do attend as part of state delegations (Mary Costabile, personal communication, January 5, 1993), but there is no information on whether they specifically speak to youth services issues or how effective they are.

The Legislation Committees of ALSC and YALSA in the past have primarily disseminated information from the ALA Legislation Assembly to their respective memberships, particularly concerning how ALA legislative activities might affect youth services. Apparently, the committees have not pushed legislative agendas of their own. The chairs of the ALSC and YALSA Legislation Committees expect that to change. At this writing, the committees are working on continuing the effort to pass the Omnibus Youth Literacy Act (Marge Loch-Wouters & Susan Roman, personal communication, January 5, 1993; Jeri Baker, personal communication, January 6, 1993). ALSC's Legislation Committee prepared a 2-hour program on lobbying for youth services librarians at the 1993 ALA summer conference.

Aside from the contributions that the youth services organizations make to the ALA through their participation in the Legislation Assembly, how frequently do children's and young adult librarians as individuals and members of library associations become involved in political activities? My impression has been that political involvement beyond writing letters to legislators is infrequent. In my case studies, no librarians participated in a state or national Legislative Day or testified before a legislative body except library directors (Willett, 1987). At the local level, the library director controls information both internally and externally and sets the political agenda for the local library (Shavit,

1986b; Willett, 1992). This tends to be carried through at the state and federal levels; those who are very active politically are library directors, rarely the rank-and-file librarians who are apt to say, "That's not my job," regardless of their function or specialization.

Searching 5 years (1988-1992) of *Library Literature*, the index for library and information studies, for articles about lobbying directed at youth librarians, I found very little. Eleven articles (excluding duplicates) discussed the White House Conference activities of the three youth services divisions of ALA in 1991 and 1992, and several of these were in *School Library Media Quarterly*, rarely read by public librarians. The annual "year-in-review" articles written by one of the editors of *School Library Journal* included some information about funding and legislation of interest to public library youth services. Beyond that, I located only five articles in youth services journals that recommended or discussed lobbying. Three of these articles, including an editorial, were in *School Library Journal*, the most popular periodical among school and public librarians serving young people, and two articles appeared in *Emergency Librarian*, a school library periodical published in Canada, which has a small circulation to public libraries. Likewise, the state library association journals had very few articles that appeared to be about legislative issues around youth services.

Beyond the remarkable political success story of the Omnibus Children and Youth Literacy Through Libraries recommendations passed by the White House Conference (see Chapter 10), there were no news stories or articles about youth librarians as political activists at the federal, state, or local levels during 1988 through 1992 in journals addressed to youth librarians. Furthermore, articles on funding and marketing youth services usually focus on existing opportunities such as LSCA and local foundations and businesses, not on fundamental legislative change (see articles by Rosenzweig, Faklis, and Hippenhammer in Edmonds, 1989).

Possibly youth librarians do not write about their political activities because frequently it is not politic to do so. To my knowledge, the youth librarians of one state successfully lobbied the state library agency to provide a consultant for youth services and to collect youth services statistics. It is desirable to maintain good relations with the state library staff, so these events have not been made objects of public scrutiny. In some instances, youth librarians may not view their work as political in nature, and it would not occur to them to write about it in that vein. Even allowing for these possibilities, though, it is hard to avoid the conclusion that youth librarians probably have been infrequent political activists. One example will suffice. In Fall 1991, I attended a Wisconsin Library Association fundraiser for a state assembly member. Of the 30 or so librarians in attendance, not one was a children's or young adult librarian. Yet this politician's speech to the group was entirely devoted to his childhood use of public libraries and the benefits his own children received from the library.

Undoubtedly, there are a number of reasons for the apparent disinterest in lobbying, aside from the political reticence of the profession as a whole (Shavit, 1986b). Youth services is a very active and intense area of the profession. In addition to the usual duties of collection management and reference demanded of all public service librarians, youth librarians are expected to design, publicize, and present programs with a high degree of frequency and to maintain liaison with community agencies, especially schools. To be politically active through an association or personally may mean a diminution of either public services or personal activities. The "canonization" of the library director as the political representative means that there may be little administrative approval or concrete support for staff political activities. Additionally, despite the political attractiveness of children and teenagers, there may be a perception that youth librarians lack political experience and are ineffective, which may have some basis in fact, if the literature is an accurate reflection of youth librarians' political activities.

The apparent disinclination to become politically active and the perception of youth librarians as politically ineffective may have been changed by the 1991 White House Conference (Jeri Baker, personal communication, January 6, 1993). Acceptance of the Omnibus Youth Literacy Act as the major recommendation of the conference is a tribute to the efficacy of the organization and lobbying skills of youth services librarians across the country, most of whom worked within their own states to see that the necessary resolutions were passed prior to the national conference. One hopes that youth services librarians understand that they have acquired not only transferable skills but supporters in their home states whose goodwill and influence should be cultivated if the provisions of the Youth Literacy recommendations are to become fact.

The strategy developed by the American Association of School Librarians (AASL) and outlined by Dianne Hopkins (1992) contains basic elements of successful political action that can be used in other contexts. The list includes communication within the organization to garner support through state affiliates and the grassroots membership, issue papers supported by research findings, representation on major committees, coordination with other units of the organization working on related issues, and coordination with other groups outside the organization with cognate interests. One must note that planning and implementing the process that led to adoption of the Omnibus Children and Youth Literacy Through Libraries Act at the 1991 White House Conference took 7 years and much hard work by hundreds of school library media specialists and youth librarians around the country. As Marilyn Miller (1992) noted, making the Omnibus Youth Literacy Act a reality will take continued effort from the same constituencies. And, it will be a fine school for political action.

RECOMMENDATIONS

Recommendation #1

One can only applaud the efforts of the ALSC and YALSA Legislation Committees to assist the associations' members to understand and act in the political milieu of which public libraries are an undeniable part. As Somerville (1989) pointed out, children and teenagers are public libraries' political capital, which they have not used to the full extent possible. In addition, the committees should encourage the publication of more articles about lobbying and other political activities in the *Journal of Youth Services in Libraries*, not only "how-to" articles, but also articles about successful and unsuccessful political activities, and reports of ALA legislative activity of interest to youth librarians. Eileen Cooke, director of ALA's Washington Office, writes a column for *School Library Media Quarterly* about legislative efforts. Perhaps she could be asked to share some of that information with ALSC and YALSA members through *JOYSIL*.

Recommendation #2

If they are not already involved, state association children's and young adult services organizations should consider their needs for legislation committees and other ways of becoming active in their association's political efforts. And they should be writing about their own political efforts and the state legislation that youth librarians should watch and in which they should become involved, in their newsletters and state association periodicals. Because more youth librarians belong to state associations than to national organizations, it is particularly important to develop strong political knowledge and ability at the state level.

Recommendation #3

Just as the state and national youth services associations have pioneered in offering continuing education at conferences around many new

Table 9.1.   Summary of Recommendations for Library Associations

---

1. The Legislation Committees of ALSC and YALSA should encourage the writing and publication of articles about political activities specifically for youth librarians in the *Journal of Youth Services in Libraries*.
2. State library association groups concerned with young people should form legislation committees and find other ways to become politically involved at the state level.
3. State and national library associations should make continuing education in political effectiveness available to youth services librarians.

---

services, the organizations should help their members and the wider profession develop skills related to lobbying and information gathering for political purposes. The program at the 1993 ALA summer conference may provide a model that can be used in other situations. Lacking activities specifically designed for them, youth librarians should attend conference sessions on political effectiveness that may be available through organizations that serve library directors, regardless of type of library.

CONCLUSION

The youth services associations representing public libraries have only recently begun to recognize their need and potential for political action, thanks to their collaboration with the school library associations during and before the White House Conference of 1991. Gathering data and lobbying require persistence, determination, and the willingness to work over a long time frame before results are seen. And then, the consequences may not be all that one hoped for, and unforeseen consequences may arise, requiring further effort.

There are no substitutes for political activity. The public library is a creature of government, which is to say, the result of political activity on the part of the 19th-century founders. Its existence depends on continued funding, particularly at the local level, but to a certain extent also at the state and federal levels. At all levels, the claims on government are many and justifiable. Athough individuals can and should make their views known to their political representatives, it is through their associations that youth services librarians have a better chance to establish the legitimacy and value of their role in the education and development of young people and state their reasonable claims on the public exchequer. Youth services needs associations that are numerically strong and leaders who are comfortable with their political roles in order to be sure that the issues are given a place on the agenda.

CHAPTER 10

Federal Government Policies

INTRODUCTION

When we began this book, public policy was defined as the things that governments choose to do or not do (Dye, 1987). Local governments, with state and federal assistance, have chosen to make available to young people collections of books, magazines, videos, sound recordings, toys, and other materials, selected and organized by persons interested in young people and their materials, who promote the use of the materials and offer guidance in their use. The goals of the policy are to improve the educational, informational, cultural, recreational, and developmental circumstances of children and young adults by offering them choices among a range of possibilities. This policy, which has a century-long history in the United States, happens within and through an institution called the public library. Throughout the book, we have documented what is known about the accomplishments, ideology, and impact of youth services, yet in the first chapter, we noted several challenges that face them today: funding restraints, structural changes in personnel, technological change, demographic change, concern for educational achievement, acceptance of young adult services, and the status of young people in our society.

The alternatives we have examined do not completely address the challenges or meet the criteria for effective library services, although they offer some possibilities for rethinking youth services to fit the last decade of the 20th century and the beginning of the 21st century. This chapter and the two that follow discuss current policies of national, state, and local governments and recommend specific new policies. Individual librarians must also take some responsibility if changes are to be made, and recommendations are made for them, as well, in Chapter 12.

FEDERAL GOVERNMENT POLICIES

The United States federal government does not have a single, formal, comprehensive policy dealing with information or libraries, although it has written policies that deal with some aspects of information and libraries. For example, Office of Management and the Budget Circular A-130 instructs federal agencies in how the public is to be given access to information the agencies publish. A number of laws, administrative regulations, and programs exist at the federal level to assist libraries and/or regulate the provision of information. Because the notion of what governments *do* as opposed to what governments *say* is central to our discussion of public policy, we examine the programs that constitute federal information policies regarding children. We do not discuss the National Libraries of Agriculture and Medicine, the National Technical Information Service, or the Government Printing Office. These entities have an impact on public libraries but very little influence on policies affecting young people. The major federal agencies that have a potential impact on public library services for children and young adults are the Library of Congress, the National Commission on Libraries and Information Science, and the Department of Education, with a few opportunities offered by other federal agencies such as the National Endowment for the Humanities.

THE LIBRARY OF CONGRESS

Children's Literature Center

The Library of Congress functions as a national library for the United States, although legally it is Congress's library. It influences youth services in four ways. One is through providing some visibility at the national and international levels for American children's literature via the Children's Literature Center within the Library. Its impact on young people is mostly indirect; it publishes an annual list of recommended children's books and provides research facilities for scholars. Exhibits, symposia, and publications disseminate the Center's work to scholars, authors and illustrators, people who work with children, and the general public. Occasional programs involve children directly, and staff also advise the media on children's books ("Children's Literature Center celebrates," 1987; Coleburn & Giordano, 1988; Coughlan & Woodrell, 1989; Dalrymple, 1991; Lamolinara, 1990). Although the work of the Center and its staff are well respected within the world of children's books, it is not well known to the general public.

National Library Service for the Blind and Physically Handicapped

The second program that involves children is the National Library Service for the Blind and Physically Handicapped (NLS). NLS is known for its Talking Books program, which mails, at no charge to NLS or the user, books and magazines on cassette tape and flexible disk and in Braille to persons with vision impairments or disabilities that prevent their using codex-form books. The service is managed through a system of regional libraries, at least one in each state and three of the territories. The federal government funds the materials, and the state governments support the regional libraries through the state library agency, the state department of education, or the state school for the blind (Marsha Valance, personal communication, July 8, 1992). Although each book is brailled or recorded by volunteers, the process is quite expensive and just 2,000 to 2,500 books are produced each year, which means that a great deal of selectivity is exercised in choosing titles (Cylke, Dixon, Hagle, & Wintle, 1989; Sharlynn Pyne, personal communication, July 8, 1992).

NLS's intention is to offer a service that is equivalent to public library services for the sighted, but clearly the blind and physically handicapped do not have access to the amount or range of print information and recreation that the sighted do. A survey completed in 1977 revealed that only 12% of those eligible made use of the service, but 48% of the eligibles knew about it (Cylke, Dixon, Hagle, & Wintle, 1989). This rate is lower than the general adult population's use of the public library, which is approximately 20% per month.

Since 1952, NLS has included children in its audience, but most of its users are over 55. NLS has made some special accommodations for children by producing picturebooks with clear acetate interleaves on which the text is brailled, allowing a sighted parent to read to a blind child or a blind parent to read to a sighted child. Some books have had tactile inserts made for them, such as raised line drawings (Cylke, Dixon, Hagle, & Wintle, 1989). NLS owns approximately 12,000 titles for young readers, a small percentage of the more than 1.1 million books in the total collection; 400 to 500 new titles for young people are selected each year, about 20% of the total (Simpson, 1991; Sharlynn Pyne, personal communication, July 8, 1992; Marsha Valance, personal communication, July 8, 1992). This figure is about 10% of the new books published for young people each year. Young people are estimated to be 20,000 of NLS's readers, a figure that is obscured by the fact that books are mailed to schools and institutions as well as individuals. More than 80% of users are adults (Sharlynn Pyne, personal communication, July 8, 1992).

For those whom it serves, NLS makes available materials that individuals could probably not afford to purchase and that would not be available on the open market because the audience is too small to be profitable. Distribution at the state level allows users to have somewhat more personal service than they would with national distribution, and personal service is a quality public libraries hope to provide. NLS is an example of vertical equity – treating those with a disadvantage in a special fashion to make them more like those without the disadvantage.

Center for the Book

Founded in 1977, the Center for the Book's purpose is to encourage the appreciation of books and reading. Until recently, it has focused on adult reading and scholarly research in reading. In Summer 1992, the Center for the Book formed a partnership with Head Start and the Association for Library Service to Children to work together in literacy projects across the country. A package of videos and a resource notebook was planned as the first project, to be available sometime in 1993. Though the intention is sound, as it combines expertise in young children with expertise in children's materials and two federal agencies with a private voluntary association, the partnership was too new at this writing to be evaluated.

Cataloging

Most of the Library of Congress's activities mentioned here reach relatively few young people. For children and young adults, the most immediate impact of the Library of Congress is through cataloging. Most children's and young adult trade books published in the United States (and many books for adults) are cataloged at the Library of Congress before they are published. Cataloging and classification information is printed in the book and shared through the Library's own programs and the various other automated shared cataloging schemes (known technically as *bibliographic utilities*) that operate internationally. Unfortunately, the subject headings that are supposed to help young people locate books by topic are at an advanced reading level. The list of headings used for children's books under the Annotated Card Program has been tested at the sixth-grade reading level, the upper end of the age range served by children's services (Moll, 1975). Many adults do not read at a sixth-grade level. Furthermore, the reading level of the subject headings is never altered to suit the reading or interest levels of the material. Russell (1991) observed that subject headings are not used consistently within a broad subject area in materials for young adults. Although subject terminology is changed periodically, the thesaurus is not updated fast enough for many professionals (Berman, 1987; Russell, 1991).

Recommendation #1

Available information does not suggest that either the Children's Literature Center or the NLS are inefficient or ineffective, though neither agency is reaching its total potential audience. Because it seems unlikely that improvements could be made without more federal dollars, no recommendations are offered for either service, even though a case could be made to increase services of both agencies. However, the system of subject headings does not encourage child development or enhance education; it does not encourage children or teenagers to become successful independent users of library catalogs. Therefore, the first recommendation is that the Library of Congress should improve the thesaurus of subject headings in two ways. The first recommended improvement is obvious: Subject headings should be applied in a consistent manner in materials for all ages. Second, the Library of Congress should establish a second set of children's subject headings at the third grade reading level in order to improve access to information in library catalogs for children under the sixth grade. This set of headings should be applied to materials for children in grade four and younger. The third grade reading level is selected because that is the approximate age when children develop concrete operations and become capable of using catalogs.

One day perhaps online catalogs will not rely on librarians' rules or subject headings, and users will be able to make inquiries using the terminology they know. When that day comes, there will be no need for standardized age-level subject headings. Having subject headings at three levels of readability (grade three, grade six, and adult) would be a step in the right direction. In automated systems, it would be possible to link the three levels, so that the user would retrieve all relevant material regardless of the reading level of the subject headings (Adeline Wilkes, personal communication, February 11, 1993). For example, whether you used "Measures" or "Mensuration" you would be given a list of the materials on that subject. Improving catalog access requires subject headings accessible to the youngest catalog users as they are at a stage of development when categorization and classification become important cognitive skills. Library catalogs have the potential to reinforce emerging intellectual abilities, but only if the cataloging is readable.

This recommendation may have some costs associated with it, as it will take the Library of Congress staff time to develop a new scheme of subject headings and procedures for applying them. However, the present thesaurus undergoes revision as it is. It is not unreasonable to ask revisers to consider a young child's subject heading list. A model is available in the work of the Hennepin County (MN) Public Library, which has developed both children's subject headings and young adult subject headings (Berman, 1987). Furthermore, assistance from the youth services divisions of the American Library Association and the Cataloging of Children's Materials Committee of the Association for Library Collections and Technical Services could be expected. Many librarians would volunteer if given a chance to do something meaningful about subject headings for young people.

NATIONAL COMMISSION ON LIBRARIES AND INFORMATION SCIENCE

The National Commission on Libraries and Information Science (NCLIS) was established by Congress in 1970 and is an agency of the Executive Branch of the federal government. It has "primary responsibility for developing or recommending overall plans for the provision of library and information services adequate to meet the needs of the people of the United States" (Stevens, 1976, p. 64). Fourteen members of the Commission are appointed by the President of the United States, and the Librarian of Congress serves ex officio. NCLIS is supposed to represent the public, all types of libraries, information producers, and the information technology industry. Of the 30 persons who served on the Commission between 1970 and 1990, only seven of them had had careers as librarians, and just one, Clara Jones, former director of the Detroit Public Library, was a public librarian (Mary Costabile, personal communication, July 10, 1990). Currently, two commissioners are school librarians and one is an academic librarian. Private sector representation remains high, and politics no doubt enters into appointments. From time to time there have been conflicts between the American Library Association and NCLIS (Berry, 1989, gives an account of the two most notable disagreements), and in the recent past NCLIS has had several turnovers in leadership.

NCLIS uses a multifaceted process in attempting to look after the nation's information needs. Over the years, it has commissioned studies (e.g., information needs of citizens, needs of libraries for shared bibliographic information, library technology, personnel needs of libraries), convened symposia (e.g., information literacy in education), and empaneled committees. In 1989, a committee met to formulate guidelines for national information policies. Sometimes commissioners travel to various parts of the country to gather information through hearings and on-site observation; in 1989 and 1990, libraries on American Indian reservations received this kind of attention. Documents and suggested policies are the products of these activities, but librarians are generally critical of NCLIS because concrete results (i.e., more favorable policies and more federal dollars for library services) have not been produced.

Until recently, NCLIS focused little attention on children. For our purposes, the major NCLIS projects were the first White House Conference on Library and Information Service (WHCLIS) in November 1979 and the second WHCLIS in July 1991.

White House Conferences

Over 3,500 people attended WHCLIS I, and the 806 delegates and alternates produced 64 recommendations. Twenty-seven delegates were under the age of 20 (Daniels, 1990). The Conference was criticized for ignoring the needs of academic, school, and special libraries and their patrons in favor of public libraries (Berger, 1989). However, no recommendations from WHCLIS I referred mainly to public libraries and only eight of them directly implied public library services to young people. (Forsee, 1989, found 14 resolutions related to services for adults in public libraries.) Resolution A-4 included out-of-school youth in the proposal to develop literacy programs in libraries. Resolutions A-5 (Access to Library and Information Services) and A-8 (Intellectual Freedom) included children and young adults among the groups mentioned as needing particular attention. The recommendation regarding the establishment of school libraries (C-3) included cooperation with public libraries' youth services. Resolution C-5 recommended that the public library supply access to information communication technology for community groups that serve young people and other special groups. C-17 recommended that state library agencies hire specialist consultants in children's services, young adult services, and adult services. E-5 recommended the establishment of an International Youth Library that would promote multicultural understanding, similar to the International Youth Library in Munich. Finally, Resolution F-2 recommended that the NCLIS, state libraries, and local library boards add young people as voting members (*Information for the 1980's*, 1980).

A number of other resolutions, such as those regarding specialized services for persons with disabilities or education of staff persons of color can be construed to include children and young adults, although young people were not specifically mentioned in the resolutions. It is difficult to gauge the impact of White House Conferences. Forsee (1989) claimed, "There were sweeping effects on the library and information community following the conference" (p. 310) and mentioned increased funding for library cooperation in the Library Services and Construction Act, higher visibility for library programs within the Department of Education, and progress in adult literacy programs.

Not everyone agreed with that assessment. Daniels (1990), in a detailed review of the first White House Conference on Libraries and Information Services for its impact on youth services in school and public libraries, concluded: "WHCLIS I had virtually no influence on the federal government and only limited effect on states in regard to school and public library services for children and young adults" (p. 39). He noted that of the 47 states that had state conferences, only one state, New Jersey, improved services to young people: New Jersey adopted state guidelines for services to children and young adults. The country did not see the development of an International Youth Library or an increase in the number of youth services consultants in state library agencies or young people serving on library boards. Increases in LSCA were short lived.

In July 1991 a second White House Conference on Libraries and Information Services was convened, after having been delayed for 2 years by the Bush administration. Before the national conference, preconferences were held in each of the 50 states, the territories, and the District of Columbia to determine issues to be brought before the entire Conference. The preamble to the law authorizing WHCLIS II included the statement that "the future of our society depends on developing the learning potential inherent in all children and youth" (quoted in Berger, 1989, p. 11), offering some hope that youth services issues would be considered. The Conference was organized to address three themes— literacy, productivity, and democracy—reflecting current and con- tinuing national preoccupations.

The three youth divisions of the American Library Association—the American Association of School Librarians (AASL), the Association for Library Service to Children (ALSC), and the Young Adult Library Services Association (YALSA)—cooperated on the creation of the Om- nibus Children and Youth Literacy through Libraries Act. AASL pro- vided the initiative and the leadership for a national political process that eventually garnered support not only from delegates to the confer- ence but from several other national organizations, such as the Children's Defense Fund, the National Parent Teachers Association, and the American Association of Retired Persons (V.H. Mathews, 1991).

School librarians and youth librarians in each state were mobilized to attend regional meetings armed with statements supporting youth services for the attendees to vote on. These efforts assured that youth services in school and public libraries would be discussed at the preconferences. Work with the ALA Executive Board resulted in ALA support for youth issues being included in the WHCLIS database. Continued lobbying before and during the conference resulted in the Omnibus Children and Youth Literacy through Libraries Act being voted the top priority among the 95 recommendations and petitions that the conference delegates finally sent on to President Bush. Those leading the effort made effective partnerships with the 13 young people who attended the conference as delegates or alternates (V.H. Mathews, 1991).

The Omnibus Children and Youth Literacy through Libraries Act comprises four titles: School Library Services, Public Library Children's Services, Public Library Young Adults' Services, and Partnership with Libraries for Youth. One feature in all four titles is the request for funding demonstration projects, sometimes targeted at specific groups. In addition, the children's services title includes provision for parent/ family education projects for early childhood, partnership activities with day-care centers, and increased funding for Head Start. The young adult title provides for demonstration grants to provide outreach services to at-risk young adults through youth-serving agencies, plus a "Kids Corps" program to provide library jobs for young adults. The partnership title requests funding for cooperative activities between school and public libraries, including a national resource-sharing network and intergenerational programs for latchkey children and young adolescents. Further partnership proposals include collaborative activities between library schools and schools of education to develop youth librarians, opportunities for development of multicultural authors, and the establishment of research funding to document how children and young adults develop information seeking and using skills.

Other proposals that, if carried out, would affect children's and young adults' use of public libraries include recommendations to increase funding for a variety of purposes: purchase of library materials, public access to information without fees, compliance with the Americans with Disabilities Act, bringing all libraries into the National Research and Education Network (NREN), multilingual and multicultural programs and staffs, resource sharing among different kinds of libraries, literacy initiatives for the disadvantaged, and expanded funding of tribal libraries. One petition asked for the retention and expansion of Library

Services and Construction Act (LSCA) funds (see later section on Department of Education) "to assist in the redefinition of library and information services to children and youth, families and communities." One recommendation asks Congress to fund a basic level of support for public library facilities and services.

A few recommendations do not call specifically for funding, such as the requests that Congress legislatively mandate ALA's Freedom to Read Statements, recognize libraries as "partners in lifelong learning" and as educational institutions, and "bring attention to" the reading needs of young people with disabilities that prevent their use of ordinary print. If Congress were to officially recognize all libraries as educational institutions, they would be able to compete for grant funding that is now available only to schools; thus, we could expect strong lobbying against libraries by schools. This would not be desirable.

Since the close of WHCLIS II, a follow-up teleconference discussing the recommendations attracted 20,000 people nationwide, and plans are afoot to monitor the progress of the recommendations. The Library Services and Construction Act was reauthorized in 1992 with increased funding (despite Bush administration proposals to make drastic cuts), NREN was amended to include libraries and passed by Congress, and the Department of Education budget line for fellowships for graduate students in library and information studies was increased with special provision for students intending to go into youth services in school or public libraries. NCLIS has held regional meetings to discuss the Omnibus Youth Literacy Act. All of these events might be attributed to the second White House Conference.

If so, its influence was short lived. In 1993, the Clinton administration, like its Republican predecessors, attempted to cut funding for several major library programs and consolidate several others administered by the Department of Education, including the Library Services and Construction Act. The cuts were rescinded only after a great deal of lobbying by librarians.

Will the WHCLIS II recommendations be funded? Probably not in the immediate or foreseeable future, given the concern over the budget deficit and other problems that may seem much more urgent than library and information services (Eileen Cooke, personal communication, July 14, 1992; Mary Jo Lynch, personal communication, July 14, 1992). The fact is, libraries are not a major political actor on the national stage. At this writing, a school library title that would carry out some of the school library provisions of Omnibus Children and Youth Literacy proposals has been added to the Elementary and Secondary Education Act. Its fate is not yet known.

What, then, is the importance for young people of White House Conferences or even the National Commission on Libraries and Information Science? The direct, short-term impact is probably small, especially if we look at NCLIS itself. It is an advisory body that can only make recommendations, not genuine policy. It is difficult to identify concrete improvements in public library services resulting from a body that mainly holds meetings and issues reports. Many librarians are skeptical of NCLIS because of its strong connection to the information industry, an industry that exists to make a profit. Public librarians, who place a high value on public access to information, are inclined to distrust the profit motive, even though libraries must have connections to producers and vendors of information for their very existence.

Although observers of WHCLIS II who were not involved in youth services viewed the conference negatively (Charles McClure, personal communication, April 2, 1993), from a youth services point of view it was a successful conference. Two aspects of WHCLIS II may have long-term consequences. First, the Omnibus Children and Youth Literacy Through Libraries Act and other recommendations make concrete suggestions about a number of the issues detailed in the first part of this book, such as programs for parents and childcare providers, latchkey children and young adolescents, and education for youth librarians. These issues are now part of the knowledge of the entire library profession and the nonlibrarian delegates. The impact may be greatest at the state and local level because of the raised awareness of citizen participants (Eileen Cooke, personal communication, July 14, 1992). The issues form part of the public record of WHCLIS II and thus, part of any national discussion about libraries and information services, as well. Over time, progress may be made on enacting the recommendations.

Second, the political processes involved may have a strong impact on youth services if children's and young adult librarians continue to utilize them. The three youth divisions of ALA have always cooperated because of common interests, historical ties, and overlapping membership. The Omnibus Children and Youth Literacy Through Libraries Act has set a mutual national agenda. The coalition building among the three youth divisions should have transferability to other projects at the national level, as well. Learning to organize a political campaign should also be transferable to state and local contexts—a successful model has been developed and tested. What remains to be seen over the next decade is how well the coalition can sustain itself and preserve the focus on youth issues. It also remains to be seen if public library youth librarians can make the transfer of national political experience to the state and local levels. If progress toward enacting the Omnibus Youth Literacy Act is to be made, it will have to be made by the concerted and continuous efforts of youth librarians, not the National Commission on Libraries and Information Science.

Recommendation #2

The second recommendation is that the National Commission on Libraries and Information Science should have wider representation of public librarians. As a body with potential to influence national library and information policies, the NCLIS should balance representation from the public sector with that from the private sector.

Recommendation #3

Because people under 18 make up half of public library users, more effort should be made to incorporate direct information from them into NCLIS decisions, including young people's testimony on subjects that affect them and seating a youth representative as a voting member of the Commission. As their participation in the White House Conferences has shown, adolescents are capable and responsible participants in the democratic process.

Recommendation #4

The fourth recommendation is that NCLIS work on ways to implement the Omnibus Children and Youth Literacy through Libraries Act, finding places in pending legislation and in legislation being reauthorized to insert the provisions of the Act. This would avoid having to find new sources of funding. NCLIS should work with the youth divisions of the American Library Association in devising the strategies for carrying out this recommendation. In other words, NCLIS should take a more active role in policy formation.

Recommendation #5

As the new national information transfer programs develop under NREN legislation, NCLIS should undertake to monitor the inclusion of public libraries and access to young people. The originator of the legislation, Vice President Albert Gore, had in mind that children would have access to the system, and as former Assistant Secretary of Education Dianne Ravitch represented Republican interest in youth admittance to national databases, the issue of young people's entry into the technology of information has some powerful allies (Eileen Cooke, personal communication, July 14, 1992).

U.S. DEPARTMENT OF EDUCATION PROGRAMS

Tacit recognition that libraries are educational institutions is given at the national level by the fact that federal library programs are administered by the Office of Educational Research and Improvement (OERI), located in the U.S. Department of Education. Two divisions of OERI are important for public libraries, the National Center for Education Statistics and the Library Programs Office. The Educational Resources Information Center (ERIC) is another federal agency that provides assistance to librarians serving children and teenagers.

National Center for Education Statistics

Federal/State Cooperative System. One of many projects of the NCLIS has been the development of national systems for gathering data about libraries through the National Center for Education Statistics (NCES). For public libraries, the Federal State Cooperative System for Public Library Data (FSCS) amasses information. Previously, the NCES collected national public library statistical information on a sporadic, irregular basis, and the 50 state library agencies gathered annual data, but each state decided what to collect and how to collect the information. Although data topics were similar, the precise variables collected differed from state to state. With leadership from the NCLIS and the American Library Association's Office for Research and Statistics, work with the Chief Officers of State Library Agencies, a division of the American Library Association, NCES, and the Library Programs unit of the Department of Education began in 1983. A pilot project with 15 states between 1985 and 1987 showed that it was possible to define standardized measures and their collection. In 1988, a Memorandum of Understanding was signed between NCLIS and NCES to continue the joint development of the system (Lynch, 1991; S. Martin, 1989). Using specially designed microcomputer software, 44 states and the District of Columbia submitted data in 1989; the resulting tables did not meet NCES standards and could not be published officially.

However, the 1990 data (41 items) were collected from all 50 states and after corrections were made, the report passed NCES review (Lynch, 1991). From this data, it was found that 75.8% of public library funding in 1990 was from local sources, 14% from state, and 1.3% from federal sources, including Library Services and Construction Act funds (see following). The rest of public library funding (8.9%) came from "other" sources, such as fines and gifts (American Library Association, 1993). It should be noted that the states continue to collect unique data items as individual state library agencies dictate.

The original plans for the Federal State Cooperative System (FSCS) did not include collecting data for children's or young adult services. Only 33 states collect data about children's services (Garland, 1992), and no states are known to collect annual data about young adult services. Because the NCES will not publish data from less than an 85% response rate, at least 43 states would have to submit data about youth services before such information could be included in the FSCS (Jan Feye-Stukas, personal communication, July 11, 1990). Through the work of Barbara Immroth and other representatives of the Association for Library Service to Children, the state data coordinators have agreed to collect two children's services variables-circulation of children's materials and attendance at children's programs-starting in 1991. The first 2 years of reporting were not expected to meet NCES standards because library staffs will have to be trained to compile data correctly, but the third year the data will be reported. This means that, starting in 1994, national children's circulation and program attendance for the previous year will be available (Mary Jo Lynch, personal communication, July 14, 1992). It should not prove to be a major difficulty to gather these data; Garland (1992) found that 89.1% of public libraries already collect data about children's materials circulation.

One of the reasons that it was possible to reach agreement on collecting the two variables for children's services was the publication of *Output Measures for Public Library Service to Children* (Walter, 1992), which established definitions of children's circulation and program attendance. Because adults are responsible for charging out many children's items and accompany children to programs, the profession has debated whether adult use of children's services should count for children's services or adult services. By stating in a nationally accepted document that adult use of children's services should be counted with children's use of the services, Walter established at least a definite opinion if not an end to the debate (Mary Jo Lynch, personal communication, July 14, 1992).

Recommendation #6

The sixth recommendation is that NCES continue to work with the state data coordinators to find ways of including young adult variables in the FSCS. Deciding on and implementing the collection of young adult variables may well be more difficult than the work on children's variables. As an example, circulation, which would appear to be a simple matter of counting, presents problems for young adult services. Even if we agree that only materials marked "young adult" are to be counted as young adult circulation, we have the problem of paperback circulation, which may not be automated in some libraries but may constitute the bulk of young adult circulation. Libraries would also have to alter their circulation software; it would be appropriate to use LSCA moneys to support the needed changes (see later section). This would accomplish several things: It would create a database for continuing research in young adult services, allow librarians to assess the contributions of young adult services to the public library as a whole, and allow librarians to compare their efforts with those of libraries in similar communities.

Office of Library Programs

Administration of the Library Services and Construction Act (LSCA) and Title II of the Higher Education Act (HEA), two major federal programs with an impact on youth services, is under the aegis of the Office of Library Programs in the Department of Education.

Higher Education Act.   HEA programs comprise fellowships for doctoral and master's level studies, training and retraining institutes, and research and demonstrations. Currently, youth services is seen by the Office of Library Programs as one of several priorities principally because of the labor shortages in the field as noted in the first chapter of this book. In recent years, HEA II-B money has gone to students pursuing doctoral studies in youth services, both for school and public libraries, and a considerable share of the fellowships for 1992–1993 funded doctoral and master's students in youth services. Approximately 26% of the master's degree fellowships and 15.4% of doctoral fellowships provided to graduate schools of library and information studies were earmarked for persons interested in children's or young adult services (calculated from data supplied by Ray Fry, personal communication, July 17, 1992). Recent HEA-funded institutes trained children's librarians to serve handicapped children and utilize evaluation techniques.

The money available through HEA Title II-B is relatively little: In 1990, the funds expended for these three programs totaled $849,557, a far cry from the $3.4 million awarded for research alone in 1967, the first year of the program. That the profession has not been able to maintain the level of research funding is partly due to cuts in federal research funds generally but may also indicate the level of importance the Department of Education assigns to librarianship. Fifteen proposals for institutes were received in 1990 and 4 were funded; 41 research and demonstration proposals were received and 5 were funded in 1990 (A.J. Mathews, 1991). Two of the research projects and one of the institutes concerned children's services; previous research and institute funding also went to youth services. We cannot claim federal neglect in regard to the HEA funds. It is important to retain the flexibility to respond quickly to the changing needs of all types of libraries when funds are so limited. Therefore, no recommendation is made about the HEA programs administered by the Library Programs Office, but only because we are being realistic about the funding possibilities.

Library Services and Construction Act.   The Library Services and Construction Act (LSCA) is the major source of federal funds for public libraries and has been in place since 1956. Currently, there are eight titles in the LSCA: public library services, public library construction, interlibrary cooperation, library services for Indian tribes and Hawaiian natives, foreign language materials, library literacy programs, evaluation and assessment of LSCA, and library learning center programs. The state library agencies distribute the moneys for services, construction, interlibrary cooperation, and foreign language materials (the latter was funded for the first time in 1991). Library Programs Office staff allocate funds for literacy and Indian library services. Indian and Hawaiian native services are funded by segregating 2% of the money appropriated for services, construction, and cooperation. The Reagan and Bush administrations attempted to eliminate funding for the LSCA; however, Congress has never allowed the act to be "zeroed out" of existence. Rural interests seem to be particularly strong in protecting it (Cooke & Henderson, 1991). Not all titles are funded in every year, particularly the titles for foreign language materials, LSCA evaluation, and library learning centers.

The Clinton administration recommended a $14 million cut in LSCA for fiscal year 1994 to be achieved by cutting out funds earmarked for construction, foreign language materials, and literacy programs. The services title would have been increased by $12 million. The administration's argument was that these parts of the LSCA had served their purposes. After intense lobbying by librarians, the rescissions were restored, with a small increase in the construction title and the loss of the foreign language materials, a net gain of only $240,000 over fiscal year 1993. Table 10.1 reports LSCA and relevant HEA appropriations for fiscal year 1993, fiscal year 1994 administration requests, and Congress's final conference report allocations.

It might seem that the federal contribution to public libraries is not very meaningful because it is so small. However, the uses to which the money is put represent some of the most creative and innovative services available, because over 60% of the money is used for demon

Table 10.1.   Funding of Federal Library Programs for Public Libraries

Program and Title	FY 1993 Appropriations (in thousands)	FY 1994 Administration Request (in thousands)	Conference Report
LIBRARY SERVICES AND CONSTRUCTION ACT			
I. Public library services	$ 83,227	$ 95,000	$ 83,227
II. Public library construction	16,584	0	17,792
III. Interlibrary cooperation	19,749	19,700	19,749
IV. Indian library services (2% of Titles I, II, and III)			
V. Foreign language materials	968	0	0
VI. Library literacy programs	8,098	0	8,098
Totals	$128,626	$114,700	$128,866
HIGHER EDUCATION ACT			
II-B. Library education	$ 4,960	$ 0	$ 4,960
II-C. Research & demonstration	2,802	0	2,802

stration projects, allowing libraries to try services and materials they have not had before. The problem is that over the years of LSCA, very little has been done in the way of evaluation, accountability, or diffusion of the results of all these demonstrations at the national level. Although Library Programs staff write occasional reports about LSCA projects in particular areas, there is no readily accessible database of the demonstrations, no way of knowing the impact on services, or even how many of the demonstrations were regarded as successful enough that public librarians adopted them as part of their basic services.

Shavit (1986b) reported that the evaluations that have been done have tended to not measure impacts or effectiveness, and when they have been critical of LSCA, they have tended to be ignored. For instance, an evaluation of the 1978 expenditures found that only 20% of the Title I funds were actually expended on the groups targeted by the Act (Shavit, 1986b). We know that services for children and young adults receive LSCA funds (although young adult projects are apt to be few in number), but we do not know the proportion of funds awarded to youth services. In 1978, 5.2% of LSCA Title I funds were spent on "Special Target Groups," which included children and teenagers with the elderly and the hearing impaired (Shavit, 1986b).

Given the lack of information about the diffusion and impact of innovations through demonstration projects, it is disturbing that the second White House Conference delegates asked for further funding of demonstration projects. If librarians cannot show that "basic" library services have an effect or are not committed to implementing successful demonstrations, it is hard to see that requests for further funding will be taken seriously.

Recommendation #7

Therefore, the seventh recommendation is that the Library Programs Office in the Office for Educational Research and Improvement undertake a study of LSCA-funded projects to determine if youth services is receiving a proportionate amount of LSCA moneys and the impact of the projects supported. This basic data is needed in order to determine if federal money is being used in ways that are congruent with the library and information needs of young people and the intention of Congress in funding the LSCA. If, as seems likely, there are inequities in funding youth services projects, the Library Programs Office, with the youth divisions of ALA, should find ways of redressing the situation, particularly through the proposals of the Omnibus Youth Literacy Act.

Educational Resources Information Center

Founded in 1966, the Educational Resources Information Center (ERIC) is actually a network of clearinghouses that are each responsible for an area of education. The library services clearinghouse is located at Syracuse University. The staff at each clearinghouse reviews and selects documents to be included in ERIC paper indexes—*Current Index to Journals in Education* and *Resources in Education*—and the online bibliographic database. Together, *CIJE* and *RIE* identify journal articles and nonpublished sources of research and practice in all areas of education. The database is also available on CD-ROM. ERIC continuously builds a microfiche database of research reports, conference papers and proceedings, and other forms of information that are not easily accessed. Currently, ERIC is developing full-text CD-ROM discs that would contain "the best" (about 10%) of ERIC documents in a compact machine-readable form. These would disseminate current education research more widely in a more readable format and ease printing paper copies of documents (Brandhorst, 1991).

As an education bibliographic and document service, ERIC is important to youth librarians as a source of up-to-date information that includes librarianship and relevant topics outside the field. For instance, articles and documents about preschool literacy development from both the education and library perspectives can be located through *RIE*. The CD-ROM database in particular is easy to search and identifies both journal articles and entries in the microfiche files.

Since its inception, ERIC has made the bibliographic records available to commercial vendors free of charge. The vendors do charge their customers for online or CD-ROM services, but because their overhead is low for ERIC, its information is less expensive than most other databases. It seems proper that this be the case, because the information in the database is gathered at public expense, and it is used to improve public services. A proposal has been made to have ERIC charge the vendors; these additional costs would undoubtedly be passed on to users, including libraries and their patrons. The share of ERIC users represented by libraries is not known, but libraries are part of a group of agencies and individuals who represent 21% of ERIC use (Brandhorst, 1990).

Recommendation #8

It is recommended that ERIC reconsider the charges to vendors because of the adverse impact it would have on libraries, students, researchers, and others who use the information. Ways to avoid charging for educational use of the database should be explored.

Recommendation #9

In 1990, Ted Brandhorst, Director of ERIC, wrote that Congress had appropriated funds for marketing and publicizing ERIC products for the first time. It is recommended that youth services librarians be the target for some of the advertising campaign to increase their awareness of the service and encourage them to access information about education and library research that can improve the educational effectiveness of their activities on behalf of children and young people.

National Endowment for the Humanities

The National Endowment for the Humanities (NEH) is also a source of support for public library activities. Funds have aided in the preservation of important collections at the New York Public Library, for example, and supplied training and speakers for many adult programs. Librarians who have used this source of funding have been warmly appreciative of it (J. Greiner, 1990). NEH "encourages libraries to design out-of-school projects for groups of young people of high school or junior high school age" ("National Endowment for the Humanities," 1991). This writer could find no recent reports of NEH projects for young adults in the literature, however. The same questions that one asks about Library Services and Construction Act funds—how much goes to youth services and what is the impact?—could be asked of the National Endowment for the Humanities public library programs for young people.

Recommendation #10

The National Endowment for the Humanities should undertake a study of their public library programs for young adults and consider ways of increasing proposals for projects involving young people at public libraries.

SUMMARY

The reader of this chapter may have found that it is difficult to get an overall view of the federal policy toward public library youth services. This is because the policy is largely unarticulated; it resides in the programs and activities of the federal government, emanating from several agencies and coordinated by none. Although the United States federal government provides a very modest amount of the funding for public libraries and none of this funding supports basic operations, the funds that are available encourage innovation in services and materials. This is particularly true of Library Services and Construction Act funds and to a lesser extent funds available from the National Endowment for the Humanities. The federal government, however, also provides services for public libraries as local institutions that have a national impact, through the research, education, statistical, and database development that occurs in the Department of Education. The Library of Congress provides leadership in the areas of cataloging, classification, children's literature, and materials for the blind and physically handicapped. The federal government has also provided opportunities to develop national agendas for libraries and information service through the National Commission on Libraries and Information Science and the White House Conferences. In many cases, however, what has been done at the federal level has taken much prodding from librarians and the library associations.

Indeed, the patchwork approach has come about partly because of the nature of governance in the United Sates and partly because librarians have gotten some of what they have asked for. Theoretically, state and local governments are to run the country, with the federal government stepping in when the interests of more than one state are involved, when a national approach would appear to better serve the purpose, or when there is a gap that no other entity is willing to take a risk to fill. Practically, it is not always easy to tell when a situation has a legitimate claim on the federal purse, and there is certainly always debate over such claims. On the other hand, librarians have not wanted a comprehensive federal presence in the funding of public libraries. They have preferred funding for the "special" things: demonstrations of new programs, contributions to library construction, services to the blind and physically handicapped, low postal rates.

With the growth of electronic networking and information transfer, the boundaries of local, state, and federal interests will be even less apparent, and the segregation of federal funding for special purposes only will become inappropriate. Those who have lobbied to have public libraries included in the NREN have recognized the increasing need to have a strong federal contribution to public library funding. Youth services librarians need to be active at the federal level to ensure that the interests of young people are included in public library programs as well as school library programs.

Remembering that the programs discussed here are not the only federal involvements in libraries but just those that have an impact on children and teenagers or on services to them, one is struck by how little attention is actually paid to public library youth services by the federal government. This is in distinct contrast to the former Soviet Union where youth libraries were supported by the national government— partly, of course, because their propaganda value was well recognized by Lenin's wife, librarian N.K. Krupskaya. American librarians touring

Table 10.2.   Recommendations for Federal Government Policies

1. The Library of Congress should develop a set of subject headings at the third-grade reading level to be used with materials written at the fourth-grade level or younger.
2. The National Commission on Libraries and Information Science should recruit more public librarians to serve on the commission.
3. The NCLIS should incorporate information from young people in its hearings and include a young person as a voting commissioner.
4. The NCLIS should work on ways to implement the Omnibus Children and Youth Literacy through Libraries Act through pending and reauthorizing legislation.
5. The NCLIS should work to ensure that young people are included in efforts to establish national information networks via NREN and other proposals.
6. The National Center for Education Statistics should work with the Chief Officers of State Library Agencies and the youth divisions of the American Library Association to identify appropriate, measurable data elements for young adult services in the Federal State Cooperative System for Public Library Data.
7. The Library Programs Office should study the proportion of Library Services and Construction Act funds being used to develop children's and young adult services and the impact of the supported projects. Improved methods of diffusion of successful projects should be developed and inequities redressed.
8. The Educational Resources Information Center should find ways of avoiding charges for its online and CD-ROM services.
9. ERIC should include public library youth services as a target group for its marketing efforts in order that librarians can be fully aware of the usefulness of the database in improving their services to young people.
10. The National Endowment for the Humanities should study its public library programs for young people, their impact, and effective methods of diffusion for successful projects.

the separate library facilities provided for children through age 15 were impressed with the reading research and cultural immersion accomplished by the children's libraries in the Soviet Union (Roman, 1989). Americans have a strong preference for making library decisions locally, yet this predilection can result in a hodgepodge of programs with no clear vision or focus.

Our national leadership in librarianship as in other fields comes from the national professional organizations and dedicated individuals, not from federal bureaucracies. The Association for Library Services to Children and the Young Adult Library Services Association will continue to supply direction and information. Sometimes the effort should be channeled through the American Library Association's Washington office, whose staff monitors legislation affecting libraries and actively lobbies Congress. At other times the grassroots approach is very effective, as in the campaign mounted for the Omnibus Children and Youth Literacy through Libraries Act passed so overwhelmingly by the second White House Conference on Libraries and Information Services. The recommendations listed in this chapter indicate areas for new and continuing monitoring by the professional organizations at the national level.

CHAPTER 11

State Government Policies

INTRODUCTION

In the previous chapter, we noted that the establishment of public libraries is not provided for in the United States Constitution and is thus reserved for the states. With the exception of Hawaii, which operates all public libraries on the islands, and Vermont, which manages regional systems for its public libraries, the states have delegated authority for public libraries to local governments (Asp, 1986). This does not mean that the states take no interest in public libraries. As also described in Chapter 10, the states administer federal grant programs under the Library Services and Construction Act (LSCA) and collect data for the Federal State Cooperative System for Public Library Data (FSCS). In addition to playing a mediating role between the federal government and local public libraries, most states provide some financial support and other services to public libraries and collect information about libraries to report to the state legislature. The department of state government responsible for these activities is called various names among the states, but the generic term for all of them is *state library agency*.

Additionally, the state governments involve themselves with public libraries through educating librarians. Because many of the schools of library and information studies that were located at private colleges and universities have closed, the education of librarians has become more and more a de facto function of state government, with 49 of the 57 (86%) ALA-accredited programs located in state or Canadian provincial institutions. About half the children's librarians in the United States have the Master of Library Science or equivalent degree (Lewis & Farris, 1990); thus, the contribution made by the states to the education of children's services personnel is considerable. No comparable figures are available for young adult librarians, but there is no reason to imagine that the private institutions educate more young adult librarians than the state-supported schools.

In this chapter, we examine the various roles played by state library agencies and library education in support of library services for children and young adults. Frequently, it is very difficult to distinguish specific impacts on youth services from impacts on the public library in general. Youth services often derive some benefit from funding or activities that are not aimed at them. For example, increased state aid might permit libraries to hire more staff for technical services, circulation, or reference, which would result in better service to young people as well as adults, but the improvement in service to youth might not be measurable. In addition, we encounter once again a dearth of factual data and research to help us generalize our observations.

STATE LIBRARY AGENCY ROLES

Depending on the situation, state library agencies may provide consultation to local government officials, library trustees, and librarians; reference service for hard-to-answer questions; service to the blind and physically handicapped; continuing education for librarians and other library staff; archives for state government; coordination of interlibrary loan and other forms of cooperation and resource sharing; planning for statewide performance measures and services; and film and video lending circuits. In the policy-making arena, state library agencies may be responsible for studies and reports on public and other types of libraries, recommending new policies, and supporting legislative initiatives in cooperation with state library associations (Kellerstrass, 1990; B. Weaver, 1990). State library agency functions may include managing a library that serves the public and the state legislature in ways analogous to the Library of Congress. State library agencies allocate state and federal financial aid and grant programs to public libraries. So varied are the activities of state library agencies that Barbara Weaver, state librarian of New Jersey, declared, "The only function that is common to all fifty state library agencies is public library development" (1990, p. 28).

State library agencies' interest in public library development has been encouraged by the LSCA, which requires state government administration (Strong, 1986; Wiegand, 1986), and many state library agencies use

LSCA moneys to partially fund their operations (Shavit, 1986a). Initially, public library development meant aiding local government to establish public library services in rural areas that did not have a library. Consultants from the state library would discuss basic issues about the nature of services, staffing, financing, legal questions, whether to invest in a building or use a bookmobile, and so forth, with local officials and interested citizens. Many states were engaged in this activity before 1956 when LSCA took effect, but federal funding ensured that all of the states engaged in public library development activities. Indeed, the legislation was designed to accommodate the states' rights interests in Congress (Holley & Schremser, 1983; Wiegand, 1986). Most parts of the country now have public library service with staff capable of handling basic library administration. The development aspect of state library work currently focuses on maintaining and improving services in public libraries in all types of communities, not just rural areas, and on "facilitating discussion and decision making among interested parties, rather than providing subject expertise" (B. Weaver, 1990, p. 30).

Direct Financial Support

Analysis of the Federal State Cooperative System data from 1990 indicated that state governments on average paid 14% of public library expenditures (American Library Association, 1993); a small proportion, indeed, but 10 times the amount provided by the federal government. It is not clear whether these figures refer only to direct financial aid to public libraries or if they include indirect support such as reimbursement to libraries for providing services to patrons who live outside the local jurisdiction. As in so many aspects of social services, the states vary greatly in the proportion of total expenditures they provide to public libraries. Table 11.1 shows 1989 total per capita expenditures by public libraries and 1989 and 1990 per capita state aid. In 1990, support to public libraries from state governments varied from $.04 per capita in Colorado and Ohio to $3.15 in Maryland. In 1989, the low figure was $.02 per capita in New Hampshire; the high was $5.60 in Georgia (*1991 State Library Agencies Financial Survey*). As a proportion of total per capita expenditures in 1989, Georgia contributed 55.3% of per capita expenditures to its public libraries, whereas New Hampshire provided only 0.14%.

The range of total per capita expenditures and per capita state aid among the various states undoubtedly reflects a number of factors beyond the cost of living. Ability and willingness to support public services of any kind vary across the country. If many or most users of the public library are the educated middle class, we would expect states

Table 11.1. Per Capita Public Library Expenditures (1989) and State Aid (1989 and 1990)

State	1989 Expenditures	1989 State Aid	1990 State Aid
Alabama	$ 8.13	$ .85	$ .20
Alaska	23.64	1.82	1.89*
Arizona	14.53	.19	.17
Arkansas	5.98	1.04	1.08
California	15.89	1.17	1.16
Colorado	18.01	.04	.04
Connecticut	22.10	.40	.42
Delaware	8.22	1.17	1.26
District of Columbia	29.46	N/A	N/A
Florida	11.93	.72	1.30
Georgia	10.13	5.60**	2.73
Hawaii	17.23	N/A	N/A
Idaho	9.84	N/A	N/A
Illinois	19.25	.88	.92
Indiana	17.95	.25	.11
Iowa	11.85	.56	.55
Kansas	15.85	.42	.50
Kentucky	7.04	.44	.46
Louisiana	11.52	N/A	N/A
Maine	12.66	.03	.19
Maryland	24.45	3.98	3.15
Massachusetts	19.18	2.76	2.13
Michigan	13.83	1.95	1.12
Minnesota	18.62	1.08	1.29
Mississippi	6.58	1.03	1.85
Missouri	13.37	.37	.40
Montana	7.56	.32	N/A
Nebraska	13.16	.12	.20
Nevada	9.65	.07	.07
New Hampshire	14.45	.02	N/A
New Jersey	21.16	1.38	1.16
New Mexico	11.34	.08	.10
New York	29.48	3.11	3.10
North Carolina	10.55	1.72	N/A
North Dakota	8.01	.76	.72
Ohio	23.34	.04	.04
Oklahoma	10.24	.59	.54
Oregon	14.74	.15	.14
Pennsylvania	10.99	1.94	N/A
Rhode Island	11.71	2.55	1.11
South Carolina	8.72	N/A	.94
South Dakota	13.09	N/A	N/A
Tennessee	7.70	1.21	1.29
Texas	8.94	.33	.31
Utah	13.64	.12	.28

(continued)

Table 11.1.   *(continued)*

State	1989 Expenditures	1989 State Aid	1990 State Aid
Vermont	12.37	N/A	N/A
Virginia	16.29	1.84	2.74
Washington	19.81	N/A	N/A
West Virginia	7.46	3.11	3.11
Wisconsin	16.53	1.80	1.95
Wyoming	19.83	N/A	N/A

Note. Copyright 1991. The Council of State Governments. Reprinted with permission from *State Library Agencies Financial Survey,*.

*Corrected figure from George Smith, Alaska State Library, personal communication, September 28, 1992.

**Corrected figure from Diana Tope, Georgia State Library, personal communication, October 2, 1992. Differences between 1989 and 1990 amounts are due to population growth and reduced state aid for public library construction.

that have large proportions of such people in their populations to spend more on public libraries; the differences between Arkansas and New York are political, cultural, social, and educational (at least), as well as financial. Shuman (1989) noticed that there are regional patterns to state aid for libraries, with the industrial, urbanized states east of the Mississippi River putting forth greater effort, in general, than other regions. The data he used for his study disclosed that in 1987-1988, five states did not contribute to local efforts to fund public libraries: Idaho, South Dakota, Vermont, Washington, and Wyoming (Shuman, 1989).

Table 11.1 may also indicate that states that have very strong traditions of local government control typically send less state aid to their libraries. Maine, Connecticut, and New Hampshire provide characteristic examples. Even though we might expect that any educational enterprise would be an exception, this is not necessarily the case. As this chapter was being written, the head of the state education agency in New Hampshire proposed that the state bow out of any regulation of public education.

Several of the southern states supply relatively large proportions of their states' public library budgets although overall expenditure is low. Arkansas, Georgia, Mississippi, North Carolina, Tennessee, and West Virginia all provided 15% or more of per capita public library expenditures in 1989. Historically, public library development in the South lagged behind other parts of the country (Carmichael, 1986), and state legislators may have felt it necessary to encourage them. In Georgia, at least, political sentiment is not against state aid, and the aid is allocated in a manner that attempts to equalize the level of services provided in poor communities with that provided in wealthier areas (Diana Tope, personal communication, October 2, 1992).

Insofar as the health of youth services depends on the health of the public library as a whole, one can only wish that state support were greater. During 1991 and 1992, however, 40 of the 50 state library agencies reported cutbacks in overall funding, frequently in the form of hiring freezes and reductions of services to libraries and individuals. State aid to public libraries fared a little better than state library agencies. Comparing the columns of per capita state aid for 1989 and 1990 in Table 11.1, 16 states cut their per capita level of support for public libraries, 18 states increased support, and 4 states maintained the same amount. Thirteen states did not report per capita aid for one or both years. In a few cases, states have gone ahead with projects to improve overall state library agency services, especially through telecommunications (*1991 State Library Agencies Financial Survey*), even in the face of revenue shortfalls, demonstrating that it is possible to overcome "The Productivity Paradox" described by Levine (1979) as one of the dilemmas of cutback management; that is, needing to increase productivity through technology but not having the financial ability to make the necessary investment.

Recommendation #1

The data given here are typical of the kind of information available about state aid to public libraries. It is agreggate data that does not tell us very much about how moneys are spent at the local level or what proportion of state effort assists youth services. The impact of state spending on public library youth services has not been measured or estimated by any research study known to the author. Therefore, the first recommendation for state governments is a study of the impact on youth services of the distribution of state aid to public libraries. Such a study would have to look at the indirect effects as well as impacts that accrue directly to youth services. Assuming that state subventions have positive effects seems fairly safe, but identifying the specific impacts that state support provides would allow youth services supporters to make their cases with more force and satisfy requirements for accountability. Although scholars would like to have such information for the nation as a whole, it is far likelier that studies would be conducted on a state-by-state basis and by a few states, rather than by all of them. This would, however, be a suitable topic for funding by the U.S. Department of Education's Office of Library Programs.

Consulting Services

The children's services survey by the National Center for Education Statistics found that 58% of public libraries did not employ any librarian with primary responsibility for children, and the earlier study of young adult services found that 89% did not have a young adult librarian. Many libraries are too small to have specialized staff; all patrons are served by generalists. However, public libraries are frequently organized into local and regional systems and have direct access to a state library agency. Those without youth services staff might be able to consult with an expert from a centralized source. The NCES found that regional children's consultants were available to 43% of public libraries, local consultants to 54% (Lewis & Farris, 1990).

The young adult study showed that 51% of libraries had access to someone with experience and training in work with young adults at their local system headquarters; 40% could call on a librarian at the regional system for advice regarding young adult services (NCES, 1988). (This was not an either/or situation; some libraries had consultants at both the local and regional levels.) Counter to common sense, libraries with a young adult librarian were more likely to have a local or regional young adult consultant. This may indicate that where there is a commitment to young adult services at the local and regional systems level, that commitment is more likely to extend to local branches, and vice versa: If young adult services are not given priority in the branches, the systems will not support them, either. Clearly, youth services is one area in which many local libraries cannot rely on internal expertise. With good reason they may look to the state library for assistance. Will they find it?

The answer is a resounding "maybe." Of the 67% of libraries with some outside consulting for children's services, 41% received support from the state library agency. Of the 51% of libraries that had outside consulting available for young adult services, 41% received young adult services support from the state library agency. In other words, less than a third of public libraries rely on their state libraries for consultation regarding children's services and less than a quarter of them expect help with young adult services. Forty-five percent of public libraries had neither a young adult librarian nor access to a young adult consultant (Lewis & Farris, 1990; NCES, 1988).

One could hypothesize a communication gap, that services from the state library agencies are available but librarians do not know about them. From the point of view of the state library agencies, then, what consulting services are available to public libraries needing assistance with youth services? In a recent dissertation, Feehan (1991) surveyed all 50 state library agencies and found that only 12 had full-time youth services consultants and four additional states had vacancies for full-time positions. Hawaii was the only state that had full-time consultants for both children's and young adult services. (It should be kept in mind that Hawaiian public libraries are entirely operated by the state government as a single library system. Therefore, the state library agency consultants may interact more closely and more frequently with local librarians than is usual in other parts of the country.) Another 24 states employed consultants who spent part of their time on youth services.

Sixteen of these part-time consultants spent less than 25% of their time on children's services and 23 spent less than 25% of their time on young adult services. Ten states had no youth services consultant: Georgia, Maine, Maryland, Michigan, Minnesota, Montana, New Hampshire, North Dakota, Washington, and Wyoming. Note that most of these states have extensive rural areas with many small towns, precisely the situations that need youth consultants at the state level because local librarians have to be generalists. In her summary of previous studies, Feehan noted that the number of consultants reported between 1957 and 1981 varied widely, partly because some of the surveys did not investigate whether the consultants worked full time or part time in youth services. However, it appears that the number of full-time state consultants reported in her study is about double that of previous findings, a heartening improvement. Nevertheless, it has to be said that those librarians who reported no youth services consulting available from their state library agency were reporting the situation accurately.

The importance of consultants is in the work that they do and their effectiveness in improving services to children and teenagers. Feehan (1991) asked respondents to describe typical work assignments in youth services. They answered with specific examples of consulting and advising in the areas of collection development and maintenance, budgeting, planning, procedures, facilities, grant writing, policy development, and mediation of disputes. From these examples, one can see that subject expertise in youth services remains a valuable commodity provided by state library agencies in some states. Consultants provided leadership for statewide activities such as planning the summer reading program and implementing continuing education. Respondents saw themselves as problem solvers, conduits of information about the national and international library scene for the librarians of their home states, and advocates for youth services within the state library agencies.

Are consultants effective at what they do? Feehan, interested in the ways in which state agency youth consultants could be considered change agents, asked the full-time youth services consultants to rate themselves on 40 questions. The answers were combined into six scales: change advocacy, leadership skills, managerial characteristics, openmindedness, personality characteristics, and change agent roles. The average rating was "high," indicating the consultants had a positive view of their ability to effect change. These results have some notable limitations: the small size of the group studied and the possible self-report bias. Because the majority of persons who serve as youth services consultants do so part time, their effectiveness is also a concern, but we cannot make generalizations about their impact beyond saying that surely having some assistance in a broad array of issues has to make a difference to the librarians and the children and young adults they serve.

Recommendation #2

It is tempting to recommend that all states should employ a full-time consultant to assist librarians with services to children and young adults. The financial situation of most states at this writing makes such a recommendation futile. However, those state library agencies that are not making any effort to assist with youth services should be reminded that in the minds of many politicians, the public library is associated with the education of children, and as we have seen, this is rightly so. A political asset is waiting to be utilized. It is recommended that a consultant in public library development at each of the state agencies be assigned to spend a portion of his or her work hours supporting youth services.

Administration of Federal Programs

As described earlier, the administration of federal programs is one of the *raisons d'etre* of state library agencies. We do not have good records of how the states have allocated the money among the various constituencies that use the public library, as noted in Chapter 10. The states devise their own allocation plans within the broad categories of the various titles of the Library Services and Construction Act. Some of the states dedicate specific amounts to particular kinds of youth services programs; Wisconsin, for instance, has a Reading Readiness category for projects to extend preschool services. In general, however, we do not know what proportions are spent on youth services and what proportions are spent on other kinds of programs, administration, and administrative improvements such as automation. Total appropriations are reported by the state library agencies and the federal government with some narrative about specific projects, but details of all the projects funded are not generally published.

The Library Programs Office publication, *LSCA Programs: An Action Report II* (Library Programs, 1989), includes reports on activities funded under Titles I, II, and III of the Library Services and Construction Act from 1982 to 1987. The writers discussed projects in literacy; services to the blind, the handicapped, the institutionalized, and the elderly; library construction; cooperative activities; and national and regional resource centers. It is possible to go through the information and find mentions of programs for young people, but an overview of the proportion of LSCA funds used for youth services is difficult to obtain. For example, the report on LSCA literacy projects mentions specific projects that served children and young adults, but gives no indication of the numbers of young people served or the proportion of literacy funds expended for serving them (Chute, 1989). Similarly, by summing figures supplied in the 1986 report of state-by-state expenditures for serving the institutionalized, the patient reader could estimate that 14.5% of $3.4 million in LSCA money was spent on behalf of institutions serving young people (Skaptason, 1989). This estimate would be an underreport because many states did not itemize grants to institutions nor specify which institutions served children or young adults. The reader has to guess from the names of institutions whether they served young people.

Recommendation #3

State library agencies should make an effort to determine if children and young adults are receiving an appropriate amount of state-controlled federal funds. Some of the considerations that might go into determining appropriate levels of federal funding in a given state include the proportion of the population under the age of 18, the prevalence and condition of public and school library services for young people, the availability of alternate forms of recreation and education within the state, the literacy and school drop-out rates, and so on. Some assessment of the needs of young people in comparison to those of adults and other special populations will be needed. No single consideration can guide the determination for all states or even a single state. Considering the concern about adequate access to technology for young people expressed in Chapter 1, particular attention should be paid to how LSCA funds are used to extend the availability of changing technology to children and young adults. When services to young people receive fewer LSCA dollars than their needs indicate, the state library agency should rectify the allocation mechanisms.

Implementing this recommendation requires collecting accurate and complete data from the local library staff who implement LSCA programs. Typically this is difficult to do unless those who must file reports see some benefit to themselves or their services. Enlisting the assistance of the children's and young adult services section of the state library association at the very beginning will make this task more acceptable. Reports need not be made every year. Sampling periodically, perhaps every 3 to 5 years, would give an adequate picture and create a database for comparing changes in allocation over time.

Support for Legislative Initiatives

Since the late 1970s, state library agencies and library professional organizations have become more politically aware and astute as a natural consequence of the fiscal situation that has required library agencies at all levels of government to compete with other departments for the ever-limited budget dollar. Descriptions of the process of dealing with state legislatures in California and New York clearly demonstrate the necessity of cooperating with state library associations and other groups in order to achieve desired ends (Shubert, 1990; Strong, 1990). Strong and Shubert also made clear that achieving legislative goals requires commitment and hard work, possibly over several years, as we noted in the discussion of lobbying in Chapter 9.

What is not clear in the record is the extent to which state library youth consultants are active in promoting legislation that would benefit youth services. Feehan (1991) discussed "policy development" as an area that the consultants are active in, but the kinds of policies being developed appear to be local public library operational policies and internal state library policies, rather than statewide laws and funding initiatives. This may be a result of the relative scarcity of full-time state library consultants for youth: People whose major responsibilities lie elsewhere do not have the time that it takes to work on political agendas for youth services, even when advising the legislature is considered a function of the state library agency.

Recommendation #4

State library youth consultants in cooperation with the state library association youth sections should provide the leadership to continue the momentum achieved by the 1991 White House Conference. They should see that the interests of children are considered in legislative initiatives undertaken by their state library agencies. Through their experience of state government, consultants have the expertise to assist youth librarians (preferably through the youth services sections of the state library association) to become involved in the state political process, identify suitable coalition partners and receptive state legislators, and cooperate with the other groups involved in developing state library policy.

In states that have no youth services consultant, it is recommended that the leadership come from the youth services division of the state library association. Although it is sometimes a poor strategy to have anyone other than the library director engaged in advocating library issues to local government, at the state level no such impediment exists; nor will local officials consider it inappropriate for an employee to lobby state government on behalf of local government.

THE ROLE OF THE STATES IN EDUCATION FOR LIBRARIANSHIP

Approximately half of the persons who identify themselves as children's librarians in the United States possess a degree called a Master of Library Science (MLS) or some variant terminology such as Master of Arts in Library and Information Studies (Lewis & Farris, 1990). No survey data exist for the qualifications of young adult librarians, and we have no information with which to make a reasonable estimate of the number of persons with graduate degrees serving young adults as their primary responsibility. For the purposes of this analysis, can we say that many youth librarians may be underqualified for their jobs? And if so, does it matter?

Although it may appear that the matter is settled, in fact there has never been complete unanimity about the necessity for the MLS. Critics point out that many people who work in libraries do a fine job without ever having attended a graduate program in library and information studies. An apprenticeship model of professional training is most suitable for a practical field, these commentators assert. Others note that some of those who have the Master of Library Science or equivalent degree are incompetent. The issue of accreditation adds a further dimension of controversy. Public librarians who have the degree usually have attended a program accredited by the American Library Association, but nonaccredited programs exist and many school librarians and some public librarians have degrees from them. These facts are frequently pointed to by those without the ALA-accredited credential as evidence that the credential itself is not worth very much. In addition, some of those who have earned the ALA degree are harshly critical of the education they received.

All of this is to state the obvious immediately: No system of professional education is without controversy, kibitzers, and critics. We need also to say that sometimes the criticism is valid. Indeed, research comparing the effectiveness of library school graduates with nonlibrary school graduates has shown graduates to have at best a relatively modest superiority over those without the degree. Some of that superiority is in areas that are intangible but important to a service orientation: giving greater satisfaction and having more commitment (Murfin & Bunge, 1988; Wert, 1980). None of the research has been conducted using youth librarians as subjects.

What the fault-finders neglect to consider is that generalizations are traps for generalizers. Those who have never attended a graduate school of library and information studies cannot know what they have missed or how their work might be made more meaningful and efficient with specialized education. Those who know only the library school that they attended (and know that school only as it was at the time they were enrolled) also have limited information. As for the incompetents, a year or two of education cannot remake a human being; likely they were incompetent before they arrived at library school. The school is at fault in admitting the incompetent but cannot be accused of producing incompetence.

As a library educator, I am unabashedly in favor of graduate level education for librarianship; no sensible reader would expect me to be otherwise. The reality of library education is that it is not nearly as poorly conceived and delivered as its detractors would have us believe, but it is not as perfect as any set of accreditation standards might leave the unwary to expect. At this point in my career, I have intimate acquaintance with four ALA-accredited programs and know faculty members from several dozen other schools. Most of the individuals involved struggle honestly with the questions that beset the profession and the situations encountered on their home campuses. In these parlous times, some of us feel we are constantly fighting the forces of chaos, of which students and graduates may be only dimly aware.

As in the case of state library youth consultants, surely something is better than nothing. But that is not an excuse to accept the status quo without looking at it. In Chapter 6, we examined the content of library education for youth librarians for clues as to their effectiveness. Research in the 1980s indicated that children's librarians had emphasized library materials, particularly children's literature, in their coursework, without a concomitant focus on child development (Greene & Cullinan, 1988; Grover & Moore, ca. 1981; Smardo, 1980). Carlson's (1985) research into programs for toddlers and preschoolers showed that the librarians designed appropriate activities for young children, but they were self-educated. That is, much of their understanding of young children had come from postgraduate reading, not from courses taken in library school.

A survey conducted in 1985 requesting information about youth services courses offered during the three academic years from 1982 to 1985 concluded that enough courses had been available for interested students. Seventy-one percent of the 38 responding schools indicated that two to four courses suitable for children's services preparation had been offered; one or two courses for young adult services had been offered at 61% of the schools. Data about the content of these courses showed that very often subjects were combined; for instance, 34% of the schools taught children's literature and audiovisual media in one course and 32% combined young adult literature with services to young adults (Allen & Bush, 1987). Greene and Cullinan (1988) found that materials and services for young children were treated in a course of their own at only one library school and that two thirds of the respondents combined early childhood with later childhood in their courses. Perusal of the raw data from a similar but unpublished survey conducted in 1991 by Priscilla Drach and J.W. Coffman confirmed the general state of course offerings noted by Allen and Bush.

What is of concern, however, is that the number of courses may not be truly adequate. Most of them are survey courses, and if, in addition to a body of literature, instructors must also discuss child and adolescent development, nonprint media, and library services, there is little room for depth in any of these areas. And, once again, it is young adult services that seems to be particularly slighted. In terms of the competencies desired by the Association for Library Service to Children and the Young Adult Library Services Association, it would seem that children's and young adult librarians can expect to learn a good deal of what they need to know through continuing education and on-the-job training.

This state of affairs contrasts with that for students preparing for careers in some other areas of librarianship. Educators can assume that students arrive in their master's programs with some knowledge of "adult" materials because a bachelor's degree is one of the minimum qualifications for admission to a graduate degree program. Most students of youth services will not have had previous formal instruction in the materials they are supposed to be able to use and recommend to clients on their first day of work, however. (The situation may be similar for those preparing for careers in technical services and library automation.) To have available to students only one course in young adult services and two in children's services is to give them a cursory background.

It was suggested earlier in this chapter that state governments should take a direct interest in the quality of education for youth services librarians and, indeed, all librarians, because that education is now largely accomplished by state-funded institutions. This could be another function of the already overworked state library agencies. Because there is no national certification for librarians comparable to medical board examinations, some of the states attempt to influence the quality of librarians through state certification. However, the rigor and purpose of the process varies. In Wisconsin, for example, persons who do not have the MLS may be certified as librarians for towns of 2,500 or fewer by passing a single undergraduate-level course in basic library operations. Other states certify public librarians by examining their MLS transcripts to see that courses required by state law have been taken. In many states, only school library media specialists are certified because the education bureaucracy uses certification as a gatekeeping mechanism for all professionals employed in public schools. Certification of school library media specialists is generally under the aegis of the state department of public instruction, not the state library agency.

Recommendation #5

Without an exam process, it is unlikely that certification does anything more than verify graduation from a school of library and information studies. The expense of designing and implementing a certification exam, plus likely opposition to taking it, make it unlikely that such an examination will be introduced without significant pressure from forces external to the profession. Thus, state-level efforts to insure quality education for youth services may have to come from volunteer efforts of youth services librarians to influence both the schools and the state governments on the schools' behalf.

In states that have publicly funded schools of library and information studies, it is recommended that ties be strengthened between the youth services sections of the state library associations and the library schools. Connections may take various forms, such as having youth librarians serve on the schools' advisory boards where they can give advice and information relevant to the educational needs of people serving children and young adults. Knowledgeable youth librarians can present testimony before university and state legislative bodies regarding the value of the school and its impact on young people.

We have become accustomed to seeing library school alumni rush to the defense of their alma maters following the announcement of a possible closure. What we need is involvement as a normal course of affairs, not only when there is a crisis. We need to view the practice of librarianship and education for the practice of librarianship as a single system in which all members have a stake, regardless of their particular location in the system. This system has linkages and connections to other systems, such as state government and the information industry, as has been discussed throughout the book. There are no cheeses standing alone.

Recommendation #6

In order for youth librarians to have the background necessary to be active on the political playing field, library educators must take responsibility for including in their courses solid information about funding and political issues regarding public libraries. In addition, students should be encouraged to take political science courses, where available and suitable, to give them an understanding of how the system works and how they might become part of the process. Many of the knowledge areas that should be allowed to have an impact on youth librarians are outside the arena of the theories and techniques of librarianship proper. Carlson showed that knowledge of child development led to more appropriately designed programs for children. Knowledge of the political process may lead to more political success at the statehouse and elsewhere.

SUMMARY

Through the state library agencies, state governments provide support and some funding to public libraries as part of their responsibilities for public library development. State library consultants can provide expertise to local librarians in the form of advice, continuing education, and legislative advocacy. In this chapter we have observed how little is actually known about the impact of state and federal aid on youth services, pointing to the need for an evaluation of the aid. I have urged closer ties among youth librarians and state consultants and more state-level political activity by children's and young adult librarians.

Further, state governments are the chief supporters of library education, giving the states a greater interest in the education of librarians than either the states or the profession have yet realized. Participation in library education and political support of library schools on the part of alumni should not wait until there is a crisis. So often the profession's criticism of its own education has resulted in nonlibrarians taking a negative view of librarians and libraries. Youth librarians may have a particular role in informing legislators and university administrators about youth's developing needs for competent use of information technologies.

Until the nation recovers from the recession, it is unlikely that direct state aid to libraries will increase. State efforts to encourage public library development may continue to emphasize the use of technology to create greater efficiency, rather than extending labor-intensive services such as personal consultation. Youth services consultants and local

Table 11.2.   Summary of Roles and Recommendations for States

1. State library agencies should undertake to study the impact of state aid on library services to children and young adults, possibly with federal funding. Studies should concentrate on both the direct and indirect impacts of the funding.

2. State library agencies that do not have a consultant with responsibility for assisting youth services in public libraries should hire such a person or rearrange the duties of existing consultants so that youth services librarians have access to a knowledgeable person on whom to rely for guidance in program design and evaluation, collections, services, funding, and facilities.

3. State library agencies should examine the proportion of Library Services and Construction Act moneys currently spent on services to children and young adults and especially on projects related to computer technology and multimedia. If children and teenagers are not well represented in these projects, funds should be reserved for youth services demonstration programs.

4. State library youth consultants and youth services divisions of state library associations should take responsibility for examining and influencing legislative initiatives supported by state libraries for their impact on services to children and young adults.

5. Youth librarians, represented by the youth services sections of the state library associations, should maintain closer connections with the library schools within their states in order to have an active role in the development of curriculum and to support the school both on-campus and in the state legislature.

6. Library educators should include political issues as part of the "basic training" of youth librarians (and anyone planning to serve in a publicly supported institution).

youth librarians will need to keep greater vigilance to be sure that the interests of children and teenagers are considered as the state and federal governments develop plans for cooperation and resource sharing. Children and young adults elicit strong, positive, emotional responses from the general public and the politicians. With planning and the help of other organizations interested in the future of young people, youth librarians can ensure that young people continue to receive the educational, informational, recreational, and cultural services they require.

CHAPTER 12

Local Librarians and Local Government Policies

INTRODUCTION

Whether we are discussing health, education, social welfare, or libraries, young people usually do not receive services directly from the state or federal government; they are served much closer to home by local agencies. Leadership and discussion at the state and national levels are necessary but not sufficient for the development of services delivered to users. Thus, children's and young adult librarians in municipal, county, and special district libraries carry on with their activities, sometimes without knowing what is being done on their behalf by state and federal governments and library associations. We know from the user studies available that young people represent at least half of the people who visit public libraries during any week and that children's materials alone account for close to 40% of public library circulation. Nevertheless, we also know that half the materials and staffing budgets are not allocated to youth services and that teenagers in particular are unlikely to find in their local public library a staff member specifically trained and designated to serve their interests and needs.

As we have previously noted, the focus of service at the local level includes the fact that public libraries receive the majority (80% or more) of their funding from local property taxes and other local sources. In interviews with public librarians in my case studies, I found they believed strongly that public library funding should come mostly from local funds because of their firm professional value of tailoring the service to the individual community (Willett, 1987). They insisted that the public library as a local service should be funded locally. However, reliance on the ability and willingness to pay of those residing in a specific geographic area means that poor and small communities will not have the level of services provided in wealthier communities.

An extreme comparison can be drawn between the Commerce Public Library and the Lassen County Public Library, both in California. For the 1991-1992 fiscal year, Commerce spent $136.87 per person, whereas Lassen County spent $3.80 (Elizabeth Gibson, personal communication, November 23, 1992). In the previous year, the Commerce Public Library served 12,000 people with 24 full-time equivalent (FTE) staff members, spent $157,600 on materials, and had total operating expenditures of $1.36 million. Lassen County, serving a population more than twice as large as Commerce, had 4.45 FTE, a total materials budget of $1,647, and operating expenditures of $142,769 (*California Library Statistics 1992*, 1992).

Although small communities pay more per person in order to provide basic services, and willingness to pay undoubtedly differs between the two communities, these are not the only reasons for the discrepancy. Nor does the situation arise because the citizens of Lassen County need their library less than the residents of Commerce. The key difference is the value of real property and the property tax and other revenues collected in the two communities. Funding for public schools suffers from the same inherent weakness in the use of property taxes as a major revenue source.

In addition to the disequalities that arise from reliance on local funding, the local point of view ignores the encroaching reality of electronic information services as well as resource sharing activities that do not depend on local ownership of information, only local access to it. Dubberly (1992) called this "shared users" because users are less and less limited to local holdings. His response is to call for greater funding involvement at the national and state levels, and still maintaining local administrative control. Under the economic theory of public goods, such funding may become more and more appropriate. However, with the current economic reality making it unlikely that federal and state funding will increase in the foreseeable future, our policy recommendations must converge on what can and should be done by local librarians and local government officials.

We began this book by describing a number of challenges currently facing youth services. These challenges and others have to be faced at the local level in order to bring meaningful changes. The challenges were: funding restraints, structural changes in personnel, ambivalence toward changing technology, demographic shifts, concern for educational achievement and literacy, and legitimacy. We also established

criteria for judging alternatives based on research in educatic
development, the standards of public goods theory set by eco...
and political and professional feasibility, all with an interest in minimizing additional costs to the taxpayer. In this chapter, we address the challenges from the local viewpoint, suggesting changes in perspective and approach.

FUNDING RESTRAINTS

Youth services librarians are sometimes advised that the way to approach local funding constraints is to write grants for state and federal funds, private foundation moneys, and local corporate philanthropy. I would certainly not discourage anyone from doing so, but the limitations of such grants must be recognized. Usually, grants such as Library Services and Construction Act funds are available for demonstrating new services, not for maintaining current operating costs, and frequently the grant is available for a limited period of time. When the period is over, the funds and the programs may disappear together, though it sometimes happens that an extremely successful or politically attractive program will be given continued funding by local government.

Money from private sector sources is also likely to be limited to specific projects and for specific purposes. Salaries, for example, may be excluded because corporations and foundations like to be able to point to the physical objects they have provided. Whether from private or public sources, grants cannot be the mainstay of youth services, although they may be godsends for particular programs—summer reading support being an example where many libraries have had successful cooperation from local businesses over several years. Survival of youth services depends on continued, regular support from the general library budget. Therefore, youth librarians must pay close attention to local economic conditions.

At the time that this is being written, the country is slowly recovering from a prolonged recession. Localities differ greatly in the degree to which the recession has had an impact on them. Reading the news columns of library periodicals such as American Libraries and Library Hotline, one might find as many positive stories of bond issues passed and services improved as negative stories of budget cuts and staff layoffs. Realistically, we cannot expect federal or state aid to public libraries to increase very much unless and until the economy improves, and local corporations have reduced their handouts. Even in periods of economic growth, local governments cannot provide all services at the levels desired by professionals or the public; resources are not infinitely expandable. Protective services (fire and police) and schools are usually seen as the most immediate priorities, and if, at any time, it becomes necessary to cut these areas, libraries and other "discretionary" services may seem much less important to the public and the politicians and so suffer even greater cuts. After the passage of Propositions 13 (California) and 2 1/2 (Massachusetts), libraries and parks suffered greater cuts than other municipal and county services (J.M. Greiner, 1984; Schwadron & Richter, 1984).

Sociologists who study organizations suggest that responding to environmental situations such as funding restraints might be handled through two general approaches. Organizations may attempt to modify the environment, or they may adapt to the environment (Perrow, 1986; Pfeffer & Salancik, 1978; Scott, 1981). For public librarians, modifying the funding environment essentially means political activity of one sort or another, whereas adaptation may provoke structural changes and altered goals.

Recommendation #1

Local youth librarians need to be aware of the funding situation of their own library and that of the local government that sponsors the library. They need to have a perspective that includes all departments of the library and they need to be an advocate for the entire library as well as youth services. This is the case because there is anecdotal evidence that library directors are more generous to youth services when support for the library as a whole is adequate. After Proposition 13, youth services in three of four case study libraries were cut, but when funds were restored, children's services was a priority area for rebuilding (Willett, 1987, 1992). On the other hand, youth services librarians need to be aware of the needs of other departments in the library. Sometimes other areas actually do need more funding than the youth departments. Compromise serves well in internal as well as external politics.

Librarians and library directors should remember the political value of active children's and young adult services. Programs that serve young people, especially those that have obvious educational value, are viewed positively by the electorate and therefore by politicians. In the most recent observation of my case study libraries, the two directors considered most successful at maintaining local government support expected department heads, including the coordinators of children's services, to provide them with evidence of effective activities to support budget requests for the library as a whole (Willett, 1992). Management-level youth librarians should ask and expect to be included in the process of designing and defending the library budget.

Recommendation #2

On the other hand, local youth services librarians need to be an advocate for their departmental budget because it is unlikely that anyone else will do this without some leadership from them. Budget requests for staff, open hours, and materials must be well supported with evidence of need because the demands for accountability are with us always. The decade of the 1980s might be dubbed the Age of Managerial Competence for all the calls for youth librarians to think of themselves as managers and not just service providers. The title of the 1986 Allerton Institute at the University of Illinois at Urbana-Champaign highlights the double focus of youth services. It was called "Managers and Missionaries: Library Services to Children and Young Adults in the Information Age."

A managerial approach emphasizes planning and evaluation, having goals and objectives, considering outcomes with a minimum of subjectivity, and avoiding blind adherence to professional ideology. Managerial competence includes the flexibility and creativity to deal strategically with unexpected change. In order to provide the data necessary for good management, youth librarians keep use statistics and evaluate their services using a variety of techniques (such as those described in Robbins, Willett, Wiseman, & Zweizig, 1990, and *Output Measures for Public Library Service to Children* by Walter, 1992). In addition, youth librarians must be aware of local conditions in schools, day care, and youth agencies both private and public, and be knowledgeable about the information contained in census and other demographic reports.

Recommendation #3

Activities that bring the youth librarian into working contact with other youth organizations and agencies are another form of political activism. Previously, we have observed the coalition building that took place within each state before the 1991 White House Conference on Library and Information Services. At the local level, coalitions and joint activities can give youth services political credit both within the library and in the local political sphere because they can result in efficient use of dollars and they create allies for the library. It is recommended that youth services librarians work with other local youth-serving organizations for mutual benefit.

Political activity does not guarantee that funds will be increased or even that reductions will be avoided. Some localities have experienced population growth or a change in population that results in greater demands being placed on library staff whose numbers may remain the same or be reduced when budgets are not allowed to grow. One adaptive response might be to reduce the variety of services offered. Another might be to change the personnel role structure of who does what in the library. As a new librarian 20 years ago, I was told that in order to maintain quality control, all programs and services had to be offered by the professionally qualified librarians or paraprofessional library assistants who had been extensively trained to provide services. Today's youth services librarians are much more open to sharing their expertise. They have realized that if that knowledge remains the sole possession of library staff, few children will receive the benefits of it—the library staff is physically unable to reach all children. I once estimated that each children's librarian serves between 2,200 and 3,300 children (Willett, 1988). Providing individual reading guidance at any meaningful level to so many children is impossible.

Recommendation #4

The current model of youth services includes the use of volunteers trained to assist within the library and the training of other adults, such as teachers, childcare providers, and parents, to provide reading guidance, reading aloud, and storytelling in other settings. Exemplary programs have been created at the Hennepin County Library in Minnesota and the Alameda County Library in California. Such efforts use librarians' time efficiently by extending their reach to many more children. However, training nonlibrarians is not a task that should be undertaken lightly or by librarians who have little experience with children. In addition, as Mahmoodi and Wronka (1989) pointed out, youth librarians must add to their repertoires knowledge of how adults learn in order to be effective trainers. The fourth recommendation is that youth librarians find ways of incorporating volunteers and training of adults into their programs in order to use their time more efficiently, and that they utilize the principles of adult education to do so.

STRUCTURAL CHANGES IN PERSONNEL

At one time in the 1980s and early 1990s, public libraries experienced a shortage of youth services librarians. Coming on the heels of funding restraints due to the economic situation, a labor shortage might be seen in some quarters as a blessing. The labor shortage was believed to have a number of causes: the low salaries paid to youth librarians, the lack of a career ladder for them, and the attractiveness of other professions and other functions in librarianship. Although large urban libraries continue to have difficulty attracting youth librarians, in many parts of the country there is actually a lack of positions available. Both situations are likely to lead to increased use of paraprofessionals, a further structural change that is coming to many aspects of the profession. Library paraprofessionals are persons with bachelor's or associate's degrees (in a variety of subjects) instead of master's degrees in library and information studies who carry out many of the basic functions of librarians. These persons receive on-the-job training to fit them for service in the particular library where they work, but they are usually blocked from advancement or more professional responsibilities without the master's degree, and they are paid less than librarians. Public libraries have employed such persons for many years.

Now, some of the more technical aspects of librarianship are becoming "deskilled" with the use of computer technology; for example, much cataloging is now done by paraprofessionals. Catalogers with master's degrees carry out functions that require greater expertise or managerial and supervisory skills, rather than doing original cataloging only (Adeline Wilkes, personal communication, October 20, 1992). Considering that the two national surveys did not distinguish between staff with and without the master's degree, many of those called children's librarians and young adult librarians are likely to be persons without the professional qualification.

A related phenomenon is the advent of the generalist librarian who serves all ages, a personnel structure that may be used to reduce costs in large libraries (Kimmel, 1981). Small libraries always have had "generalists" because many of them employ a single librarian. Considering that only half the country's libraries have designated staff for children and only 11% have young adult staff, realistically, quite a lot of young people are served by generalists. In 45% of libraries without a young adult librarian, young adults are served by generalists (NCES, 1988). Both the paraprofessional and the generalist professional are unlikely to have education in the aspects of youth services that youth librarians see as crucial: knowledge of books and other materials for specific age groups, knowledge of children and young adults, design and implementation of services and activities for different ages, advocacy and public relations, and professional development (Association for Library Service to Children, 1989; "Young adults deserve the best," 1982).

The foregoing chapters should have indicated that the complexities of public library services to young people require staff with more qualifications than simply liking young people and enjoying the books published for them. Kimmel (1981) pointed out that when the Baltimore County Public Library converted to a generalist approach (among other structural changes), the former youth specialists were available to design activities and train other librarians how to serve children and young adults. She said, "To ignore client differences in collection development, merchandising techniques, and staff training and development is to ignore three hundred years of study and concern" for children and teenagers (p. 301). It is, however, unlikely that financially strapped local governments can be persuaded to hire more children's and young adult librarians, assuming that they could be found. Therefore, a structural change is needed to accommodate the financial restraint and the labor shortage.

Recommendation #5

If we accept the premise that the generalist and the paraprofessional will remain the service providers for many of the nation's young people, then we must see that these persons are trained to supply as high a quality of service as possible. What is needed is a position of youth services trainer in the regional libraries. Some regional library systems already have a position that encompasses some training or consulting for youth services. For example, Wisconsin regional library services include someone who is a liaison for youth services; the persons holding these positions do not all have youth services experience, however. The NCES young adult services survey (1988) found that regional youth consultants were often located in regions that had professional young adult librarians, perhaps because the existence of young adult librarians indicates an acknowledgment on the part of library administrators that young adult services requires as much direction and expertise as services to children or adults.

Small libraries, especially rural libraries, need that expertise and direction, as well. As positions at regional library headquarters become available, it is recommended that they be filled with persons with youth services experience who should be given the mandate to implement comprehensive training programs for library employees who serve young people but lack skills and formal education in the areas needed. Persons who have been employed as children's librarians for a few years but may not be ready to serve as administrators in charge of children's departments might be ideal candidates for such positions. They will have skills and experience to share and will gain from the exposure to many different libraries and communities. Regional positions will allow for the development of a career step on the way to administration without taking the dedicated youth services person away from youth services. Effective regional youth librarians may be able to demonstrate the value of having a professional to serve young people to public library directors reluctant to push their local authorities for such a position.

Recommendation #6

Although we have shied away from making recommendations that would result in increased funding, the salary issue must be faced. Although we have the factual data to support the finding that youth services librarians are paid less than public librarians in other functions (Lynch & Myers, 1986; Lynch, Myers, & Guy, 1984, 1991), we do not have research data to indicate that low salaries keep otherwise interested persons from entering youth services. There may be a general correlation between income and ability, but it is also true that many capable people select occupations they like, giving salary a lower priority. So, we have no reason to expect that the lower salaries are due to less ability among youth services librarians than other groups of librarians. Although the public sector does not respond as quickly as the private labor market, any shortage of youth librarians may ultimately result in gradually raising salaries as library directors find they have to compete for a smaller pool of qualified applicants.

Further, if the only reason for paying a children's or young adult librarian less than a reference librarian or cataloger is that young people are valued less than adults, that is age discrimination. Local governments with civil service personnel departments usually avoid this by not having separate classifications by function – a Librarian I is a Librarian I regardless of department or specific job duties – but the studies by Lynch, Myers, and Guy indicate that it happens anyway. Analysis of the various tasks done by librarians might well show that beginning youth librarians have more encompassing job demands and more managerial responsibilities than entry-level librarians in other departments. It is recommended that local governments and librarians work toward equity in compensation for children's and young adult librarians, recognizing that work with young people requires not only unusual personal and communication skills but also a broad knowledge of human development and organizational ability. The consequences of inadequate remuneration may be inadequate service to a population in the process of developing the human capital of the future.

AMBIVALENCE TOWARD CHANGING TECHNOLOGY

Just as technology affects the structure of job responsibilities for catalogers, for youth services librarians, use of technology increases the scope of their duties, introduces new publics to their services, provides tools for managing the work of the youth services staff, and creates challenges for spending acquisitions budgets. I have suggested that librarians are ambivalent about technology. Ambivalence may characterize librarians' willingness to use technology for their own work but not to make it available for young patrons, or to accept wholeheartedly one aspect of a technology although rejecting another aspect. The principle technologies discussed in Chapter 1 were computers and television.

Computers

Administrative use of computers allows librarians to monitor more easily various aspects of their services, such as circulation, and perform statistical tests on other data; for instance, calculating the average attendance at a series of preschool story hours. The advantages of this type of computer application are obvious and quite uncontroversial. However, computer systems do require regular upgrading, and can place a strain on library capital improvements budgets. Other areas where there seem to be more problems include microcomputers for public use, access to the rapidly developing information infrastructure, and online cataloging for young people.

Recommendation #7

It was pointed out in Chapter 1 that less than 30% of public libraries made personal computers and software available to the public (Lewis & Farris, 1990). Although many children had access to computers at school, not all do, and less than 25% of children and teenagers had computers at home (Kominski, 1991). Middle-class white children were more likely than other children to have computers at home. Clearly there is an opportunity for public libraries to redress an inequality by working to make microcomputers, software, and Internet access available for young people in libraries everywhere.

Public libraries should do so because computers can help them fulfill their mission to provide information, education, recreation, and culture to their communities. Much of the software that is available has educational value and much of it is imaginative in design, allowing for the use of parallel processing skills and the practice of reading (Greenfield, 1984; Sewell, 1990). Even computer games provide young users with computer readiness skills, such as knowledge of keyboards. As IBM and Apple work to make their operating systems compatible, the variety of applications for education, information, and entertainment will increase.

The Internet, an international network of electronic networks, has been growing exponentially; vast amounts of information are available online for anyone with the equipment and the knowledge to use it. Librarians worry that their role may diminish in this new environment, but this will only happen if librarians do not acquire expertise in the changing technology. Many librarians have or are developing expertise (McClure, Ryan, Lauterbach, & Moen, 1992). During 1992 and 1993, a large number of electronic discussion groups for librarians were started on the Internet, some of which are designed for youth librarians, such as KIDLIT and PUBYAC. Other discussion groups for children are available, such as KIDSPHERE. These groups are in addition to files of information on a great many subjects.

Youth librarians should work to expand access to computers, computer networks, and software to young people in less advantaged areas of their communities in particular, because these are the children and teenagers who may have less access at home and at school. Initial equipment and software are often available on a grant basis from the manufacturers or through other grant projects, such as LSCA grants. If grants are not available, other means should be found to make available to children and teenagers high-quality microcomputers with a range of capabilities. Computers are the intellectual tools of today as well as tomorrow, and young people must become adept at applying them and implementing the various cognitive strategies required for sophisticated computer use, just as they are taught to apply various cognitive strategies in reading.

In addition, young people, particularly secondary students who are learning in their high school libraries about some of the online and CD-ROM products available for bibliographic searching, will come to view any library without such services as inadequate if not obsolete. If students in grades kindergarten through 12 are permitted access to the National Research and Education Network (NREN), as Vice President Albert Gore has proposed, then their use of the public library may change drastically unless the public library is a place where youngsters can gain entry to the NREN and instruction in its use.

Youth librarians will also have to face the consequences for their materials budgets and collection development strategies. For the immediate future, the book will not be supplanted; however, a different distribution of priorities will need to be developed to accommodate a wider repertoire of sources providing information, education, culture, and recreation. Librarians must also begin to prepare for the eventual transition away from books with paper pages, just as they moved from clay tablets and parchment rolls in the past. It is not too difficult to see that the recent development of personal notebook technology could lead to electronic handheld books.

Recommendation #8

A second area of concern about computer technology centers around the shift to online catalogs. Although researchers are attempting to design online cataloging systems appropriate for children's developing abilities (Walter & Borgman, 1991), only one commercially available system has been designed specifically for children, the Kid's Catalog. Anecdotal evidence suggests that several systems in use in schools can be used by children below high school age, but the limited systematic research done with such systems has found that children have more difficulty with them than librarians may think (Edmonds, 1987; Solomon, 1991). It is recommended that youth services librarians work with vendors and systems designers at any library that is planning to implement or upgrade an online catalog. Familiarity with children is required for the development of catalogs that are sensitive to their needs for easily understood catalog screens and help systems. Very likely a catalog that a fourth grader can use will also suit the needs of the general adult patron as well, because many adults are not entirely comfortable with catalogs, whether online or in card form. It may be necessary to maintain children's card catalogs side by side with online versions that contain the entire library's holdings, at least for young children's use. Edmonds, Moore, and Balcom (1990) theorized that physical manipulation of cards may aid the searching of children in the concrete operations stage (approximately ages 7 to 12).

Television

The second technology that arouses some ambivalence on the part of youth librarians is television. On the one hand, many librarians condemn commercial broadcast television, joining the crowd of antitelevision crusaders who believe that television is responsible for a host of social ills from illiteracy to violent crime. On the other hand, librarians purchase videotapes to circulate in their libraries, and in 1991 the Association for Library Service to Children inaugurated the Andrew Carnegie Medal for Excellence in Children's Video, named after the 19th century philanthropist who funded thousands of public libraries in the English-speaking world. Perhaps librarians simply participate in the ambivalence about television in the larger society. There is, at any rate, more than a tinge of elitism in a group that appears to say that one form of television is better than another.

People evaluate particular shows for their individual merits on the basis of production, content, and whether or not the show meets the viewer's personal taste. Whether the program is delivered over the airwaves or via VCR makes little difference to the quality or viewer satisfaction, just as a paperback book delivers the same content as a hardcover edition. As there are various kinds of reading matter to meet a variety of tastes and needs, so there are many kinds of viewing available for the insatiable American consumer to choose, and nearly everyone could identify a specific television program they would prefer to a particular book.

Recommendation #9

It is recommended that librarians take a broader perspective and a more tempered approach to the subject of television. A thoughtful examination of the research literature on the subject of television, rather than the popular press, will reveal that there is much about television viewing's effects that is not known at the present time. Although recreational television seems to fill the interest niche that comic books do, it appears to have had little effect on "serious" reading (D.R. Anderson & Collins, 1988; Himmelweit, Oppenheim, & Vince, 1958). Researchers are cautious about the possible desensitizing or traumatizing effects on children of viewing televised violence, however.

Taking a historical perspective will allow librarians to understand that popular media have always been suspect to cultural elites. At the turn of the century, for example, novels were the subject of controversy among some librarians who feared they would cause the young to become dreamy and unrealistic (West, 1988). Librarians should realize that little is known about the actual effects of reading. If reading has the power to produce good effects, such as self-education, we must also recognize its power to do harm. One South African researcher has found that some adult readers of fiction become addicted to it in the sense that they have the mental and physiological reactions of substance abusers (Nell, 1988). Perhaps those 19th-century librarians were right to fear fiction! Nevertheless, our society is founded upon the belief that individuals have the right and the ability to choose which influences to follow and which to ignore. Librarians like to hand the responsibility for helping children make adequate choices to their parents, but if the public library is an educational institution, perhaps librarians should do more for both parents and young people.

A moderate view of television would recognize that children over the age of about 6 are capable of evaluating and selecting the television shows they watch (P. Palmer, 1986). Children should be given opportunities to express preferences and responses to all forms of communication media (books, television, radio, newspapers, etc.) in order to encourage critical thinking as well as response. Neither reading nor watching television is a simple, passive act. Each is a complex phenomenon deserving of study, consideration, and discussion among people of all ages. Part of the study and consideration of video and broadcast television by young people in public libraries might be directed at allowing children and teenagers to discuss and produce videos as well as view them, just as some libraries encourage teenagers to read, respond, and write by producing young adult book review magazines for their peers. These activities are more positive than the "Turn off the Television" campaigns launched by some librarians.

DEMOGRAPHIC SHIFTS

In Chapter 1, we identified three major demographic trends affecting services for youth: the increase in working mothers (and other changes in family lifestyle), the decreasing proportion of young people in the population, and the increasing proportion of ethnic and racial minorities. Librarians are quite aware of these demographic challenges because the impact of them is visible every day the library is open and because they are discussed in the media. These trends are affecting many aspects of contemporary life, not just libraries. Because of their visibility, local librarians have made efforts to deal with these trends, taking preschool programs to day-care centers, nursery schools, and Head Start programs; developing and increasing collections and services to minority groups; and passing the Omnibus Youth Literacy through Libraries recommendations at the White House Conference in 1991. A number of libraries have active after-school programs to accommodate those children whose parents use the library for afternoon childcare and those children who choose to be in the library after school. The recommendations to be made about coping with demographic shifts are largely common sense ideas that can be tailored to suit the local community.

Changes in Family Lifestyles and Circumstances

In addition to the changes already achieved by youth services, the entire library needs to consider how the pattern of family life has changed and what the new pattern means for use of the library not only by young people but also by adults. Time has become as vital and as limited a resource as money in our society, and time is the principal direct cost of public library use (Van House, 1983), a fact foreseen by the great Indian librarian S.R. Ranganathan (1964), whose "Five Laws of Library Science" include "Save the time of the reader." In families where both parents or the single parent work and children are in school and/or childcare, the normal business hours and usual services of public libraries may not allow much access. In fact, this is the case with all households with persons who work, whether or not there are teenagers or children. Flexibility and creativity in hours will assist library users to make efficient use of their time (Hennessy, 1985).

A further consideration in economic terms is competition. In this country, many commercial establishments, such as grocery stores, pharmacies, bookstores, and video stores, are open 24 hours per day. Library hours in a culture that is open around the clock may seem unduly limited and exclusionary. As the reader will recall from the discussion on economics, unlike other public services, there are a variety of viable and attractive substitutes for some of the services offered by the public library—bookstores, video stores, newsstands, drug stores, grocery stores, and so on, offer reading, viewing, and listening—but at a direct cost to the consumer. Substitutes for garbage pickup, utilities, postal service, policing, fire protection, mosquito abatement, national defense, and so forth are less easily provided by individuals for themselves.

Recommendation #10

In order to remain competitive for the services for which people can find substitutes and to provide access to its unique services, it is recommended that the public library change its hours to suit the lifestyles of people in the community. It is not always easy to know what hours are most suitable, and one expects that they will vary from community to community and even from neighborhood to neighborhood, according to the lifestyles of the community. Branches of the Madison (WI) Public Library are open on Friday nights, for example. On one side of town these are popular hours and children's programs offered on Friday nights have high attendance, but on the other side of town Friday evenings are not as busy as some other times. On any day of the week, evening hours are busier generally than the daytime (Barbara Dimick, personal communication, December 14, 1992).

Elieson and Dowd (1992) attempted to establish correlations between the hours of local businesses and library use hours at a small public library but were unable to do so. They concluded that patron preference surveys and actual use patterns may be the best means of determining hours. However, unless libraries experiment with varied hours, actual use patterns and surveys of current users may only confirm the status quo.

Sunday open hours have been successful in some libraries, which report that Sunday circulation over 4 hours is equal to the circulation during 8 hours on other days of the week. Sunday use by students and by family groups is also reportedly high (cited in Hennessy, 1985), indicating that Sunday hours may have a strong positive impact on the library's ability to encourage the development of young people. Staff unwillingness to work on Sundays seems to be the chief obstacle to more libraries opening on that day. Understandably, library employees, like the rest of the population, view Sunday as a day of "free" time. However, there are a variety of ways of negotiating staffing for Sundays that share the burden among staff, as businesses do, and library employees should recognize that Sunday hours and other less conventional hours may allow the library to achieve more of its mission of universal access.

Recommendation #11

It has been noted previously that changes in parental availability during the day have meant that young children are in day care and so not available for the kind of in-library preschool story hours provided since the 1940s. Older children may be in need of after-school care. Youth librarians have adapted by taking story hours to day-care centers, training childcare providers and teachers to use library materials with children, and cooperating with a variety of agencies to provide after-school activities. Another change for some families has been increased homelessness. Youth librarians in Milwaukee, Wisconsin, and DeKalb County, Georgia, have responded by providing outreach services (such as storytelling and deposit collections) to homeless shelters and meal sites. Some librarians have seen the changed family situation as one that offers many opportunities to reach more children and parents than ever before; however, such services are not universally available. It is recommended that youth librarians everywhere review policies, procedures, and use patterns to determine what adjustments and changes may be needed to fit services to the current reality.

Changing Ethnic and Racial Composition

Another major demographic change in the United States' population concerns the change from a largely European-origin population to a far more racially and ethnically mixed people. Accompanying the change in numbers has come the realization that the United States has never truly been a melting pot, that even as immigrant groups have adapted to a form of government and society that derives from English and European roots, they have retained some unique values and cultural practices that diverge from those of other citizens. The resulting pluralism and diversity are the subjects of intense debate in the scholarly press under the guise of political correctness. They appear in changing school curricula that emphasize tolerance and sensitivity to all groups and in the passage of English-only laws. And they occur in the concerns voiced by some commentators: Is there an American culture? If so, what is it? If not, how can we have political unity amidst cultural diversity? Are all values and value systems created equal?

It is not my purpose here to attempt to answer these queries but to point out that they are exciting questions that truly test our way of life in the United States (and the communal life of other countries with large immigrant or multiracial populations). They are also questions for which libraries of all kinds, but especially school and public libraries, are uniquely suited to assist in the search for answers. Librarians can make a contribution here because of our professional attitudes toward collections and services and in the way we staff our libraries. Since 1939, American librarians have publicly committed themselves to supporting intellectual freedom; that is, the obligation to make available material on a wide range of views and issues, including unpopular ones. School and public libraries extend this commitment to young people as well as adults, allowing them to explore beyond the material presented in the classroom.

Recommendation #12

The collection aspect of pluralism may be fairly well in place among librarians, at least intellectually, but multicultural services and staff seem to be lagging behind. Improved services would undoubtedly follow if more members of minority racial and ethnic groups were represented in the profession. Recruitment of minorities continues to be a challenge, possibly because librarians are perceived to have low salaries and low social prestige and possibly because members of minority groups have had few opportunities to see role models from their groups. Although library schools, the federal government, some of the states, and the minority organizations among the professional associations have scholarship and recruitment programs, there is a general perception that many professional librarians go to library school after serving as paraprofessional and clerical staff in libraries (Beaudin, Fisher, Knowles, & Morita, 1990; Caywood, 1991).

Librarians are their own best recruiters. Not only should they encourage talented minority staff with whom they work, librarians and trustees should find concrete ways of assisting such persons through scholarships, internships, and released time for graduate education. Additional minority professionals would not only improve services to ethnic populations, they would provide role models for young people by demonstrating that minorities can take visible leadership positions in the community and are not relegated to clerical and paraprofessional positions. Bandura's (1986) research in social learning suggests the importance of role models. A task force of the Association of College and Research Libraries called to develop strategies for recruiting minorities to academic libraries recommended "participation in youth programs to arouse interest in librarianship at an early age" (Beaudin et al., 1990, p. 1017). If academic librarians recognize the need to begin recruiting early, so should public libraries, which have much greater access to young people themselves. School librarians have also recognized the value of early recruitment. Many of the state organizations for school librarians have chapters for high school students (Betty Carter, personal communication, January 15, 1993).

Recommendation #13

We must also reckon with social class differences in library use. The techniques needed to serve lower class populations may be different than those that reach middle-class residents, irrespective of race. Outreach and marketing efforts may require more mobile services, rather than expecting that people will come to the library. The models of outreach services developed in the 1960s and 1970s are still viable and are still used in some places and could be used in others. There are newer models, such as working with social service agencies and community organizations, all of which require the library staff to leave the library. At the same time, the library cannot abandon the services expected by the middle class because this group has been the public library's main political and financial support for more than a century. Librarians should continue to develop extension services for ethnic and low-income communities while maintaining conventional library services at branches and main libraries. Local librarians may face difficult choices in terms of staffing and service provision, such as forgoing preschool story hours at the library in favor of training parents and day-care workers to provide story hours, leaving collections and reference services for all ages as the main services of stationary buildings.

Changing Proportion of Children in the Population

In 1980, persons under the age of 18 represented 28.0% of the total U.S. population; in 1990 they were 25.57% of the population (U.S. Bureau of the Census, 1992). These figures represent a continuation of a historical trend toward an older median age for the country; only the baby boom interrupted the progression. At the same time, the percentage of the population that is over 65 is increasing. The Census Bureau projects that both trends will continue through 2080 as will the trends in the growth of racial and ethnic minorities discussed earlier. It should be noted that the proportion of under-20s among the Hispanic and African-American populations will remain approximately one third. Accurately predicting the future that far ahead is extremely difficult, especially because birthrates and immigration rates are sensitive to unpredictable factors such as economic and political events. For planning purposes, the data are useful, however.

Those who think that young people will become less important as library clients are not aware that at no time in the next 40 years is the population of under-20s expected to drop below 53 million, even by the lowest of the Census Bureau's projections (Spencer, 1984). If those numbers are not enough to make young people noticeable as a group, it should be remembered that children and young adults use the public library to a proportionately greater extent than their elders. Furthermore, children's and young adult services have a political value needed to maintain support for the public library today and in the future. In addition, the contribution that youth services makes to education gives an economic value to the public library that may be greater than that provided by services to adults (Getz, 1980). The research evidence presented in Chapter 6 suggests that youth librarians are not able to reach as many children and young adults as could benefit from their services. Fewer young people in the population may only mean that a larger proportion of them may be reached by youth services in the future.

Recommendation #14

Therefore, it is recommended that youth services be maintained and, where financially possible, augmented. In order to do this, youth librarians must be able to market their services with research and theoretical background demonstrating the educational and economic value of public library services to young people. Further, youth services librarians must study the education, economics, and demographics of their particular communities in order to show the library director, the library board of trustees, the public, and the local government how their services fit not just the national or state pictures but also the local one. Quoting national data is not as helpful at the local level as information that applies to the community that funds the services. The presence of home schoolers and the use of the whole language method in local classrooms could be additional sources of support for strong youth services.

Recommendation #15

As the proportion of the population over 65 increases, public library services to senior citizens will become more important, and rightfully so.

It would not be helpful for youth services to compete with services for the elderly. Creative ways of avoiding competition may involve innovative services that bring the two age groups together (Cart, 1992; Willett, 1988), such as asking senior citizens to volunteer for reading programs and tutoring services for young people or training teenaged volunteers to read aloud or perform for elderly shut-ins.

CONCERN FOR EDUCATIONAL ACHIEVEMENT AND LITERACY

Since the early 1980s, we have been hearing from the popular media that America's schoolchildren are not achieving at the levels of students in other developed countries or at the levels of American students in the 1950s and 1960s, particularly in mathematics and science. Reading achievement is also a matter of concern. In 1987–1988, only 41.8% of 17-year-olds read at the adept level and only 4.8% could be considered advanced readers (Snyder & Hoffman, 1991). In addition, 23 million adults are estimated to be illiterate (National Commission on Excellence in Education, 1983), and 20% of the over-25 population had not finished high school (Snyder & Hoffman, 1991). High school dropout rates were 12.5% in 1989 and over 40% for Hispanics between the ages of 20 and 34 (Snyder & Hoffman, 1991).

We must be concerned about these figures because they presage a difficult time ahead for the nation. As the national economy becomes ever more dependent on technology, workers will be needed who are capable of operating and maintaining the sophisticated electronic systems that characterize today's manufacturing and service industries. Reading, mathematics, and logic skills will be in greater demand. If the demographic scenario described earlier comes to pass with fewer young people available for the work force, one consequence may be a scarcity of workers overall. If those workers are not capable of performing the tasks needed, then economic productivity will fall.

The educational ground that must be made up is considerable, and the schools need all the support they can get. What should be the role of the public library under these circumstances? As noted in Chapter 1, the public library is legally an educational institution, though the general public and the educational establishment may not always recognize it as such. Traditionally, public libraries have provided collections to schools in one form or another for over 100 years. Many librarians do not think of themselves as educators in a formal sense, though most recognize and value the role they and library collections play in informal, self-directed learning for people of all ages. On the other hand, youth librarians find themselves giving formal instruction to parents and caregivers in promoting early childhood reading experiences and family literacy. Children's librarians play the role of school librarians with home-schooled children. The research evidence shows that a large proportion of reference work with children and young adults involves assisting them with homework assignments.

Recommendation #16

Youth librarians take pride in the fact that their knowledge and skills are of value for formal as well as informal learning. It has not always been easy to convince teachers that librarians are fellow professionals, however, and school librarians and youth librarians have been known to have territorial disputes (Dyer, 1978). With the development of multitype library systems (which include public libraries along with school, academic, and special libraries), cooperation and shared users are becoming the norm. This requires a more holistic view of library users. Considering the educational needs of today's young people, a focus on the young user as an individual who is also a learner, no matter what the immediate request may be, might serve to create a new context for youth services. I do not mean to suggest that public library youth services should become narrowly concentrated on supporting the curricula of local schools or give up their emphasis on recreational reading. Youth librarians should remember that social learning theory shows us that learning takes place in many circumstances and is under the control of the learner. Librarians must ask themselves, "What are young people learning from the way I deal with them? What will they take away from an encounter with me that they can usefully apply to other situations?"

It is appropriate to note that in Canada school librarians are called teacher-librarians, a term that seems more accurately descriptive of the work actually done by school library media specialists and also by youth librarians in public libraries. That title emphasizes an interpersonal function, rather than an orientation to media and materials. At its best, the teaching done in public libraries shows young people much more than how information is organized and retrieved. Youth librarians should be living embodiments of the passion for knowledge.

Recommendation #17

As social learning and child development theories suggest, the learning that takes place in libraries is not limited to the cognitive or intellectual realm. Recognition of the possibilities for libraries to enhance social, emotional, and physical development will encourage youth librarians to design buildings, collections, policies, and services for the whole person as well as all people. It is especially difficult for librarians to recognize the potential for and positive value of encouraging social development and self-esteem in adolescents. Many librarians are comfortable with the concept of library-as-sanctuary for young people and adults, as long as those seeking sanctuary are quiet and do not interfere with others' use of the library (Cart, 1992). But teenagers are not always quiet, and they need places where they can be noisy and work in groups as well as quiet places for individual work.

Recommendation #18

A further need that adolescents have is access to information about situations and conditions that affect them intimately yet are controversial. Today, any topic related to sexuality (AIDS, pregnancy, contraception, etc.), drugs, or suicide could be considered in that category. Accurate and timely information on these subjects may be the difference between life and death for teenagers. Because young people are required to attend school, it is sometimes difficult for teachers to present a variety of views or a full range of alternative responses to a situation. Public opinion may be loudly divided on whether contraception should be taught as part of educating young people about sex, for example. The public library, however, is a voluntary use institution; no one is coerced into using it or accepting the views of the creators of any materials present in the library. Nevertheless, public libraries do receive complaints, sometimes of virulent emotional intensity, about materials. Very often, availability to children or young adults is the crux of the issue.

To protect young people's access to controversial information, two courses of action are recommended: (a) better communication with the public, local library trustees, and public officials about the reasons for standing by the American Library Association's Library Bill of Rights and Freedom to Read Statement; and (b) recognition of the responsibility to help young people assess the accuracy and validity of materials. The latter may be done informally, as part of assisting young people with homework or personal requests, or as part of formal bibliographic instruction. The former may require presentations or be accomplished through institutional policy development that involves a spectrum of individuals participating. In both arenas, the youth librarian's role as an educator is clear. It is important to do both things in order that the library be understood as an institution that is responsive to the concerns of the community as well as individual desires.

LEGITIMACY AND ACCEPTANCE

Throughout this book, I have compared repeatedly the difference in status between children's services and services to young adults: the lack of personnel assigned to young adult services, the fewer programs offered them, and the lack of research about them as library users (other than as students). Even though 25% of persons using public libraries are between the ages of 12 and 18 (National Center for Education Statistics, 1988), their needs and interests are not given the same recognition as older and younger people. I view this as a problem of acceptance and legitimacy. The situation of young adult services within librarianship is somewhat analogous to the position of librarians in the larger society. Sociologists classify librarians, teachers, pharmacists, and some other occupations as *semiprofessions* or *marginal professions* (Pavalko, 1988), partly on the basis of the status accorded to these occupations by the general society. Within librarianship, young adult services has been marginalized.

Recommendation #19

As noted in Chapter 1, young adult librarians believe that the larger society holds a negative perception of the teenager that influences how librarians view young adults. Adolescents may be seen as an abnormal population to be controlled or as virtual adults needing the same kinds of services that out-of-school adults need. Both views indicate a lack of knowledge and understanding of adolescent development. It is recommended that all librarians directly serving the public in public libraries be required to demonstrate an understanding of human development, including the adolescent period. Personnel departments might approach the situation through interview and written examination questions or through requiring courses in the subject on transcripts submitted with job applications. Job announcements and advertisements should stipulate the requirement, as well.

Recommendation #20

Because legitimacy and acceptance are bestowed by others and not acquired solely through internal merit, young adult librarians must continue to work for recognition of themselves and their clients. The positive approach to the situation is to demonstrate that one is not only an advocate for the adolescent but also for the library and its clientele in their entirety, with an understanding of the challenges facing other departments and the importance of their clients. In other words, recognition is reciprocal. Providing activities for teenagers as volunteers and employees within the library demonstrates that they can make a contribution to the library, thus helping change perceptions of the adolescent as a problem or as just another adult.

Recommendation #21

Children's librarians should also take some responsibility for promoting young adult services. This is not because children's librarians are asked to take on young adult services in the absence of a young adult librarian—the NCES study (1988) indicated that only in 12% of the libraries without a young adult librarian were young adult services handled by the children's librarian. The problem for children's librarians is the diminished effectiveness of their own efforts if the continuity of service is not maintained. Young adults are more mobile and have a greater number of options for spending their nonschool hours than children. If they discover that on their "graduation" from the children's room, the library staff they are now expected to deal with knows few of the materials of interest to them beyond reference materials for homework purposes, the library may lose them as patrons when they leave school.

Reference librarians, children's librarians, or generalist librarians cannot be expected to know young adult materials and interests in depth because they usually have another priority for their professional development. The children's librarian's goal of developing future library users and supporters is not best served unless there are staff adequately trained to serve young adults. Only 19% of the libraries surveyed by NCES (1988) required staff serving young adults to take continuing education or professional development courses in the area. Where it is impossible to add specialized staff, out of self-interest, children's librarians should press for more in-service training in young adult services.

SUMMARY AND CONCLUSIONS

In this chapter we have returned to the challenges described in Chapter 1 with the intention of making recommendations to address each of them, consonant with the criteria of enhancing development and education, meeting the tests of public goods theory, and retaining the good will of professionals and politicians. The challenges were funding restraints, labor shortages, technological changes, demographic changes, needs for increased education and literacy, and legitimacy and acceptance of young adult services.

The recommendations here are couched in fairly global terms as if the expectation was that all libraries everywhere should attempt to implement all of them. In fact, not all of the recommendations apply to all public libraries. Some libraries may be doing many or most of the recommended activities; as unlikely as it seems, some communities may be unaffected by demographic changes, labor shortages, funding restraints, or any of the other challenges. But librarians should not take it for granted that the challenges do not apply to their communities or their users. For a number of years, the Public Library Association has recommended that librarians periodically undertake a process of planning and role setting (C.R. McClure et al., 1987). The concept derives from the perspective of Lowell Martin who noted that the idea that public libraries can be all things to all people is not practicable because library resources are finite. His notion was to "concentrate and strengthen" by focusing on the roles that would make the most difference to the individual community (L.A. Martin, 1983).

Recommendation #22

Martin identified eight roles, subsequently adopted by C.R. McClure et al. (1987): community activities center, community information center, formal education support center, independent learning center, popular materials library, preschoolers' door to learning, reference library, and research center. Although only one of these roles specifically applies to young people, all of the roles can be used by youth services. C.R. McClure et al. (1987) recommended that libraries use a planning procedure that can be more or less elaborate as time and resources allow, but important parts of the process are including members of the local community and "looking around" at the community before selecting the roles that the library will pursue as its primary and secondary priorities. Because the need for change is great and because the changes recommended throughout this chapter and in other chapters are numerous, it is recommended that librarians implement a planning and role setting process before making major alterations in their services to children and adolescents.

Table 12.1. Roles and Recommendations for Librarians and Local Government

1. Youth librarians should be knowledgeable about the financial situation of the library and the budget process. They should provide library directors with information and ammunition to support budget requests to local authorities.

2. Youth librarians should be able to defend their own departmental budget requests with evidence of need. A managerial approach and information gathering will supply the data needed.

3. Youth librarians should create coalitions with other local youth-serving agencies to optimize use of available dollars and create community allies for youth services and the public library.

4. Because youth librarians will continue to work with adults who are parents, teachers, and day-care providers, they need to become knowledgeable in the methods of adult education.

5. Regional public library systems should employ youth services trainers/consultants with the experience and knowledge to help generalists and paraprofessionals on the frontlines of library services to provide superior service to young people. It is further recommended that these positions not be additional positions but come from restructuring jobs within the systems as position vacancies occur.

6. Local governments should recognize the consequences of not paying competitive salaries to attract competent youth services librarians.

7. Youth librarians should work to see that microcomputers, appropriate software, and network access are available in public libraries everywhere, particularly in areas where few young people have access to computers at school or at home. This should include adjusting budget priorities.

8. Youth services librarians should work with the designers of automated catalog systems in order to assure that children and young people will be able to use the systems. As necessary, youth librarians should maintain card catalogs because young people are more successful at their use of them than at using automated catalogs.

9. Youth services librarians should become more knowledgeable about the research regarding young people and television. Rather than seek to turn young people away from television, youth librarians should learn how to use it and encourage thoughtful viewing and video production by young people.

10. Public librarians should adjust library hours to accommodate the needs of working parents and other clients.

11. Youth librarians should review their policies, procedures, and services in regards to possible changes in their communities' lifestyles that may require changes in library services.

12. Librarians and trustees should provide concrete means of assisting minority paraprofessional and clerical employees to attend graduate school to obtain the Master of Library Science or equivalent degree.

13. Public librarians should design services appropriate for ethnic and low-income communities and concentrate materials loans to middle-class clients at stationary branch and central libraries.

14. Youth librarians should use the research findings regarding the youth services' role in education and economics, backed up with local data, to market their services.

15. Public librarians should encourage the interaction of senior citizens and young people through volunteer services and programming.

16. Youth librarians should remember that each encounter with a young person is a "teachable moment" in which to demonstrate how information is organized and to convey enthusiasm for learning.

(continued)

Table 12.1. *(continued)*

17. Public librarians should accept that the public library mission for children and teenagers includes enhancing social, emotional, and physical development when designing facilities, policies, services, and collections. Buildings should allow for adolescent peer interaction as well as individual quiet study.

18. The youth librarian's role as educator includes communicating with the public, library trustees, and public officials why the intellectual freedom stance of librarians includes young people, and educating young people to assess critically the materials in the library.

19. Public libraries should require that all librarians serving the public demonstrate an understanding of human development, including the period of adolescence as a condition of employment.

20. Young adult librarians should take a positive approach to improving their status and the status of adolescents within the library through the kinds of interactions they have with other staff and through presenting teenagers as capable, interesting people who can make a contribution to the library.

21. Children's librarians should take some responsibility for promoting the employment of young adult librarians and in-service training for other staff who deal with young adults in order to maintain continuity of service for young people and a greater likelihood of approaching the goal of continued library use and support.

22. Public librarians should implement the procedures in *Planning and Role Setting for Public Libraries* in order to determine the most appropriate and viable roles for the library, following the philosophy of "concentrate and strengthen."

CHAPTER 13

Discussion and Conclusion

AN OVERVIEW

About 100 years ago, public librarians first opened their doors to children; about 70 years ago, librarians began to recognize that adolescents should have library services tailored to their needs and interests. At their inception, these services were examples of innovative public policies emanating from the bureaucrats who administered libraries, unlike public libraries themselves, which citizens invented. We can call public libraries and public library services to young people public policies because they are activities that governments have chosen to provide (Dye, 1987). Largely locally funded services with supplemental funding from state and federal governments, libraries derive their legal support from permissive, not mandatory legislation, leaving them vulnerable to changes in policy.

Library services to youth are embedded in a susceptible institution founded in the 19th century to furnish adults with books. It is really not at all surprising that in the late 20th century youth services find themselves challenged by changes in funding availability, new labor and population patterns, evolving media and technologies, reforms in education, and challenges to their legitimacy. I do not mean to suggest that Armageddon is about to arrive, engulfing and destroying youth services as we know them. Rather, the need seems to be an understanding of what facets of the past retain their value in the present and what modifications in goals and activities are needed in order to serve the present and allow accommodation to the future.

I have chosen the vehicle of public policy analysis as a means of making an assessment of youth services because it permits a multidisciplinary perspective, which is necessary in order to evaluate a human services delivery system as complex as public libraries. Because libraries have many goals and serve a varied clientele, even very small libraries and those that concentrate on one or two PLA roles can be said to be complex organizations. Over the decades that public libraries have existed, librarians have defined the policy at the same time as they have defined their profession. Keeping in mind that no public policy does all it was meant to do, the ultimate question that has to be asked of any policy is to what degree it does what it was intended to do. The mission statements of public library organizations have included education, information, culture, and recreation, with youth services adding enhancement of development, socialization, lifelong interest and skills in reading and information searching, and creating something called "the library habit," or perpetuation of library use (Chelton, 1990).

Therefore, we have looked at youth services through the lenses of child development, social cognitive theory, a model of the development of reading, history, and descriptive and evaluative research. These particular points of view were used because they are relevant to answering the question of whether public library youth services have the intended effects. In addition, the microeconomic theory of public goods was employed because any use of public funds should be justifiable under the tests of this theory in order to be considered worthy of public funding.

After looking at the theories and the evidence, there are only a few things that we can say definitely. We know a reasonable amount about what libraries make available to children and young adults on an individual basis in the way of collections (largely books), reference and reader's advisory services, activities (particularly story hours and summer reading programs), and staff. Basically, these things are the policy; they represent what is purchased through the expenditure of public funds. By their nature, it seems likely that the things libraries furnish to their young users do what is intended, but firm evidence of outcomes is lacking for most services. We also lack data about the quality and currency of collections and staff. Because they have written about their experiences, we know that for some individual young people the public library makes a great deal of difference; it is a refuge and a place to learn about themselves and the world (Cart, 1992; Toth & Coughlan, 1991). It seems very likely that library use in childhood is a strong precursor to library use in adulthood. On the basis of individual testimony and the evidence that young people use the public library to complete the requirements of their formal schooling, youth services meet the tests of public goods theory because they contribute to the production of human capital.

There are some areas in which libraries are not doing what they might to foster development of children and youth, cataloging for younger children being one example. The most striking example, however, is service to young adults. For all variables that have been collected, young adult services has less attention paid to it than service to children or adults: fewer librarians and programs; smaller, less varied collections; and less research attention. The development of people in transition from childhood to adulthood is relatively neglected by most public libraries in the United States. Early adolescence is a stage of life that is susceptible to intervention by adults. The positive attitude toward libraries carefully built by children's services may be lost in early adolescence. However, we cannot be sure about this or much else in youth services. The alert reader has no doubt noticed the number of times that I have said, "There is no research on this topic, but the theory says. . . ." Many of the recommendations relate to specific research that could be carried out as part of policy reviews by various government agencies, but other kinds of studies are needed as well.

RESEARCH NEEDS

Specific areas needing research include young people as library users, quality of reference service by youth librarians, the association of activity programs with circulation and other kinds of use, political activities of youth librarians, and a task analysis of youth librarians. One of the missing research pieces is basic user studies. Public library use by adults has been studied, but researchers have not identified all the relevant variables that encourage or determine adult use. We know next to nothing about the use children and teenagers make of the library, except for the fact that many use it for school assignments and some use it for recreational reading. We do know that recreational reading occupies little of the average child's time, and this has not changed over generations. Hence, one has to question whether youth librarians have had much success in encouraging the habit of reading. More research is needed in how children and young adults use libraries and whether libraries aid and abet the development of information and cognitive processes. Only within the last 7 or 8 years researchers have begun applying child de- velopment theories to their studies of public library youth services. Stud- ies by Carlson (1985) in toddler programs, by Edmonds, Moore, and Balcom (1990) in catalog use, and by Eaton (1991) in locational skills are examples of studies based on theories of development.

We also do not know if library use by children and young adults follows the same pattern that adult use does. The behavior of children and young adults in the library has not been observed systematically. Low-income areas have low use of public libraries generally, but do children and young adults in low-income neighborhoods use their libraries less, more, or as much as low-income adults? Do they use libraries as much or for the same purposes as young people in more affluent areas? Do they have the same preferences for materials? Level of education is a significant factor in adult public library use—what difference does parental education make in library use by children and young adults? How are teaching methods in local schools related to public library use by students?

Public librarians have paid little attention to the issue of social class, preferring to believe that the library is "available freely for all," when in fact, its adult users are largely middle class. Heath's (1983) ethnographic research among lower class African-American and white residents of two southern communities revealed that both groups taught their preschool children something about language and reading, believing it would help them with school. In fact, however, neither group understood what would be required by the school, and few of the children were successful academically. Research is needed to discover how public librarians can avoid reinforcing class differences and provide a bridge to the larger world for all children.

It is likely that proximity to home plays a part in children's use of the library; what is the optimum distribution of public libraries to encourage maximum use by young people? What do children and young adults think and feel about their use of public libraries? Answers to these questions would allow librarians to tell funding agencies more exactly what the library does for young people and our society. Furthermore, knowing the answers to these questions would allow us to design, with focused cooperation from community members, the most meaningful services and activities.

Youth librarians expend a great deal of energy and creativity on activity programs—preschool story hours, crafts, author visits, summer reading programs, and the like. What are the outcomes for the children and teenagers who attend the programs? If older children's reading skills do not deteriorate over the summer, but math and science skills do, perhaps summer programs should have a different focus, with reading being encouraged for children under the fourth grade and a science focus for older children. How do activity programs influence other variables such as circulation and public perception of the value of the library? What do young people think about these programs and the librarians who serve them? Some of these questions are not susceptible to study with the methods currently available, but some of them are. Again, answers could help librarians design the most beneficial and effective services for users.

In addition to studying users in a variety of ways, youth librarians need further study. In Chapter 6, it was observed that reference librarians accurately answer questions about 60% of the time, and the Connecticut Research Documentation Project (Hektoen, 1981) found that children's staff frequently gave wrong answers, though no percentages were published. How accurate are youth librarians compared to reference librarians, and if there is a difference, what accounts for it? Does possession of the MLS make a difference to reference accuracy or other measures of quality? What rate of reference accuracy is reasonable and possible, and how can librarians achieve maximum accuracy and efficiency in reference services to young people?

Reference services are only one activity of youth librarians. To give some direction and understanding of what librarians serving children and teenagers do, ALSC and YALSA have determined competencies for librarians working with children and young adults in any kind of library. We do not know how many youth librarians meet them or which competencies are in most need of development. Another approach to the issue would be to conduct a task analysis following the daily work of actual youth librarians. Such a task analysis would determine which tasks are most frequent and which least frequent and the skills and education necessary for carrying them out. A task analysis would give the profession more concrete data on the skills most useful to youth librarians in addition to the professionally determined competencies. The impact on library education both for master's degree students and for continuing education could be considerable. If, as I suspect, the work of youth librarians was found to require a greater number of skills and a greater development of managerial ability than, for example, general reference work, a task analysis could also lead to greater respect for youth librarians.

Another area needing study is the political activities of youth librarians. From the literature, it would appear that few youth librarians are involved in lobbying; however, it may be the case that their activities are simply not written about. And, too, it is likely that the activities around the 1991 White House Conference may change the perception of youth librarians and the perception of others about youth librarians as effective political campaigners. Time and research will tell if my contention that services to young people are politically very attractive is correct.

There are enough possible research questions listed here to keep several doctoral students and academic researchers busy. One should also not ignore the need for replication of previous research. It is fairly typical of research in librarianship that studies are not replicated. One study can only be considered suggestive; it is the accumulation of evidence over studies in different situations and by different hands that lends weight to conclusions and leads to theory building. For example, Fasick's studies of children's use of Canadian public libraries have, as yet, no counterpart studies done in the United States. The question of child-accessible catalog formats deserves a great deal more study, especially as research findings and the observations of practitioners do not agree. Virtually every study of youth services mentioned in this book is unique, with the exception of the research on summer reading programs, and even there more outcome-oriented research would be welcome. There is a great need for studies based in child development theories and learning theories.

A HOLISTIC VIEW OF YOUNG LIBRARY USERS

One of the purposes of this book has been to bring information and theory from a variety of academic disciplines to bear on the analysis of public library youth services. The fields chosen were those deemed relevant to youth services based on the services' stated goals. They were also chosen to convey the notion that library users must be considered in light of the complexity of their entire lives, not simply as users of libraries. Probably few individuals decide to use the library just for itself; a need or desire for something that the library has prompts the use. Libraries are the means to particular ends, not ends in themselves. In fact, in many cases (but not in all), the library is only one of several possible means to a similar end. For many adults, other sources (such as friends or professionals) may be more attractive because of their knowledge of the seeker and their understanding of the problem (Krikelas, 1983).

If we think of the public library from the user's point of view as *part* of an individual's process of acquiring information, education, recreation, and culture, then it becomes easier to understand why Dervin (1977) believed that the situations in which people find themselves may have more to do with their information use than the demographic variables on which librarians generally base their services. When individuals present themselves at the library, their queries may or may not relate to ethnicity, gender, or age. Until he tells someone what he wants, the Asian-American 7-year-old who approaches the reference desk cannot be presumed to prefer books on Chinese New Year over videos about dinosaurs.

On the other hand, demographic characteristics identify some of the common conditions and situations that humans beings find themselves in. These traits plus individual tastes and situations have an impact on the content and format of information sought. For instance, people between the ages of 5 and 18 usually find themselves in some kind of educational program. Therefore, public librarians need to know about the curricula of local schools and the prevalence of home schooling in their communities in order to adjust collections and services to probable as well as actual requests, because, as researchers have consistently found, young people expect to use the public library to complete requirements of their formal education. However, school children do not spend all their lives in school, and their interests vary widely. They bring their personalities, upbringing, social roles, and all the rest of their lives with them when they come to the public library, not just their personas as people enrolled in an educational system.

Demographic characteristics allow librarians to predict some of the questions and interests of users, but it is not possible to be truly prepared for all questions. Unusual and unpredictable questions are the great pleasures of librarians (or they ought to be), whether asked by children, teenagers, or adults. When librarians accommodate various user conditions and situations, including age, language, disabilities, and ethnic and racial background as well as class, they say to everyone, "These conditions and situations are normal and we respect them." Beyond collections and services, visual clues let people know immediately if they are welcomed (McDonald & Willett, 1990). Such things as toys and child-oriented graphics in children's rooms and posters of popular musicians in young adult areas not only help young people identify "their" place in what can be a large and confusing building, they also tell young people that their culture (in a broad sense) is accepted. If, however, individuals sense that their uniqueness is not respected as well as their group membership, they may find library use frustrating and either turn to alternative sources of information and recreation or give up their search.

The physical and human interactions that people use as clues to whether or not the library is a place for themselves are changing. We have already noted the increasing availability of electronic information from home, school, and office. As we add Dubberly's (1992) concept of "shared users" (access to books and other media regardless of institutional ownership), and the usefulness of mobile services designed for specific communities, we move further and further away from the image of the library as a building containing graphic records of knowledge and the locus of services accessing those records. Because this image is several thousand years old, it will be difficult to relinquish entirely, and it is likely that both building-centered and remotely generated electronic services will continue to coexist. The library building may continue to meet interests in physical containers of recorded knowledge such as books and videos. Library buildings will likely continue to provide privacy and security (Cart, 1992) and meet the expectations of the traditional middle-class clientele for materials and face-to-face services, if for no other reason than to preserve good relations with the class that has traditionally supported the public library.

In an electronic environment lacking the visual and aural elements, however, users do not have to reveal their age, gender, social class, or race. Librarians will have to work with individuals without some of the information about the patron carried by demographic variables. If access to electronic formats is provided to all those who want it, we may see less segregation of information and ideas based on age and other such characteristics. Potentially, library service will focus on the question, the search, and the user's reception of the answer, as it does now. However, the librarian's preconceptions, which may aid or obfuscate the search, will diminish though perhaps not disappear. Access to sexually explicit material, for example, is likely to remain an area of concern in a global electronic environment in which some countries are more permissive than the United States about pornography on the network. As research data about the information search process accumulates, librarians will become ever more sophisticated at assisting inquiry, and they may not miss the loss of demographic information.

UNINTENDED CONSEQUENCES

Because no one can predict all the outcomes that a public policy will have, every policy has unintended consequences. Public libraries are physical spaces whose uses are not solely determined by public policy. Once a public space is created in a democratic society, it is difficult to control how people choose to use it, even when bureaucrats have defined "appropriate use" through internal institutional policies. People may designate their own ends for which library use is a means, and this has unpremeditated results. For young people, the intent of visiting a library may be to gather information for a school assignment, to find a video for recreational viewing, to meet friends, or to talk to a library staff member. Even for the young person who finds a physical or psycho-logical sanctuary at the public library, it is not the library that is sought, but the safety, which may not be available elsewhere.

Many of these uses are unintended consequences of a policy meant to provide entirely different services. Neither librarians nor policymakers intended to furnish safe havens or social gathering spots. (In fact, for some librarians and politicians, recreational materials and services are not as important as educational and informational services, and they have difficulty justifying the amount of time and money spent on recreation, especially for adults.) Although the intended outcomes of the policy of providing library services to young people are little studied, the consequences of unintended uses for the user are hardly recognized, let alone researched.

Despite their unintended nature, there are likely to be socially valuable outcomes associated with some of these uses. For instance, using the library as a meeting place or as a sanctuary means that while they are in the library at least, young people are somewhat safer than on the street and they may be refining social and intellectual skills, even if librarians perceive them as disruptive. Of course, unpleasant or harmful outcomes are possible for users and society, also, though perhaps less likely than positive ones. We need research to identify the unintended uses that young people make of the public library and their outcomes because then we will be able to decide whether the library can or should take appropriate action regarding these uses, whether another institution should step in, or whether we need a new institution to provide services specifically for young people to meet the needs that they themselves have identified, however tacitly.

We can theorize why the public library is attractive to young people for personal purposes that may have little to do with intended library use. For instance, adult supervision of young people is minimal but available in the public library, leading to a perception of both safety and privacy. The public library also offers access without direct cost and anonymity, because staff generally know little about individual patrons. These characteristics have consequences for libraries and librarians that have been clear for decades — not only young people but the homeless and indigent have made use of public libraries for purposes not intended by the founders — but what are their consequences for children and adolescents?

CONCLUSION

Even though we may not know if the intended outcomes occur or if the unintended consequences are harmful or benign, we do know that the policy of providing individual access to information, education, recreation, and culture in the form of graphic records through the public library is used by millions of young North Americans every year. This can be construed as a form of registering approval or "voting with the feet." Despite the identified difficulties, all of the alternatives examined proved less satisfactory than making incremental changes to the current system, which is in itself a measure of the public library's success with young people. Public library youth services fill a particular niche in the ecology of education, economics, and personal development, the shape of which is only just beginning to come clear.

Providing public library services is also embedded in the social conscience of that segment of society that recognizes that the vulnerability of children and teenagers requires the responsibility of all adults toward them. Those without children are not absolved of this responsibility, because all adults owe their education and well-being to the anonymous people who funded public services during their youth. Each generation must be able to say to those behind it, "We have done our best for you."

References

ACC and AMA warning over CCT for libraries. (1992). *Library Association Record, 94*, 154.

Allen, Melody Lloyd, & Bush, Margaret. (1987). Library education and youth services: A survey of faculty, course offerings, and related activities in accredited library schools. *Library Trends, 35*, 485–508.

American Library Association. (1993a). *ALA handbook of organization 1993/1994 and membership directory*. Chicago, IL, and London, UK: Author.

American Library Association, Washington Office. (1993b, February 1). *The essential federal role in support of libraries*. Washington, DC: Author.

Anderson, Craig R., & Ford, Catherine M. (1986). Affect of the game player: Short-term effects of highly and mildly aggressive video games. *Personality and Social Psychology Bulletin, 12*, 390–402.

Anderson, Daniel R., & Collins, Patricia. A. (1988). *The impact on children's education: Television's influence on cognitive development* (Office of Research Working Paper No. 2). Washington, DC: Office of Educational Research and Improvement, U.S. Department of Education.

Anderson, Dorothy J. (1987). From idealism to realism: Library directors and children's services. *Library Trends, 35*, 393–412.

Anderson, Richard Chase, Hiebert, Elfrieda H., Scott, Judith A., & Wilkinson, Ian A.G. (1985). *Becoming a nation of readers: The report of the Commission on Reading*. Washington, DC: National Institute of Education.

Anderson, Richard Chase, Wilson, Paul T., & Fielding, Linda G. (1986). *Growth in reading and how children spend their time outside school* (Tech. Rep. No. 389). Champaign: University of Illinois at Urbana-Champaign, Center for the Study of Reading. (ERIC Document Reproduction Service No. ED 275 992)

Asp, William G. (1986). The state of state library agencies. In Charles R. McClure (Ed.), *State library services and issues: Facing future challenges* (pp. 17–49). Norwood, NJ: Ablex.

Association for Library Service to Children. (1989). *Competencies for librarians serving children in public libraries*. Chicago, IL: American Library Association.

Avallone, Susan. (1985). A survey finds microcomputer use in academic and public libraries is still in. . .the trial "by" error phase. *School Library Journal, 31*(9), 126–127.

Bandura, Albert. (1986). *Social foundations of thought and action: A social cognitive theory.* Englewood Cliffs, NJ: Prentice-Hall.

Beaudin, Janice, Fisher, Edith Maureen, Knowles, Em Claire, & Morita, Ichiko. (1990). Recruiting the underrepresented to academic libraries. *College & Research Libraries News, 51,* 1016–1022, 1024–1028.

Becker, Henry Jay. (1989). The effects of computer use on children's learning: Limitations of past research and a working model for new research. *Peabody Journal of Education, 64*(1), 81–110.

Beentjes, Johannes W.J., & Van der Voort, Tom H.A. (1988). Television's impact on children's reading skills: A review of research. *Reading Research Quarterly, 23,* 389–413.

Bell-Gredler, Margaret E. (1986). *Learning and instruction: Theory into practice.* New York: Macmillan.

Benedict, Linda Clark. (1988). In search of. . .standards for youth services in the Pioneer Library System of New York State. *The Bookmark, 46,* 176–177.

Benne, Mae. (1977). *The central children's library in metropolitan public libraries.* Seattle: School of Librarianship, University of Washington.

Berger, Patricia W. (1989). Toward a national information policy. *The Bottom Line, 3*(2), 11–17.

Berman, Sanford. (1987). The terrible truth about teenlit cataloging. *Top of the News, 43,* 311–320.

Berry, John N., III. (1989). Put NCLIS out of its misery! Use budget for deficit reduction or depository libraries. *Library Journal, 114*(18), 4.

Blake, Fay M., & Perlmutter, Edith L. (1977). The rush to user fees: Alternative proposals. *Library Journal, 102,* 2005.

Boadway, Robin W. (1979). *Public sector economics.* Cambridge, MA: Winthrop.

Bodnar, John (1985). *The transplanted: A history of immigrants in urban America.* Bloomington: Indiana University Press.

Bogue, Donald Joseph. (1985). *The population of the United States: Historical trends and future projections.* New York: The Free Press.

Bolt, Nancy. (1988). Standards for public libraries. In Virginia G. Young (Ed.), *The library trustee: A practical guidebook* (4th ed., pp. 105–110). Chicago, IL: American Library Association.

Book industry trends. (1991). New York: Book Industry Study Group.

Boylan, Anne M. (1988). *Sunday school: The formation of an American institution.* New Haven, CT: Yale University Press.

Boylan, Patricia, Fifer, Ricki, Gellert, Roberta, & Rubinstein, Roslyn. (1983). Young adult service in New York state public libraries: An interim report. *The Bookmark, 41*(2), 122–128.

Brandhorst, Ted. (1990). Educational Resources Information Center. In Filomena Simora (Comp. & Ed.), *The Bowker annual: Library and book trade almanac* (35th ed., pp. 157–160). New York: Bowker.

Brandhorst, Ted. (1991). Educational Resources Information Center. In Filomena Simora (Comp. & Ed.), *Library and book trade almanac* (36th ed., pp. 199–222). New Providence, NJ: Bowker.

Braverman, Miriam. (1979). *Youth, society and the public library.* Chicago, IL: American Library Association.

Broderick, Dorothy M. (1974). Further reflections on the CCLD report. In John Gordon Burke & Gerald Shields (Eds.), *Children's library service: School or public?* (pp. 67–75). Metuchen, NJ: Scarecrow.

Brown, Freddimae, & Mashinic, Ann. (1983). Public, school and community college library services combined in Houston public library branch. *Public Libraries, 22,* 91–92.

Bruno, Rosalind R. (1987). *After school care of school age children: December 1984* (Bureau of the Census, Current Population Reports, Special Studies, Series P-23, No. 149). Washington, DC: U.S. Government Printing Office.

Budd, John M. (1989). It's not the principle, it's the money of the thing. *Journal of Academic Librarianship, 15,* 218–222.

Bureau of Labor Statistics. (1989). *Handbook of labor statistics.* Washington, DC: U.S. Department of Labor.

Burke, John Gordon (1974). Where will all the children go? In John Gordon Burke & Gerald R. Shields (Eds.), *Children's library service: School or public?* (pp. 9–35). Metuchen, NJ: Scarecrow. (Original work published 1971)

CACL Committee on Reference Materials for Children. (1984). Children's reference services survey. *Canadian Library Journal, 41*(2), 16–18.

California library statistics 1992. (1992). Sacramento, CA: Library Services Bureau, California State Library.

California State Library. (1979). *Survey of California public libraries, 1979–80: Before and after Proposition 13.* Sacramento: Author. (ERIC Document Reproduction Service No. ED 183 180)

Carlson, Ann D. (1985). *Early childhood literature sharing programs in libraries.* Hamden, CT: Library Professional Publications.

Carlson, Ann D. (1991). *The preschooler and the public library.* Metuchen, NJ: Scarecrow.

Carmichael, James V. (1986). Atlanta's female librarians, 1883–1915. *The Journal of Library History, Philosophy, and Comparative Librarianship, 21,* 376–399.

Cart, Michael. (1992, April 30). *Here there be sanctuary: The public library as a refuge and retreat.* Denton, TX: School of Library and Information Studies, Texas Woman's University.

Casper, Cheryl A. (1980). Subsidies for library service. In Allen Kent, Harold Lancour, & Jay E. Daily (Eds.), *Encyclopedia of library and information science* (Vol. 29, pp. 221–228). New York: Marcel Dekker.

Caywood, Carolyn. (1991). At the page stage. *School Library Journal, 37*(1), 45.

Caywood, Carolyn. (1992). Libraries, release 2.0. *School Library Journal, 38*(6), 60.

Center for Survey & Marketing Research, University of Wisconsin-Parkside. (1989). *A study to assess public utilization, perceptions and needs relative to the Arrowhead Library System.* Kenosha, WI: Author.

Chall, Jean S. (1983). *Stages of reading development.* New York: McGraw-Hill.

Chatman, Elfreda A. (1987). The information world of low-skilled workers. *Library and Information Science Research, 9,* 265–283.

Chelton, Mary K. (1987). Evaluation of children's services. *Library Trends, 35,* 463–484.

Chelton, Mary K. (1990). Evaluating the impact of federally funded public library youth programs. In Betty J. Turock (Proj. Dir.), *Evaluating federally funded public library programs* (pp. 55–65). Washington, DC: Office of Educational Research and Improvement, U.S. Department of Education.

Childers, Thomas, & Van House, Nancy A. (1989). Dimensions of public library effectiveness. *Library and Information Science Research, 11,* 273–301.

Children's Defense Fund. (1988). *A call for action to make our nation safe for children: A briefing book on the status of American children in 1988.* Washington, DC: Author.

Children's Defense Fund. (1992). *The state of America's children 1992.* Washington, DC: Author.

Children's Literature Center celebrates partnership of books and television. (1987). *Library of Congress Information Bulletin, 46,* 474.

Chute, Adrienne. (1989). Literacy activities. In Library Programs, *LSCA programs: An action report II* (pp. 3–14). Washington, DC: Office of Educational Research and Improvement, U.S. Department of Education.

Citrin, Jack. (1984). Introduction: The legacy of Proposition 13. In Terry Schwadron & Paul Richter (Eds.), *California and the American tax revolt: Proposition 13 five years later* (pp. 1–69). Berkeley: University of California Press.

Cohn, Elchanan, & Geske, Terry Garland. (1990). *The economics of education* (3rd ed.). Oxford, UK: Pergamon.

Coleburn, Jacqueline, & Giordano, Peter. (1988). Window on Japan: Children, books, and television. *Library of Congress Information Bulletin, 47*, 126–128.

Commission on Reading. (1985). *Becoming a nation of readers.* Washington, DC: National Institute of Education.

Committee on Standards for Work with Young Adults in Public Libraries. (1960). *Young adult services in the public library.* Chicago, IL: Public Library Association, American Library Association.

Cook, Ruth Cathlyn. (1952). A dozen summer programs designed to promote retention in young children. *Elementary School Journal, 52*, 412–417.

Cooke, Eileen D., & Henderson, Clarence Clenard. (1991). Legislation and regulations affecting libraries in 1990. In Filomena Simora (Comp. & Ed.), *Library and book trade almanac* (36th ed., pp. 199–222). New Providence, NJ: Bowker.

Coughlan, Margaret N., & Woodrell, Kathy. (1989). Children's Literature Center suggests books for young readers. *Library of Congress Information Bulletin, 48*, 267–268.

Cram, Laura. (1984, Fall). "Young adult services guidelines" for Virginia. *Public Libraries, 23*, 90–92.

Crowley, Terence, & Childers, Thomas. (1971). *Information service in public libraries: Two studies.* Metuchen, NJ: Scarecrow.

Cylke, Frank Kurt, Dixon, Judith M., Hagle, Alfred D., & Wintle, M. Justin. (1989). Blind and physically handicapped, library services. In Allan Kent (Exec. Ed.), *Encyclopedia of library and information science* (Vol. 44, Suppl. 9, pp. 27–64). New York: Marcel Dekker.

Daines, Guy. (1991a). CCT reply time cut to minimum. *Library Association Record, 93*, 807.

Daines, Guy. (1991b). Tender trap reopens for public libraries. *Library Association Record, 93*, 578.

Dalrymple, Helen. (1991). A conversation with children's book collectors. *Library of Congress Information Bulletin, 50*, 487–488.

Daniels, Bruce E. (1990). We hereby resolve that library services to youth will be a part of WHCLIS II. *School Library Journal, 36*(8), 38–41.

Darling, Richard L. (1968). *The rise of children's book reviewing in America, 1865–1881.* New York: Bowker.

Davidson, Judith. (1988). Adolescent illiteracy: What libraries can do to solve the problem—A report on the research of the project on adolescent literacy. *Journal of Youth Services in Libraries, 1*, 215–218.

DeProspo, Ernest R., Altman, Ellen, & Beasley, Kenneth E. (1973). *Performance measures for public libraries.* Chicago, IL: American Library Association.

Dervin, Brenda. (1977). Useful theory for librarianship: Communication, not information. *Drexel Library Quarterly, 13*(3), 16–32.

Dixon, Judith, & Dowd, Frances Smardo. (1993). Should public libraries program for babies? A national survey of children's coordinators. *Public Libraries, 32*, 29–36.

Dodge, Christopher. (1989). *TV: Beware! A list of sources on taming the one-eyed monster.* Minneapolis: Minnesota Library Association Social Responsibilities Round Table.

Doll, Carol A. (1985). A comparison of children's collections in public and elementary school libraries. *Collection Management, 7*, 47–59.

Dominick, Joseph R. (1984). Videogames, television violence, and aggression in teenagers. *Journal of Communication, 34,* 136–147.

Donelson, Kenneth, & Nilsen, Aileen P. (1989). *Literature for today's young adults* (3rd ed.). Glenview, IL: Scott, Foresman.

Dowd, Frances Smardo. (1989). The public library & the latchkey problem: A survey. *School Library Journal, 35*(11), 19–24.

Dowd, Frances Smardo. (1991). *Latchkey children in the library & community: Issues, strategies, and programs.* Phoenix, AZ: Oryx.

Downen, Thomas W. (1979). YA services: 1993. *Top of the News, 35,* 347–353.

Dubberly, Ronald A. (1992). Paradigms, paradox, and possibilities: The role of federal funding in an effective public library future. In Alphonse Trezza (Ed.), *The funding of academic and public libraries: The critical issue for the '90s* (pp.32–47). New York: G.K. Hall.

Dye, Thomas R. (1987). *Understanding public policy* (6th ed.). Englewood Cliffs, NJ: Prentice-Hall.

Dyer, Esther R. (1978). *Cooperation in library services to children.* Metuchen, NJ: Scarecrow.

Eaton, Gale. (1991). Lost in the library: Are spatial skills important in shelf searches? *Journal of Youth Services in Libraries, 5,* 77–86.

Edmonds, Leslie. (1987). The birth of a research project. *Top of the News, 43,* 323–325.

Edmonds, Leslie. (1989). *Managers and missionaries: Library services to children and young adults in the information age.* Urbana-Champaign: University of Illinois, Graduate School of Library and Information Science.

Edmonds, Leslie, Moore, Paula, & Balcom, Kathleen M. (1990). The effectiveness of an online catalog. *School Library Journal, 36*(10), 28–32.

Edwards, Margaret A. (1974). *The fair garden and the swarm of beasts* (rev. and expanded ed.). New York: Hawthorn.

Elieson, Victoria, & Dowd, Frances Smardo. (1992). Closed again? The dilemma of the small public library. *Public Libraries, 31,* 158–163.

Erdahl, Jeanne. (1975). Public library service to children in Illinois: A survey. *Illinois Libraries, 57,* 13–23.

Estabrook, Leigh S., & Heim, Kathleen M. (1980). A profile of ALA personal members. *American Libraries, 11,* 654–659.

Estabrook, Leigh S., & Horak, Chris. (1992). Public vs. professional opinion on libraries: The great divide. *Library Journal, 117*(6), 52–55.

Exter, Thomas. (1987). How many Hispanics? *American Demographics, 9*(5), 36–39, 67.

Fair, Ethel M. (1945). Who are the readers in a summer reading club? *Library Journal, 70,* 523–524.

Falcigno, Kathleen, & Guynup, Polly. (1984). U.S. population characteristics: Implications for libraries. *Wilson Library Bulletin, 59,* 23–26.

Farrell, Diane. (1977). Children's services—Unexplored issues and no answers. *PLA Newsletter, 16,* 7, 14.

Fasick, Adele M. (1978). *What should libraries do for children? Parents, librarians and teachers view materials and services in the South Central Regional System (Ontario).* Hamilton, Ontario: South Central Regional Library Board.

Fasick, Adele M., & England, Claire. (1977). *Children using media: Reading and viewing preferences among the users and non-users of the Regina Public Library.* Regina, Saskatchewan: Regina Public Library.

Feehan, Patricia Ellen. (1991). State library agency youth services consultants: Their potential as agents of change. *Dissertation Abstracts International, 52,* 3466A. (University Microfilms No. 9207946)

Fenwick, Sara I. (1976). Library service to children and young people. *Library Trends, 25,* 329–360.

53 applicants for 148 jobs. (1986). *American Libraries, 17*, 324.

Figueredo, Danilo H. (1990, Summer). How librarians came to lobby: A brief history. *New Jersey Libraries, 23*, 4-6, 8-10.

Financing our public library service: Four subjects for debate. (1988). London: Her Majesty's Stationery Office.

Fitzgibbons, Shirley. (1982). Research on library services for children and young adults: Implications for practice. *Emergency Librarian, 9*(5), 6-17.

Fitzgibbons, Shirley, & Pungitore, Verna. (1989). Educational roles and services for public and school libraries. *Indiana Libraries, 8*(1), 3-56.

Fletcher, William I. (1876). Public libraries and the young. In Department of the Interior, Bureau of Education, *Public libraries in the United States: Their history, condition and management* (pp. 412-418). Washington, DC: U.S. Government Printing Office.

Flum, Judith G. (1988). The path to empowerment for young adult library services. *Library Trends, 37*, 4-18.

Flum, Judith G., & Weisner, Stu. (1993). America's youth are at risk: Developing models for action in the nation's public libraries. *Journal of Youth Services in Libraries, 6*, 271-282.

Forsee, Joe B. (1989). For adult use: The effects of White House Conferences on Library and Information Services. *RQ, 28*, 309-312.

Foster, Carol D., Jacobs, Nancy R., & Siegel, Mark A. (1989). *Growing up in America.* Wylie, TX: Information Plus.

Gambee, Budd L. (1978). Hewins, Caroline Maria (1846-1926). In Bohdan S. Wynar (Ed.). *Dictionary of American library biography* (pp. 240-243). Littleton, CO: Libraries Unlimited.

Garland, Kathleen. (1989). Children's materials in the public library and the school library media center in the same community: A comparative study of use. *Library Quarterly, 59*, 326-338.

Garland, Kathleen. (1992). Children's services statistics: A study of state agency and individual librarian activity. *Public Libraries, 31*, 351-355.

Garrison, Dee. (1979). *Apostles of culture.* New York: Free Press.

Gerbner, George, Gross, Larry, Morgan, Michael, & Signorielli, Nancy. (1984). Facts, fantasies and schools. *Society, 21*(6), 9-13.

Gerhardt, Lillian N. (1992a). Average book prices'92. *School Library Journal, 38*(3), 130.

Gerhardt, Lillian N. (1992b). Cause for alarm and action. *School Library Journal, 38*(6), 4.

Getz, Malcolm. (1980). *Public libraries: An economic view.* Baltimore, MD: Johns Hopkins University Press.

Giacquinta, Joseph B., & Lane, Peggy Ann. (1990). Fifty-one families with computers: A study of children's academic uses of microcomputers at home. *Educational Technology Research and Development, 38*(2), 27-37.

Giblin, John C. (1981, March). The key is economics. *Ohio Media Spectrum, 33*, 4-7.

Gibson, Rose C. (1986). Blacks in an aging society. *Daedalus, 115*, 349-371.

Goals, Guidelines, and Standards Committee. (1979). *The public library mission statement and its imperatives for service.* Chicago, IL: Public Library Association.

Goddard, Haynes C. (1971). An economic analysis of library benefits. *Library Quarterly, 41*, 244-255.

Goldhor, Herbert. (1985). Public library spending jumps 11.5%; circulation up 1.9%. *American Libraries, 16*, 484.

Goldhor, Herbert, & McCrossan, John. (1966). An exploratory study of the effect of a public library summer reading club on reading skills. *Library Quarterly, 36*, 14-24.

Grannis, Chandler B. (1991a). Book sales statistics, 1989 and 1990: Highlights from the AAP annual survey. In Filomena Simora (Ed. & Comp.), *Library and book trade almanac* (36th ed., pp. 434-435). New Providence, NJ: Bowker.

Grannis, Chandler B. (1991b). Book title output and average prices: 1990 preliminary figures. In Filomena Simora (Ed. & Comp.), *Library and book trade almanac* (36th ed., pp. 423–433). New Providence, NJ: Bowker.

Gratch, Bonnie. (1978). *Final report of the Pioneer Library System: LSCA #78–19 Central Library young adult study project.* Rochester, NY: Rochester Public Library. (ERIC Document Reproduction Service No. ED 174 203)

Graybill, Daniel. (1987). Developmental changes in the Rosenzweig Picture-Frustration Study, Children's Form. *Child Study Journal, 17,* 89–96.

Greaney, Vincent. (1980). Factors related to amount and type of leisure time reading. *Reading Research Quarterly, 15,* 337–357.

Greene, Ellin, & Cullinan, Bernice E. (1988). Educating librarians to serve early childhood. *School Library Journal, 34*(11), 54.

Greenfield, Patricia Marks. (1984). *Mind and media: The effects of television, video games and computers.* Cambridge, MA: Harvard University Press.

Greiner, John M. (1984). *The impacts of Massachusetts' Proposition 2 1/2 on the delivery and quality of municipal services.* Washington, DC: The Urban Institute.

Greiner, Joy. (1990). The role of the National Endowment for the Humanities in public libraries. *Public Libraries, 29,* 331–337.

Gross, Elizabeth Henry, & Namovicz, Gene Inyart. (1963). *Children's service in public libraries: Organization and administration.* Chicago, IL: American Library Association.

Grover, Robert, & Moore, Mary Kevin. (ca. 1981). *Children's services in California public libraries.* Children's Services Chapter, California Library Association & School of Library and Information Management, University of Southern California.

Handman, Gary. (1991). The short life and ignominious death of ALA Video and Special Projects. *American Libraries, 22,* 997.

Hare, Paul G. (1988). Economics of publicly provided private goods and services. In Paul G. Hare (Ed.), *Surveys in public sector economics* (pp. 68–101). Oxford, UK: Basil Blackwell.

Harrington, Janice N. (1985). Reference service in the children's department: A case study. *Public Library Quarterly, 6*(3), 65–75.

Harris, Michael H. (1976). Public libraries and the decline of the democratic dogma. *Library Journal, 101,* 2225–2230.

Harris, Michael H. (1984). *History of libraries in the western world* (3rd rev. ed.). Metuchen, NJ: Scarecrow.

Heath, Shirley Brice. (1983). *Ways with words: Language, life, and work in communities and classrooms.* Cambridge, UK: Cambridge University Press.

Heilbroner, Robert L., & Thurow, Lester C. (1982). *Economics explained.* Englewood Cliffs, NJ: Prentice-Hall.

Hektoen, Faith H. (1981). *The Connecticut research documentation project in children's services.* Hartford: Connecticut State Library.

Hennessy, Frank. (1985). A defense of opening the public library on Sunday. *Library Journal, 110*(8), 25–26.

Hewins, Caroline M. (1893). Report on reading of the young. *Library Journal, 18,* 251–253.

Heyns, Barbara. (1978). *Summer learning and the effects of schooling.* New York: Academic Press.

Himmelweit, Hilde, Oppenheim, Abraham Naftali, & Vince, Pamela. (1958). *Television and the child.* London: Oxford University Press.

Holcombe, Randall G. (1992). Introduction: Library funding and the concept of federalism. In Alphonse Trezza (Ed.), *The funding of academic and public libraries: The critical issue for the '90s* (pp.1–14). New York: G.K. Hall.

Holley, Edward G., & Schremser, Robert F. (1983). *The Library Services and Construction Act:*

An historical overview from the viewpoint of major participants. Greenwich, CT: JAI Press.

Hopkins, Dianne McAfee. (1992). The road to Washington: Youth strategies to impact the White House Conference. *School Library Media Quarterly, 20,* 138–141.

Horning, Kathleen T., & Kruse, Ginny Moore. (1989). Introduction. In Kathleen T. Horning, Ginny Moore Kruse, & Deanna Grobe, *CCBC choices 1988* (pp. 1–3). Madison, WI: Friends of the CCBC, Inc.

Horning, Kathleen T., & Kruse, Ginny Moore. (1990). Introduction. In Kathleen T. Horning, Ginny Moore Kruse, Deanna Grobe, & Merri Lindgren, *CCBC Choices 1989* (pp. 1–5). Madison, WI: Friends of the CCBC, Inc.

Horning, Kathleen T., Kruse, Ginny Moore, & Lindgren, Merri V. (1991). Introduction. In Kathleen T. Horning, Ginny Moore Kruse, & Merri V. Lindgren, *CCBC Choices 1990* (pp. 1–5). Madison, WI: Friends of the CCBC, Inc.

Hunt, M. Louise, & Davitt, Alice A. (1937). Do children have time to read? *Wilson Bulletin for Librarians, 12,* 91–93.

Immroth, Barbara. (1989). Improving children's services: Competencies for librarians serving children in public libraries. *Public Libraries, 23,* 166–169.

Information for the 1980's: Final report of the White House Conference on Library and Information Services, 1979. (1980). Washington, DC: U.S. Government Printing Office.

International Research Associates, Inc. (1968). *Access to public libraries.* Chicago, IL: American Library Association.

Jenkins, Cynthia. (1990). The political process and library policy. In E.J. Josey & Kenneth D. Shearer (Eds.), *Politics and the support of libraries* (pp. 45–51). New York: Neal-Schuman.

Kahle, Brewster. (1991, December 28). *Electronic publishing and public libraries.* Newsgroup: mail.wais-discussion. Message-Id: 9112290435. AA08138quake.Think.COM.

Kaser, David. (1980). *A book for a sixpence: Circulating libraries in America.* Pittsburgh, PA: Beta Phi Mu.

Kellerstrass, Amy Louise Sutton. (1990). *The state library agencies: A survey project report 1989* (9th ed.). Chicago, IL: Association of Specialized and Cooperative Library Agencies.

Kimmel, Margaret Mary. (1981). Baltimore County Public Library: A generalist approach. *Top of the News, 37,* 297–301.

Kinnaman, Daniel E. (1990, March). What's the research telling us? *Classroom Computer Learning,* pp. 31–35, 38–39.

Kitchens, James A., & Bodart, Joni. (1980). Some libraries do everything well! An example of school/public library cooperation. *Top of the News, 36,* 357–362.

Kominski, Robert. (1991). Computer use in the United States: 1989 (U.S. Bureau of the Census Current Population Reports Special Studies, Series P-23, No. 171). Washington, DC: U.S. Government Printing Office.

Krikelas, James. (1983). Information-seeking behavior: Patterns and concepts. *Drexel Library Quarterly, 19*(2), 5–20.

Kuhlthau, Carol C. (1991). Inside the search process: Information seeking from the user's perspective. *Journal of the American Society for Information Science, 42,* 361–371.

Kulik, Chen-lin C., & Kulik, James A. (1991). Effectiveness of computer-based instruction: An updated analysis. *Computers in Human Behavior, 7,* 75–94.

Lamolinara, Guy. (1990). Literacy time capsule to be opened in 2089. *Library of Congress Information Bulletin, 49,* 411.

Lance, Keith Curry, Welborn, Lynda, & Hamilton-Pennell, Christine. (1992). *The impact of school library media centers on academic achievement.* Denver: Colorado Department of Education, State Library and Adult Education Office.

Lange, Janet M. (1987–1988). Public library users, nonusers, and type of library use. *Public Library Quarterly, 8,* 49–67.

Learmont, Carol L., & Van Houten, Stephen. (1989). Placements and salaries 1988: Steady on. *Library Journal, 115*(17), 46–52.

Learmont, Carol L., & Van Houten, Stephen. (1990). Placements and salaries 1989: The demand increases. *Library Journal, 116*(17), 37–44.

Leigh, Carma. (1982). Remembrances on the occasion of LSCA'S 25th anniversary. *The ALA yearbook: A review of library events 1981.* Chicago, IL: American Library Association.

Leigh, Robert D. (1950). *The public library in the United States.* New York: Columbia University Press.

Lesser, Charlotte, LiBrizzi, Rose Marie, Stephenson, Hester. (1985). Survey of children's services by Area Children's Librarians' Network. *New Jersey Libraries, 18*(1), 20–21.

Levin, Marc A. (1988). Government for sale: The privatization of federal information services. *Special Libraries, 79*, 207–214.

Levine, Charles H. (1979). More on cutback management: Hard questions for hard times. *Public Administration Review, 39*, 179–182.

Levy, Frank, Meltsner, Arnold J., & Wildavsky, Aaron. (1974). *Urban outcomes: Schools, streets and libraries.* Berkeley: University of California Press.

Lewis, Laurie, & Farris, Elizabeth. (1990). *Services and resources for children in public libraries, 1988–1989* (NCES 90–098). Washington, DC: Office of Educational Research and Improvement, U.S. Department of Education.

Library acquisition expenditures, 1989–1990: Public, academic, special, and government libraries. (1991). In Filomena Simora (Ed. & Comp.), *Library and book trade almanac* (36th ed., pp. 379–387). New Providence, NJ: Bowker.

Library expenditures by state and local governments, 1984–1985. (1988). In Filomena Simora (Ed. & Comp.), *The Bowker annual of library and book trade information* (33rd ed., p. 392). New York: Bowker.

Library Programs. (1989). *LSCA programs: An action report II.* Washington, DC: Office of Educational Research and Improvement, U.S. Department of Education.

Library reaches out. (1988). *California Library Association Newsletter, 20*(3), 2.

Locke, Jill L. (1988). The effectiveness of summer reading programs in public libraries in the United States. *Dissertation Abstracts International, 49*, 3539-A. (University Microfilms No. 8905226)

Loehr, William, & Sandler, Todd. (1978). On the public character of goods. In William Loehr & Todd Sandler (Eds.), *Public goods and public policy* (pp. 11–37). Beverly Hills, CA: Sage.

Long, Harriet G. (1969). *Public library service to children: Foundation and development.* Metuchen, NJ: Scarecrow.

Lynch, Mary Jo. (1991). New, national, and ready to fly: The Federal State Cooperative System (FSCS) for Public Library Data. *Public Libraries, 30*, 358–361.

Lynch, Mary Jo, & Myers, Margaret. (1986). *ALA survey of librarian salaries, 1986.* Chicago, IL: American Library Association, Office for Research and Office for Library Personnel Resources.

Lynch, Mary Jo, Myers, Margaret, & Guy, Jeniece. (1984). *ALA survey of librarian salaries, 1984.* Chicago, IL: American Library Association, Office for Research and Office for Library Personnel Resources.

Lynch, Mary Jo, Myers, Margaret, & Guy, Jeniece. (1991). *ALA survey of librarian salaries, 1991.* Chicago, IL: American Library Association, Office for Research and Office for Personnel Resources.

Lyon, David. (1988). *The information society: Issues and illusions.* Oxford, UK: Polity Press, in assoication with Blackwell.

MacRae, Duncan, Jr. (1981). Combining the roles of scholar and citizen. In Ron Haskins &

James J. Gallagher (Eds.), *Models for analysis of social policy: An introduction* (pp. 103–152). Norwood, NJ: Ablex.

MacRae, Duncan, Jr., & Haskins, Ron. (1981). Models for policy analysis. In Ron Haskins & James J. Gallagher (Eds.), *Models for analysis of social policy: An introduction* (pp. 1–36). Norwood, NJ: Ablex.

MacRae, Duncan, Jr., & Wilde, James A. (1979). *Policy analysis for public decisions.* North Scituate, MA: Duxbury.

Madden, Susan B. (1991). Learning at home. *School Library Journal, 37*(9), 23–25.

Mahmoodi, Suzanne H., & Wronka, Gretchen. (1989, November). *Children's services librarians teaching ADULTS.* Paper presented at the Library of Congress symposium, Learning Opportunities for Children: Libraries and Partners, Washington, DC.

Martin, Lowell A. (1963). *Students and the Pratt Library: Challenge and opportunity* (No. 1 in the Deiches Fund Studies of Public Library Service). Baltimore, MD: Enoch Pratt Free Library.

Martin, Lowell A. (1969). *Library response to urban change: A study of the Chicago Public Library.* Chicago, IL: American Library Association.

Martin, Lowell A. (1983). Urban libraries in the sunbelt. *Public Libraries, 25,* 79–84.

Martin, Susan K. (1989). National Commission on Libraries and Information Science. In Filomena Simora (Ed. & Comp.), *The Bowker annual: Library and book trade almanac* (34th ed., 1989–90, pp. 101–104). New York: Bowker.

Massachusetts Municipal Association. (1982). *Report on the impact of Proposition 2 1/2.* Boston: Author.

Mathews, Anne J. (1991). U.S. Department of Education library programs, 1990. In Filomena Simora (Comp. & Ed.), *Library and book trade almanac* (36th ed., pp. 223–287). New Providence, NJ: Bowker.

Mathews, Virginia H. (1991). Countdown to a vote: The story behind the WHCLIS youth services resolution. *School Library Journal, 37*(11), 34–39.

McClure, Charles R., Owen, Amy, Zweizig, Douglas L., Lynch, Mary Jo, & Van House, Nancy A. (1987). *Planning and role setting for public libraries.* Chicago, IL: American Library Association.

McClure, Charles R., Ryan, Joe, Lauterbach, Diana, and Moen, William E. (1992). *Public libraries and the INTERNET/NREN: New challenges, new opportunities.* Syracuse, NY: School of Information Studies, Syracuse University.

McClure, Robert F., & Mears, F. Gary. (1984). Video game players: Personality characteristics & demographic variables. *Psychological Reports, 34,* 148–156.

McDonald, Lynn, & Willett, Holly. (1990). Interviewing young children. In Jane Robbins, Holly Willett, Mary Jane Wiseman, & Douglas L. Zweizig (Eds.), *Evaluation strategies and techniques for public library children's services* (pp. 115–130). Madison: School of Library and Information Studies, University of Wisconsin-Madison.

McKenzie, Richard B. (1979). The economist's paradigm. *Library Trends, 28,* 7–24.

McMullen, Haynes. (1985). The very slow decline of the American social library. *The Library Quarterly, 55,* 207–225.

Medrich, Elliott A., Roizen, Judith, Rubin, Victor, & Buckley, Stuart. (1982). *The serious business of growing up: A study of children's lives outside school.* Berkeley: University of California Press.

Miller, Marilyn L. (1992). The road ahead: Imperatives for implementation of the Omnibus Children and Youth Literacy Through Libraries Act. *School Library Media Quarterly, 20,* 158–161.

Moen, William E., & Heim, Kathleen M. (1988). The class of 1988: Librarians for the new millenium. *American Libraries, 19,* 858–860, 885.

Moll, Joy Kaiser. (1975). Children's access to information in print: An analysis of the vocabulary (reading) levels of subject headings and their application to children's books. *Dissertation Abstracts International, 36,* 586-A. (University Microfilms No. 75-17,462)

Moon, Eric. (1963). The student problem strikes. *Library Journal, 88,* 736-738.

Munson, Amelia H. (1950). *An ample field.* Chicago, IL: American Library Association.

Murfin, Marjorie E., & Bunge, Charles A. (1988). Paraprofessionals at the reference desk. *Journal of Academic Librarianship, 14,* 10-14.

Murray, Betty-Kay Williams. (1985). Regina Public Library's survey of young adults. In Andre Gagnon & Ann Gagnon, *Meeting the challenge: Library service to young adults* (pp. 55-65). Ottawa, Ontario: Canadian Library Association.

Musgrave, Richard Abel. (1986a). On merit goods. In *Public finance in a democratic society: Vol. 1. Social goods, taxation, and fiscal policy* (pp. 34-40). New York: New York University Press. (Original work published 1959)

Musgrave, Richard Abel. (1986b). Provision for social goods. In *Public finance in a democratic society: Vol. 1. Social goods, taxation, and fiscal policy* (pp. 41-58). New York: New York University Press. (Original work published 1969)

Musgrave, Richard Abel. (1986c). Public finance, now and then. In *Public finance in a democratic society: Vol. 1. Social goods, taxation, and fiscal policy* (pp. 89-101). New York: New York University Press. (Original work published 1983)

Musgrave, Richard Abel, & Musgrave, Peggy B. (1976). *Public finance in theory and practice* (2nd ed.). New York: McGraw-Hill.

National Center for Education Statistics. (1988). *Services and resources for young adults in public libraries.* Washington, DC: Office of Educational Research and Improvement, U.S. Department of Education.

National Commission on Excellence in Education. (1983). *A nation at risk: The imperative for educational reform.* Washington, DC: U.S. Department of Education.

National Endowment for the Humanities support for libraries, 1991. In Filomena Simora (Comp. & Ed.), *Library and book trade almanac* (36th ed., pp. 288-297). New Providence, NJ: Bowker.

Nell, Victor. (1988). *Lost in a book: The psychology of reading for pleasure.* New Haven, CT: Yale University Press.

Neuman, Susan B. (1984). Reading performance. *Society, 21*(6), 14-15.

Neuman, Susan B. (1986). The home environment and fifth-grade students' leisure reading. *Elementary School Journal, 86,* 334-343.

Neuman, Susan B. (1988). The displacement effect: Assessing the relation between television viewing and reading performance. *Reading Research Quarterly, 23,* 414-440.

Nielsen, Linda. (1987). *Adolescent psychology: A contemporary view.* New York: Holt, Rinehart & Winston.

1991 state library agencies financial survey. (1991). Prepared by the Council of State Governments for Chief Officers of State Library Agencies. Lexington, KY: Council of State Governments.

North Carolina Department of Cultural Resources, Division of State Library. (1983). *North Carolina's libraries: Their role: Statements of mission and purpose.* Chapel Hill, NC: Author.

Number of book outlets in the United States and Canada. (1991). In Filomena Simora (Ed. & Comp.), *Library and book trade almanac* (36th ed., pp. 446-447). New York: Bowker.

Ohio Library Association. (1979). *A survey of children's services in Ohio public libraries.* Columbus, OH: Author.

Owens, Major R. (1990). The Congressional legislative process and library policy. In E.J. Josey & Kenneth D. Shearer (Eds.), *Politics and the support of libraries* (pp. 23-31). New York: Neal-Schuman.

Palmer, Carole. (1991). Public library circ static, spending up 11.5%. *American Libraries, 22,* 659.

Palmer, Patricia. (1986). *The lively audience: A study of children around the TV set*. Sydney, Australia: Allen & Unwin.

Palmour, Vernon E., Bellassai, Marcia C., & DeWath, Nancy V. (1980). *A planning process for public libraries*. Chicago, IL: American Library Association.

Pavalko, Ronald M. (1988). *Sociology of occupations and professions* (2nd ed.). Itasca, IL: F.E. Peacock.

Perrow, Charles. (1986). *Complex organizations: A critical essay* (3rd ed.). New York: Random House.

Pfeffer, Jeffrey, & Salancik, Gerald R. (1978). *The external control of organizations: A resource dependence approach*. New York: Harper & Row.

Piaget, Jean. (1967). *Six psychological studies*. New York: Vintage Books.

Pifer, Alan, & Bronte, D. Lydia. (1986). Introduction: Squaring the pyramid. *Daedalus, 115*, 1–11.

Pitman, Randy. (1990). Video in libraries. In *The ALA yearbook of library and information services* (pp. 248–249). Chicago, IL: American Library Association.

Postman, Neil. (1982). *The disappearance of childhood*. New York: Delacorte.

Powell, Ronald R., Taylor, Margaret T., & McMillen, David L. (1984). Childhood socialization: Its effect on adult library use and adult reading. *Library Quarterly, 54*, 245–264.

Public Library Association. (1967). *Minimum standards for public library systems, 1966*. Chicago, IL: American Library Association.

Public Library Association. (1979). *The public library mission statement and its imperatives for service*. Chicago, IL: American Library Association.

Public Library Association. (1985). *Statistics of public libraries, 1981–82*. Chicago, IL: American Library Association.

Ranganathan, Shiyali Ramamrita. (1964). *The five laws of library science* (2nd ed.). New York: Asia Publishing House.

Ratner, Carl. (1991). *Vygotsky's sociohistorical psychology and its contemporary applications*. New York: Plenum.

Razzano, Barbara Will. (1985). Creating the library habit. *Library Journal, 110*(30), 111–114.

Razzano, Barbara Will. (1986a). *Public library services to children and young adults in New Jersey*. Trenton: New Jersey State Library.

Razzano, Barbara Will. (1986b). Young adult services in New Jersey public libraries: A status report. *New Jersey Libraries, 19*(2), 5–7.

Redd, William H., Jacobsen, Paul B., Die-Trill, Maria, Dermatis, Helen, McEvoy, Maureen, & Holland, Jimmie C. (1987). Cognitive/attentional distraction in the control of conditioned nausea in pediatric cancer patients receiving chemotherapy. *Journal of Consulting and Clinical Psychology, 55*, 391–395.

Reinking, David, & Wu, Jen-Huey. (1990). Reexamining the research on television & reading. *Reading Research and Instruction, 29*(2), 30–43.

Rhees, William Jones. (1967). *Manual of public libraries, institutions, and societies, in the United States, and British provinces of North America* (University of Illinois Graduate School of Library Science Monograph Series No. 7). Champaign: University of Illinois Graduate School of Library Science. (Original work published 1859)

Richardson, Selma K. (1978). *An analytical survey of Illinois public library services to children*. Springfield: Illinois State Library.

Richman, Harold A., & Stagner, Matthew W. (1986). Children in an aging society: Treasured resource or forgotten minority? *Daedalus, 115*, 171–189.

Riechel, Rosemarie. (1991). *Reference services for children and young adults*. Hamden, CT: Library Professional Publications.

Roback, Diane. (1990, August 31). Children's book sales: Past and future. *Publishers Weekly*, pp. 30–31.

Robbins, Jane, Willett, Holly, Wiseman, Mary Jane, & Zweizig, Douglas L. (Eds.). (1990). *Evaluation strategies and techniques for public library children's services.* Madison: School of Library and Information Studies, University of Wisconsin-Madison.

Robinson, Charles. (1992). The public library vanishes. *Library Journal, 117*(5), 51–54.

Rollock, Barbara. (1978). Services of large public libraries. In Selma K. Richardson (Ed.), *Children's services in public libraries* (pp. 92–97). Champaign: University of Illinois at Urbana-Champaign, Graduate School of Library Science.

Roman, Susan. (1989). U.S.-U.S.S.R. bonding. *American Libraries, 20,* 1000–1002.

Rozek, Jane. (1990). A small-scale investigation of the overlap of school and public library collection development. *Illinois Libraries, 72,* 161–163.

Rubin, Victor, Medrich, Elliott A., Lewittes, Hedva, & Berg, Mary. (1980). *Children's out-of-school services and the urban fiscal crisis.* Berkeley: University of California, Children's Time Study. (ERIC Document Reproduction Service No. ED 222 588)

Russell, Martha A. (1991). Inconsistencies in subject headings in young adult resources. *Journal of Youth Services in Libraries, 5,* 87–92.

Sabine, Gordon, & Sabine, Patricia. (1983). *Books that made a difference: What people told us.* Hamden, CT: Library Professional Publications.

Sattley, Helen R. (1974). Run twice as fast. In John Gordon Burke & Gerald Shields (Eds.), *Children's library service: School or public?* (pp. 36–54). Metuchen, NJ: Scarecrow. (Original work published 1971)

Schauer, Bruce P. (1986). *The economics of managing library service.* Chicago and London: American Library Association.

Schramm, Wilbur, Lyle, Jack, & Parker, Edwin B. (1961). *Television in the lives of our children.* Stanford, CA: Stanford University Press.

Schutte, Nicola S., Malouff, John M., Post-Gorden, Jane C., & Rodasta, Annette L. (1988). Effects of playing videogames on children's aggressive and other behaviors. *Journal of Applied Psychology, 18,* 454–460.

Schwadron, Terry, & Richter, Paul (Eds.). (1984). *California and the American tax revolt: Proposition 13 five years later.* Berkeley: University of California Press.

Scott, Anne Firor. (1986). Women and libraries. *Journal of Library History, Philosophy, and Comparative Librarianship, 21,* 400–405.

Scott, W. Richard. (1981). *Organizations: Rational, natural, and open systems.* Englewood Cliffs, NJ: Prentice-Hall.

Selnow, Gary W. (1984). Playing videogames: The electronic friend. *Journal of Communication, 34,* 148–156.

The 17th annual Legislative Day. (1991). *American Libraries, 22,* 481.

Sewell, David F. (1990). *New tools for new minds: A cognitive perspective on the use of computers with young children.* New York: St. Martin's.

Shavit, David. (1986a). Funding of state library agencies. In Charles R. McClure (Ed.), *State library services and issues: Facing future challenges* (pp. 62–71). Norwood, NJ: Ablex.

Shavit, David. (1986b). *The politics of public librarianship* (New Directions in Information Management, No. 12). New York: Greenwood.

Shera, Jesse H. (1949). *Foundations of the public library: The origins of the public library movement in New England 1629–1855.* Chicago, IL: University of Chicago Press.

Shoham, Snunith. (1984). *Organizational adaptation by public libraries.* Westport, CT: Greenwood.

Shubert, Joseph F. (1990). State policy in New York. In E.J. Josey & Kenneth D. Shearer (Eds.), *Politics and the support of libraries* (pp. 77–86). New York: Neal-Schuman.

Shuman, Bruce A. (1989). Effort and regionalism as determinants of state aid to public libraries. *Public Libraries, 28,* 301–307.

Silver, Linda. (1980). Show me – A management approach to programs for children. *Ohio Library Association Bulletin, 50*(4), 29–31.

Simpson, Jerome D. (1991). The sound of many voices: Library access for the print impaired. *School Library Journal, 37*(11), 61.

Skaptason, Trish. (1989). Library services to the institutionalized. In Library Programs, *LSCA programs: An action report II* (pp. 39–72). Washington, DC: Office of Educational Research and Improvement, U.S. Department of Education.

Skinner, Vicki. (1989). Public library standards. *Texas Library Journal, 65,* 104–105.

Sleezer, Catherine M. (1987). I found the perfect public library. *Minnesota Libraries, 28,* 333–335.

Smardo, Frances A. (1980). Are librarians prepared to serve young children? *Journal of Education for Librarianship, 20,* 274–284.

Smardo, Frances A., & Curry, John F. (1982). *What research tells us about storyhours and receptive language.* Dallas, TX: Dallas Public Library and North Texas State University.

Smith, Frank. (1982). *Understanding reading: A psycholinguistic analysis of reading and learning to read* (3rd ed.). New York: Holt, Rinehart & Winston.

Snyder, Thomas D. (1987). *Digest of education statistics.* Washington, DC: Center for Education Statistics.

Snyder, Thomas D., & Hoffman, Charlene M. (1990). *Digest of education statistics.* Washington, DC: National Center for Education Statistics.

Snyder, Thomas D., & Hoffman, Charlene M. (1991). *Digest of education statistics 1990.* Washington, DC: National Center for Education Statistics.

Solomon, Paul. (1991). Information systems for children: Explorations in information access and interface usability for an online catalog in an elementary school library. *Dissertation Abstracts International, 52*/06A, 1927.

Somerville, Mary. (1989). Slaying dragons: Overcoming obstacles to excellence in youth services. *School Library Journal, 35*(9), 32–35.

Spencer, Gregory. (1984). *Projections of the population of the United States by age, sex, and race: 1983 to 2080* (Current Population Reports: Population Estimates and Projections, Series P-25, No. 952). Washington, DC: U.S. Bureau of the Census.

Statistics of public and private school library media centers, 1985–1986 (with historical comparisons from 1958–1985. (1987). Washington, DC: Center for Education Statistics, U.S. Department of Education.

Stevens, Charles H. (1976). National Commission on Libraries and Information Science. In Allan Kent, Harold Lancour, & Jay E. Daily (Eds.), *Encyclopedia of library and information science* (Vol. 19, pp. 64–84). New York: Marcel Dekker.

Stokey, Edith, & Zeckhauser, Richard. (1978). *A primer for policy analysis.* New York: W.W. Norton.

Strong, Gary E. (1986). Impact of the federal government on state library services. In Charles R. McClure (Ed.), *State library services and issues: Facing future challenges* (pp. 50–61). Norwood, NJ: Ablex.

Strong, Gary E. (1990). State policy in California. In E.J. Josey & Kenneth D. Shearer (Eds.), *Politics and the support of libraries* (pp. 52–69). New York: Neal-Schuman.

A survey of libraries in the United States (Vol. 3). (1927). Chicago, IL: American Library Association.

Taylor, Robert S. (1986). *Value-added processes in information systems.* Norwood, NJ: Ablex.

Television Bureau of Advertising. (1991, February). *Trends in viewing.* New York: Author.

Terrie, E. Walter, & Summers, F. William. (1987). *Libraries improve Florida's education.* Tallahassee: Florida Department of State, Division of Library and Information Services.

Thomas, Fannette H. (1990). Early appearances of children's reading rooms in public libraries. *Journal of Youth Services in Libraries, 4,* 81–85.

Tolman, Marvin N., & Allred, Ruel A. (1991). *The computer and education: What research says to the teacher* (2nd ed.). Washington, DC: National Education Association.

Torres-Gil, Fernando. (1986). The Latinization of a multigenerational population: Hispanics in an aging society. *Daedalus, 115*, 325–348.

Toth, Susan A., & Coughlan, John (Eds.). (1991). *Reading rooms.* New York: Doubleday.

U.S. Bureau of the Census. (1975). *Historical statistics of the United States: Colonial times to 1970.* Part I. (Bicentennial ed.). Washington, DC: Author.

U.S. Bureau of the Census. (1986). *Statistical abstract of the United States: 1987* (107th ed.). Washington, DC: Author.

U.S. Bureau of the Census. (1990). *How we're changing: Demographic state of the nation: 1990* (Current Population Reports Special Studies, Series P-23, No. 170). Washington, DC: Author.

U.S. Bureau of the Census. (1991). *Government finances: 1988–89* (Series GF-89-5). Washington, DC: U.S. Government Printing Office.

U.S. Bureau of the Census. (1992). *1990 census summary tape file 1C: Population and housing characteristics.* Washington, DC: U.S. Government Printing Office.

U.S. Department of Education. (1986). *What works: Research about teaching and learning.* Washington, DC: Author.

Usdan, Michael D. (1984). New trends in urban demography. *Education and Urban Society, 16*, 399–414.

Van House, Nancy A. (1983). *Public library user fees: The use and finance of public libraries* (Contributions in librarianship and information science, No. 43). Westport, CT: Greenwood.

Van House, Nancy A., Lynch, Mary Jo, McClure, Charles R., Zweizig, Douglas L., & Rodger, Eleanor Jo. (1987). *Output measures for public libraries* (2nd ed). Chicago, IL: American Library Association.

Walter, Virginia A. (1992). *Output measures for public library service to children: A manual of standardized procedures.* Chicago, IL: American Library Association.

Walter, Virginia A., & Borgman, Christine L. (1991). The Science Library Catalog: A prototype information retrieval system for children. *Journal of Youth Services in Libraries, 4*, 159–166.

Watts, Doris Ryder, & Simpson, Elaine. (1962). Students in the public library. *Wilson Library Bulletin, 37*, 244–256.

Wayland, Shirley. (1975). Measuring the preschool program. *Illinois Libraries, 57*, 24–26.

Weaver, Barbara. (1990). What on earth is a state library? Issues in state library management. *Wilson Library Bulletin, 65*(2), 28–30.

Weaver, Frederick Stirton, & Weaver, Serena Arpene. (1979). For public libraries the poor pay more. *Library Journal, 104*, 352–355.

Wert, Lucille M. (1980). The M.L.S. and job performance. *North Carolina Libraries, 38*, 10–13.

West, Mark I. (1988). *Children, culture, and controversy.* Hamden, CT: Archon Books.

White, Lawrence J. (1983). *The public library in the 1980s: The problems of choice.* Lexington, MA: Lexington Books.

Wiegand, Wayne A. (1986). The historical development of state library agencies. In Charles R. McClure (Ed.), *State library services and issues: Facing future challenges* (pp. 1–16). Norwood, NJ: Ablex.

Wilder, Philip S., Jr. (1970). *Library usage by students and young adults* (Rep. No. Four of the Indiana Library Studies). Bloomington: Indiana State Library.

Willett, Holly Geneva. (1987). Services and resources in California public libraries in fiscal year 1977–78 and fiscal year 1982–83. *Dissertation Abstracts International, 48*, 241-A. (University Microfilms No. 87–11180)

Willett, Holly G. (1988). The changing demographics of children's services. *Journal of Youth Services in Libraries, 2,* 40–50.

Willett, Holly G. (1992). Public library directors in the organizational environment: Four case studies. *Library and Information Science Research, 14,* 299–339.

Williams, Robert V. (1986). Public library development in the United States, 1850–1870: An empirical analysis. *Journal of Library History, Philosophy, and Comparative Librarianship, 21,* 177–201.

Winn, Marie. (1985). *The plug-in drug* (rev. ed.). New York: Viking.

Wisconsin Department of Public Instruction, Division for Library Services. (1981). *A report of the first statewide survey of children's services in public libraries of Wisconsin.* Madison, WI: Author. (ERIC Document Reproduction Service No. ED 212 259)

Young Adult Library Services Association. (ca. 1992). Member survey. Unpublished raw data.

Young adults deserve the best: Competencies for librarians serving youth. (1982). *School Library Journal, 29*(1), 51.

Zigler, Edward F., & Finn-Stevenson, Matia. (1987). *Children: Development and social issues.* Lexington, MA: D.C. Heath.

Zipkowitz, Fay. (1991). Placements and salaries 1990: Losing ground. *Library Journal, 116*(18), 44–50.

Zweizig, Douglas L. (1993). The children's services story. *Public Libraries, 32,* 26–28.

Zweizig, Douglas L., & Dervin, Brenda. (1977). Public library use, users, uses: Advances in knowledge of the characteristics and needs of the adult clientele of American public libraries. In Melvin J. Voight & Michael H. Harris (Eds.), *Advances in librarianship* (Vol. 7, pp. 232–255). New York: Academic Press.

Zweizig, Douglas L., Johnson, Debra Wilcox, & Robbins, Jane. (1990). *Evaluation of adult library literacy programs: A structured approach.* Chicago, IL: American Library Association.

Zweizig, Douglas L., & Rodger, Eleanor Jo. (1982). *Output measures for public libraries.* Chicago, IL: American Library Association.

Author Index

Subject Index